FIVE GREAT FRENCH COMPOSERS

PLATE I   Debussy

FIVE
GREAT FRENCH COMPOSERS

Berlioz

César Franck

Saint-Saëns

Debussy

Ravel

THEIR LIVES AND WORKS BY
DONALD BROOK

Biography Index Reprint Series

 BOOKS FOR LIBRARIES PRESS
FREEPORT, NEW YORK

INTERNATIONAL STANDARD BOOK NUMBER:
0-8369-8079-4

LIBRARY OF CONGRESS CATALOG CARD NUMBER:
77-160916

PRINTED IN THE UNITED STATES OF AMERICA

CONTENTS

CONTENTS

SAINT-SAËNS

DEBUSSY

RAVEL

LIST OF PLATES

INTRODUCTORY NOTE

T HE purpose of this book is to provide a set of compact biographies of five of the greatest figures in French music. The annotations on their works are for the general interest and guidance of the reader, and do not pretend to be complete analyses, for they have been severely condensed on account of the acute shortage of paper. It is intended for the " ordinary listener " as well as the student of music, and for that reason technicalities have been avoided as far as possible.

DONALD BROOK.

London,
Autumn 1945.

Berlioz

I

IN the days of the great Romantic Revival in Paris, three figures were conspicuous as the leaders of French culture : Victor Hugo, the famous poet and novelist ; Delacroix, the eminent painter ; and Hector Berlioz, that highly emotional composer whose *Faust, Carnaval romain* and *Symphonie fantastique* may be numbered among the concert hall favourites of to-day. The importance of Berlioz in the music of France can scarcely be over-rated, for although some critics are a trifle sceptical about the artistic value of his works, it cannot be denied that his music has strong national characteristics which withstood the cosmopolitan influences at work in the *salons* of his day. His friendship with such writers as Balzac, Gautier and Dumas probably had some effect upon him, though not, of course, to such an extent as his love for the immortal works of Shakespeare, Goethe and Beethoven.

He was born on December 11th 1803 at La Côte-Saint-André, a small town near Grenoble, in the south-eastern part of France, son of a cultured, broadminded physician of the type that toil almost incessantly with little thought for reward : the sort of man that becomes progressively more rare as civilisation tends to clothe the smash-and-grab instinct with bland respectability. As he was educated chiefly at home by this benevolent doctor it is not surprising that he grew up to be a sensitive boy, passionately sincere, and quite unprepared for the finesse of French social life at that time. He was brought up as a Catholic, for his father, a free-thinker, had promised his mother that this should be done. Throughout his childhood, however, his mother's influence was comparatively slight.

The great consolation, power and charm of music was revealed to him when he was twelve years of age, shortly after an intensely emotional experience : he had fallen desperately in love with a beautiful eighteen-year-old girl named Estelle, a granddaughter of Madame Gautier. She obsessed him so completely that he was quite overcome. He made no attempt to hide his feelings, indeed it would have been futile to make the effort, for everybody was aware of his infatuation, including, of course, the girl herself, who treated the whole matter as a huge joke. The poor boy was extremely distressed, and unlike his more hardened companions, could find no way of escape from the anguish that tore at him day and night. He avoided all company, and when restlessness drove him from the house would spend hour after hour alone in the fields. At last, music helped him to sublimate the emotions that had gained control of him, but the lovely features of Estelle remained imprinted upon his mind, and he never forgot her. As we shall see in due course, she came into his life again later, and there can be no doubt that this first romance—a most common occurrence in the lives of children of twelve or thirteen—played a far more important part in the shaping of his character than is usually the case. Mere childish infatuations, as they are so often called, can be of the utmost significance in the development of the more temperamental type of personality : a fact well known to the psychologist.

II

Berlioz could already play the flageolet and flute at sight, and as he seemed keenly interested in wind instruments, his father engaged a musician named Imbert to give him regular music lessons. Imbert was afterwards replaced by a more accomplished man named Dorant, who also taught Berlioz to play the guitar. On this instrument the boy became so proficient that eventually Dorant admitted that Berlioz could play it better than he could himself.

The urge to compose soon asserted itself in this most temperamental boy, and he spent many hours wrestling with the problems he had found in a "simplified" treatise on harmony only to discover, at length, that like so many other textbooks, it had been written exclusively for those who already understood the subject. This, however, did not deter him. He wrote a number of duets and trios, all with incredible basses and dubious harmony, and ultimately picked up the art of writing chords and tolerable progressions by listening attentively to quartets played by local amateurs, and by working laboriously through a more explicit textbook by Catel.

Then he wrote a six-part *pot-pourri* on a collection of Italian airs in his possession, and composed a quintet for flute and strings which he performed with the assistance of his teacher and three friends. His father heard them playing but did not share their enthusiasm for the composition, though this was perhaps due to the fact that he was inclined to restrain his son's enthusiasm for music, being afraid that it would interfere with his preparation for a career. He did not wish the boy to become a musician, and for that reason dissuaded him from learning to play the piano. Nevertheless, music continued to flow from the youthful pen—most of it being of a melancholy nature, for the wound made by the girl who had laughed at him was still causing pain. He even tried to get it published. Typical of his enthusiasm are two letters, still preserved, inviting the publishers to engrave at their own expense a *pot-pourri concertant*, of which he would require a number of copies for his own use. He exhorts them to reply as quickly as possible, and adds that while they are doing the work he can let them have some songs as well. Both firms politely refused the honour of publishing his work.

The question of his career could no longer be evaded, and his father was most insistent that he should enter the medical profession. Berlioz protested that the very thought of tending sick people, of working in a hospital, and worst of all, of performing operations, made him feel quite ill ; but his father was inexorable, and tried to inspire him with his own zeal for humanitarian work. The boy loved his father, and did not wish to disappoint him, but he had been reading bio-graphies of Gluck and Haydn, and could think of nothing more wonderful than a life devoted to music. Moreover, he had recently seen a large sheet of blank manuscript paper ruled with twenty-four staves waiting for a composer's pen to turn it into a full orchestral score. He had never before seen a score, and the sight of this sheet gave him just a vague notion of the thrill of writing for a large ensemble; it seized upon his imagination and filled him with a burning ambition.

He continued to hesitate, and finally, his father, knowing that he longed to possess an up-to-date flute, told him that if he would agree to study osteology, he would give him the finest flute that money could buy. At this he acquiesced, but for many weeks afterwards he felt nauseated at the thought of working among the sick and dying. After preliminary studies at home, Berlioz and his cousin Alphonse Robert, set out for Paris as medical students in the autumn of 1821.

Barely eighteen years of age, Berlioz, a red-headed youth of rather less than average height, sensitive and artistic, found himself flung into the life of the Hôpital de la Pitié. Compared with the palatial,

3

pleasant and scrupulously-clean institutions of to-day, this hospital was little better than a filthy charnel-house—in fact, it was quite typical of the French infirmary of that period. The first shock came soon after their arrival, when he and his cousin were asked to go to the dissecting chamber to work upon a corpse. As soon as he entered the room, Berlioz was transfixed with horror : it was littered with fragments of human limbs, organs of the body were dripping dismally with blood . . . horrible faces and cloven heads . . . and in the corners of the room huge rats were gnawing at unwanted human remains thrown to them by the students. As soon as he could recover his senses, he took a flying leap out of the window and ran back to his lodgings. The nausea continued for over twenty-four hours, during which time he decided that he would rather die than enter the career that had been forced upon him.

A few days later, after many hours of persuasion from his cousin, he consented to return to the hospital and to make one more attempt to endure its horrors. Strangely enough, the feeling of disgust on this second occasion produced only a sensation of coldness, and he was able to take part in the work. In time he became as callous as the rest of the students, but he found little to interest him in his work.

Life as a student in Paris had its compensations of course, and Berlioz took full advantage of them. His first visit to the Opéra was like a glimpse of heaven ; the splendour of it, the richness of the singing and the perfection of the orchestra all provided a glorious escape from the sordid life he had been compelled to lead. Then he discovered that the library of the Conservatoire, with its vast collection of music, was open to the public, and he frequented it more and more. The absurdity of preparing for a career for which he was quite unsuited continually worried him, and all the while, the exhilarating world of music seemed like a promised land waiting to receive him. The operas of Gluck were among his first discoveries, and he became so absorbed in the study of this composer's scores that he frequently went without meals.

A performance of Gluck's *Iphigénie en Tauride* made him decide to become a musician, so he wrote to his father on the same evening announcing his decision and begging him not to oppose it. When the reply came it was full of assurances that in time he would see the folly of his ways : a somewhat intolerant epistle that started prolonged and acrimonious correspondence between father and son.

4

In the library of the Conservatoire, Berlioz met Gerono, a pupil of Jean Lesueur, who offered to introduce him to his teacher so that he could perhaps gain admission to the composition class. Berlioz needed no persuasion, and set out one morning to meet the eminent musician with the score of a cantata he had written on Millevoye's poem *Le Cheval Arabe*. Lesueur received him kindly and went through this work with him. Finally, he returned it to him with the remark : "There is a fair amount of power and dramatic feeling in your work, but you don't know how to write music : your harmony is one mass of mistakes. Ask Gerono to teach you our principles of harmony, and then as soon as you have mastered them sufficiently to follow me, I shall be pleased to take you as a pupil."

The enthusiasm of Berlioz was such that within a few weeks he had acquired from Gerono a working knowledge of the whole of Lesueur's system, which was based upon Rameau's out-of-date theory, and in due course he became one of Lesueur's most ardent followers. In later life he realized how useless this study of an obsolete system had been, indeed he had to unlearn all that Lesueur had taught him and start again from the beginning, yet he always spoke kindly of his first master, and rarely recaptured the happiness of those student days when he would sit in blissful admiration while Lesueur's somewhat naïve imitations of Italian music were being performed.

While he was working with Lesueur, Berlioz also attended a series of literary lectures given by Andrieux, a prominent member of the French Academy, and on one occasion wrote to this professor asking if he could supply him with a libretto. Andrieux replied kindly, regretting that at the age of sixty-four he was in no mood to write the sort of poetry that Berlioz would want : a Requiem would have been more to his taste.

Ever since his premature love affair, Berlioz had treasured Florian's idyll *Estelle et Némorin*, so he then asked his friend Gerono, who dabbled in poetry, to dramatize it. This was done, and in due course Berlioz set it to music, but fortunately it was never performed in public, because the music was just about as bad as the amateur poet's text.

Shortly afterwards, Masson, the director of music at the church of Saint-Roch, asked him to write a Mass for Holy Innocents' Day, a festival for which an orchestra of no less than a hundred instrumentalists was to be engaged. He threw himself into this work, and at length presented the finished score to Lesueur for approval. After praising the passages that most resembled his own style, Lesueur used his influence to persuade Valentino, the leader of the Opéra, to conduct it. Meanwhile, the choristers of Saint-Roch were given the task of writing out the parts.

On the day appointed for the full rehearsal, Berlioz arrived with the conductor to find that little more than a dozen members of the orchestra had bothered to be present. Masson was full of apologies. The conductor sighed, tapped his desk, and started. The choir and orchestra thereupon produced the most horrible noise imaginable, and within a few minutes the whole rehearsal had to be abandoned. The choristers had scamped their writing, and consequently the parts were full of mistakes. Berlioz, who had been longing to hear his work performed by a large orchestra and choir, was heartbroken.

Although his attitude towards entering the medical profession had not changed, he had continued his preparation for it, and it should now be recorded that in January, 1824 he became *bachelier ès sciences physiques*.

His next task was to revise the Mass he had written for Saint-Roch, and to get it performed adequately, as few young composers can continue to make progress unless they hear at least one or two of their works performed. The latter undertaking proved to be the more difficult of the two, but eventually he met a talented and enthusiastic amateur named Augustin de Pons who lent him twelve hundred francs to pay a hundred and fifty musicians from the Théâtre-Italien and the Opéra to do justice to the Mass at the church of Saint-Roch on July 10th, 1825. Valentino conducted, and it was a tremendous success: the more enlightened musical circles immediately recognizing young, turbulent genius. Describing the performance to a friend, Berlioz wrote :-

"... When I heard the *crescendo* at the end of the *Kyrie*, my breast swelled out like the orchestra, the throbs of my heart followed the blows of the timpanist's stick. I don't know what I was saying, but at the end of this piece Valentino said to me : 'My friend, you must try to keep quiet if you don't want me to lose my head'.

"In the *Iterum venturus*, after having proclaimed by all the world's trumpets and trombones the arrival of the Supreme Judge, the choir of human souls trembling with fear gives voice ; O God ! I floated on this agitated sea ; I swallowed these waves of sinister vibrations ; I wanted to commit to no one the charge of gunning my auditors, and having announced to the sinners by a last volley of brass that the moment of tears and of gnashing of teeth had arrived, I gave such a blow on the gong that the whole church trembled. It is not my fault if the women, above all, did not believe themselves at the end of the world . . .

"Nothing was more curious than the moment it was all over. In two minutes I was surrounded, crushed, overwhelmed by the artists, the executants and the auditors who filled the church. . . . Compliments fell like hail. . . . Finally, I escaped and went to my master . . . 'Come, let me embrace you ; you will be neither a doctor, nor an apothecary, but a great composer ; you have genius. I tell you so because it is true ; there are too many notes in your Mass, you have let yourself be carried away, but through this bubbling of ideas no intention has failed to hit its mark, all the scenes are true ; the effect is inconceivable . . .' "

It should be noted that a second performance of this Mass was given a few years later at the church of Saint-Eustache when the orchestra and chorus of the Odéon offered their services gratuitously. Berlioz conducted himself and made two discoveries : that conducting a large ensemble was more difficult than he had anticipated, and that the Mass was immature. After the performance he destroyed most of the score, retaining only a few fragments which he used in later compositions. Several of his other early works were committed to the flames at the same time, including the opera *Estelle* and an oratorio.

He had by that time completed another work, *La Révolution grecque* (words by his friend Humbert Ferrand) which he had taken, upon Lesueur's recommendation, to Rodolphe Kreutzer, who was the principal conductor at the Opéra, in the hope of getting it performed at the *Concerts spirituels* in Passion Week. Kreutzer alas ! had received him with undisguised rudeness and had replied with contempt : "My good fellow, we can't perform new pieces at these concerts of sacred music. We haven't time to prepare them. Lesueur is quite aware of that." A few days later Kreutzer had met Lesueur and asked "What would become of *us* if we were to help on young fellows like that ?" It is worth noting that *La Révolution grecque* is the only one of Berlioz's early works that has survived.

Berlioz was admitted to the Conservatoire at about that time, though if Cherubini, the ill-tempered Director, had interviewed him he would probably have refused to accept him, because in the previous year he had ordered the young medical-student to be thrown out of the library for using the wrong entrance.

The relations between Berlioz and his parents continued to be a little strained, so he decided to go home for a short holiday to try to convince his father that music was the only profession he could enter. At first, Dr. Berlioz refused to consider his son's natural inclination, but after a few days he gave his consent on condition that the project should be abandoned if there were no definite signs of success at the end of a limited period. It seems that the reception of the Mass had made little impression upon him. The young student agreed readily, but when his mother heard of the arrangement she was extremely angry, for she believed, as many good Catholics did in those days, that secular music and the theatre were sure ways to eternal damnation. "I curse you ! " were her parting words.

Back in Paris he resumed his studies with Lesueur and also entered Reicha's class for counterpoint and fugue at the Conservatoire. At the same time he accepted a few private pupils to whom he taught singing, the flute and the guitar, in the hope that he would be able to repay the money that Augustin de Pons had lent him, for little could be saved out of the small allowance he received from his father. Within a few months he had reduced his debt by six hundred francs, chiefly as a result of the most stringent economy. He had taken a cheap little room on the fifth floor of a house on the corner of the Rue de Harley and the Quai des Orfèvres, and instead of dining at a restaurant, tried to satisfy himself each day with a principal meal consisting of only dry bread and raisins, prunes or dates. During the summer months he used to take his frugal meal to the little terrace on the Pont Neuf, and eat it at the foot of the statue of Henry IV while reading translations of Thomas Moore's poems.

Before the remainder of the debt could be paid off, Pons found himself urgently in need of the money, and observing his friend's privations, decided to write to Dr. Berlioz for it instead. The physician had expected his son to win some substantial prize during that term, and when he received the letter from Pons he was extremely annoyed. He paid the debt, and then wrote to his son threatening to stop his allowance if he persisted in wasting his time at music. But freed of the debt, Berlioz resolved that if necessary he would exist upon the fees paid by his pupils, and refused to be intimidated. He was living the life that was common to many a student of the arts, and loved it. Besides, his friend Humbert Ferrand had written a libretto for him, *Les Francs-Juges*, and he was deeply engrossed in setting it to music.

But at the approach of winter his meagre diet proved inadequate, and he required firewood and warmer clothes. There was but one thing to do : to find a job. After various unsuccessful attempts he heard that the Théâtre des Nouveautés was about to open with a season of opéra-comique and vaudevilles, so he sought the manager for an appointment as a flute player in the orchestra. But there was no vacancy. He asked if he could be tried for the chorus. The manager shook his head, took his name and address and promised to write if anything turned up. About a week later he was invited to compete for an appointment as a bass singer in the chorus. He went to the Freemasons' Hall in the Rue de Grenelle St. Honoré, and found six others, including a blacksmith, a weaver and a broken-down actor, also awaiting the ordeal. When his turn came, Berlioz was asked by the manager what songs he had brought. "Nothing" he replied.

"Nothing ?" the manager echoed, "Then what do you intend to sing ?"

"Anything you like. Have you no music here ?"

"No" the manager replied, "Besides, I don't suppose you can read at sight ?"

"Pardon me, I can read *anything* you care to give me."

The manager stared incredulously, and then explained that they had no music whatever. Could he sing anything from memory ? Berlioz could : he strung off a list of operas that staggered both the manager and the accompanist. In the end, he sang *Elle m'a prodigué* from Sacchini's *Œdipe*, and got the job.

Berlioz then made another acquaintance, Antoine Charbonnel, who was studying chemistry, and they decided to live together in two little rooms in the Rue de la Harpe. Antoine did the cooking, and they lived "like two princes—in exile" on thirty francs each a month.

As soon as he began to write orchestral works on a large scale, Berlioz discovered that he was handicapped by his limited knowledge of instrumentation : neither Lesueur nor Reicha knew how to orchestrate effectively. By getting to know a friend of Gardel, the eminent ballet-master, Berlioz often secured free tickets for the pit at the Opéra, and whenever he could gain admission he would take a score with him and study the orchestral parts before the curtain rose and during the intervals in order to supplement the study of orchestration that he was making on his own account. He always acknowledged that the works of Beethoven, Weber and Spontini helped him most when he was studying this subject.

It was at about this time that Berlioz tried to win a prize at the Conservatoire with a scena for full orchestra on the subject of the death of Orpheus. A mediocre pianist had to play the entries on a piano before the adjudicators. When he attempted the entry submitted by Berlioz he was unable to get through the *Bacchanale*, and without giving the work another thought, the pundits promptly disqualified it as being "unplayable" !

Overcome with indignation and despondency, Berlioz contracted a serious illness, which perhaps accounted for his father's decision to restore his allowance. His first action during convalescence was to resign his position at the Théâtre des Nouveautés, for he had become utterly weary of the distressing type of music performed there. This meant complete freedom to spend any number of evenings at the Opéra, where he was apt to make himself conspicuous if any liberties were taken with the works of the old masters.

Ernest Legouvé's first impression of Berlioz was gained when the latter made a scene in the opera house during a performance of *Der Freischütz*. In the middle of the *ritornell* in Kaspar's aria, the young student jumped up and bawled at the orchestra : "Not two flutes, you rascals !—two piccolos ! Oh, you brutes !" He was trembling with indignation, and with his great waving mop of hair, looked like some strange half-demented creature. On another occasion he was astonished to find that cymbals were being played during the first dance of the Scythians in *Iphigénie en Tauride* where Gluck had scored only for strings. He waited for the momentary pause at the end of the dance and then shouted to the conductor : "There are no cymbals there : who has dared to correct Gluck ?"

One can well imagine how Berlioz felt when a horrible adaptation of *Der Freischütz* called *Robin des Bois* was performed at the Odéon to introduce Weber to the Parisian music lover. When Weber heard it, he wrote an indignant letter to the newspapers. To this the perpetrator of the outrage had the audacity to reply that it was very ungrateful of Weber to attack him, who had done so much to "popularize" the opera, for it was entirely due to the "modifications" that the performance had been a success !

III

O<small>N</small> September 11th 1827 Berlioz went to the Odéon for the production of *Hamlet* by Charles Kemble's company from England. The genius of Shakespeare was revealed to him that evening with the vividness of a flash of lightning : it shook and overpowered him to a degree that induced a curious state of mind—he felt restless and dispirited, and being unable to work, went wandering for hours about the streets of Paris.

A few days later he went to see the same company in *Romeo and Juliet*, and on this occasion other emotions, too, were stirred ; for the woman who had played Ophelia in *Hamlet*, the tall, charming Harriet Smithson, now entranced him as Juliet. Dazzled by this beautiful actress, with whom he had fallen in love at sight, he became all the more despondent, for he could not help comparing her talent and glittering success with what he considered to be his own failure. For a month or two he seemed almost in a stupor, and then suddenly he resolved to give a grand concert of his own works—somehow, he felt, it *could* be done—to show this lovely actress that he, too, was an artist.

With wild enthusiasm he started copying out the parts of the works he had chosen—they included the *Scène héroïque* (*La Révolution greque*), a part of *Les Francs-Juges*, and *La mort d'Orphée* which had been pronounced unplayable—and saved every *centime* he could towards the cost of engaging a chorus. He was fairly certain of getting the services of the orchestra for nothing, but there remained the difficulty of obtaining permission to use the hall of the Conservatoire from the Superintendent of Fine Arts, and the consent of Cherubini, the Director.

The Superintendent agreed after persuasion from several influential friends of Berlioz, but Cherubini did everything within his power to frustrate the project. Nevertheless, the concert was held, but the inadequately rehearsed orchestra and singers did anything but justice to the more difficult items. The hall was almost empty, and the only real satisfaction the composer got was a favourable notice by Fétis, the illustrious musicologist, who declared in the *Revue musicale* that the precocious talent of Berlioz inspired in him a lively interest. "M. Berlioz has the happiest of gifts . . . he has genius. His style is forceful and animated. His inspirations often have charm ; but more often still, the composer, carried along by his young and ardent imagination, exhausts himself in combinations of an original and passionate intention . . . '' This report is of special interest when we consider that in later years Fétis frequently opposed Berlioz.

A week or so later, Berlioz wrote to Ferrand about the performance of the overture to *Les Francs-Juges* at the rehearsal for the concert : "Scarcely had the orchestra heard that terrifying solo for trombones and ophicleide for which you wrote the words for Olmerick in the third act, when one of the violins exclaimed : 'Ah ! ah !, the rainbow is the bow of your violin, the winds play the organ and the elements beat time ! ' Whereupon the whole orchestra seized upon an idea whose extent they in no way understood. The day of the concert . . . I was seated at the side of the drummer, who, holding my arm and gripping it with all his might, could not help crying convulsively at intervals : 'It's superb ! It's sublime, my friend ! . . . It's terrifying ! It's enough to turn one's brain ! ' With my other arm I tore at my hair : I longed to be able to cry out, forgetting that it was my own work : 'How monstrous, colossal, horrible ! . . . ' ''

Such was the first effort Berlioz made to prove himself to the musical coteries of Paris, and in particular to Harriet Smithson. But the actress was not even aware that the concert had been given, nor did she know of the existence of the young composer !

Soon after his "discovery" of Shakespeare, Berlioz, who had always reverenced the name of Gluck, became aware of the genius of Beethoven, whose works revealed "a new world of music" to him in much the same way as Shakespeare had shown him "a new universe of poetry." In the face of violent hostility, Habeneck and his new Société des Concerts had begun performing the Beethoven symphonies, and it was to hear the immortal Fifth that Berlioz took Lesueur, who like the other professors, had refused to patronize the "new music." Lesueur admitted afterwards that he had been profoundly moved, and added "Such music ought not to be written".[1] Berlioz replied that he need have no fear of there ever being too much of it.

When Humbert Ferrand and two friends started the *Revue européenne*—a review devoted to politics, religion, art and whatnot—they asked Berlioz to become their music critic. This he did, chiefly to flay the pro-Rossini critics employed by certain other journals, and to ridicule their "blasphemous" views on the artistic integrity of Gluck.

---

[1] In his *Mémoires*, (Lévy, Paris : 1870), Berlioz explains this remark as a confession of regret, envy, dread of the unknown, and impotency.

In the summer of 1828 Berlioz entered again for the competition at the Conservatoire, hoping to win the Prix de Rome so that he could at last make an impression upon Harriet Smithson. He received the second prize for his *scène lyrique* entitled *Herminie*, a very pleasing work which was not published until many years after his death. It is rather amusing to note that he often expostulated about the absurdity of allowing the painters, sculptors, architects and engravers of the Académie des Beaux-Arts to vote on the merit of the musical entries, yet it was due entirely to the votes of these gentlemen that he won the prize ! The musicians among the adjudicators had been in favour of awarding the prize to another of Reicha's pupils.

It was presumed generally that he would win the first prize in the following year, so when the competition came round again, Berlioz decided to write without restraint—without bothering too much about the reactionary prejudices of the examiners. The subject set for the candidates was the death of Cleopatra, and the setting by Berlioz was both strikingly original and appropriate, but the adjudicators decided to make no award that year because they felt that a young composer with such radical ideas in music should not be encouraged. Boïeldieu, one of that enlightened body, met Berlioz on the following day and asked him why he had thrown away the prize when it was so easily within his reach. The jury, he said, wanted music that was graceful and soothing. The young composer then reminded Boïeldieu that Cleopatra, having poisoned herself, died in agonizing convulsions !

Berlioz had by that time made the acquaintance of the genius of Goethe, for he had read Gérard de Nerval's translation of *Faust* (1827) and had been so fascinated by it that the book had been his constant companion for months. This prose translation contained some songs that he had set to music under the title *Huit scènes de Faust* and had published in the spring of 1829. He sent two copies of his score to Goethe on April 10th with a letter declaring : "*Faust* having been for several years past[1] my habitual reading, continual meditation upon this astonishing work (although I could see it only through the mist of translation) has at length put a spell upon my mind : musical ideas have formed themselves in my mind around your poetic ideas, and although I was firmly resolved not to unite my feeble tones to your sublime ones, little by little the temptation grew so strong, the attraction so powerful, that the music for several scenes was completed almost without my being aware of it."

[1] Typical of Berlioz is this slight exaggeration.

Berlioz then goes on to say that he has published the score, and asks Goethe to accept it as homage. The German poet passed the score on to Carl Friedrich Zelter (1758-1832) with a request that he should send Berlioz a friendly acknowledgement. Zelter— the man who tried to improve Bach's *St. Matthew Passion*, by the way—described it to Goethe as a "musical miscarriage, the result of an abominable incest."

It was just after this incident, when the young composer was still under the spell of Shakespeare and Goethe, that he completed his famous *Symphonie fantastique*, which had been taking shape for some time in his mind. His unrequited passion for Harriet Smithson inspired this work, which indeed is autobiographical, and although we do not know much about his relations with this actress, it seems that she had given him some encouragement but had been a trifle afraid of his wild impulsiveness.

Coming to the year 1830, we find Berlioz writing to his friend Ferrand on February 6th telling him that Miss Smithson is in London, yet seems quite near to him, and that once more he is plunged into interminable and inextinguishable passion for her. In another letter, dated April 16th, however, he speaks of having discovered frightful but indisputable truths about her which had aided his recovery.

The *Symphonie fantastique (Épisode de la Vie d'un Artiste)* caught the imagination of the directors of the Théâtre des Nouveautés and they agreed to give a performance of it. Berlioz invited about eighty musicians to augment the fifty players normally engaged at the theatre, and was given an assurance that accommodation would be provided for them. To his dismay, he discovered when they had all assembled for the rehearsal that the space provided was utterly inadequate and that nothing like enough music desks had been brought in. The project had to be abandoned, but not before the orchestra, despite their confusion, had played the *Bal* and the *Marche au supplice* to show the directors what they were missing.

IV

FERDINAND HILLER, a friend of Berlioz, knew an extremely beautiful girl of nineteen named Marie (Camille) Moke, and without thinking of the consequences, told her about Berlioz's extraordinary passion for Miss Smithson in terms that left no doubt in the girl's mind about his friend's fiery temperament. He then added very foolishly that of course a man like Berlioz would not fall in love with a girl of her type.

The effect of this remark upon an alluring and conceited young Parisienne is not difficult to guess, and she lost no time in ensnaring the young composer. We are told that at first he tried to resist her, but yielded at length, and then threw himself with all the ardour of youth into this *affaire*. In later years he was obstinately reticent about his relations with her, though he admitted that they ran through the whole gamut of passion, which, considering the fact that she offered herself quite brazenly, is not surprising. Berlioz was keen to marry her, but her mother, hoping for a more wealthy suitor, did nothing to encourage them, and with the July Competition at the Conservatoire in view, the composer did not try to hasten matters.

That year—1830—he won the Grand Prix de Rome with *Sardanapale*, but knowing the mentality of the academicians, he did not write the conflagration scene until after he had secured the prize. This intensely dramatic scene, by the way, was a complete fiasco at the first performance, for the horns, drums and cymbals all missed their cues at the climax. Berlioz was so incensed that he flung his score right into the middle of the orchestra, knocking over two of the music desks and causing a general mêlée. The scandalized academicians gasped in horror—but Berlioz had got his prize and would not have hesitated in telling them where to go had they tried to reprimand him.

The Grand Prix carried with it, among many other benefits, an award of three thousand francs a year for five years, and free maintenance in Rome while the winner pursued a further course of study there. The latter was compulsory, and although Berlioz did not want to leave Paris, he was obliged to go. Before he went, however, he was able to give a public concert at which both *Sardanapale* and the *Symphonie fantastique* were adequately performed. Liszt was present and met Berlioz for the first time. Shortly afterwards the great composer-pianist made his brilliant arrangement of the *Symphonie fantastique* for piano.

Berlioz became formally engaged to Mlle. Moke, and then after a short visit to his parents proceeded to Rome. His first three weeks there were filled with anxiety at receiving no correspondence whatever from his *fiancée*. Then, unable to bear the strain any longer he decided to return to Paris, but a short illness detained him at Florence on the way. It was here that he received a letter from the girl's mother calmly announcing her daughter's marriage to Camille Pleyel, the pianoforte maker. Seething with rage he made plans to murder Mlle. Moke, her husband and her mother, and then to commit suicide. But after having armed himself with two or three pistols, bottles of laudanum and strychnine, appropriate disguise and so forth, he suddenly changed his mind and returned to Rome !

There he met Mendelssohn, who for some reason took a dislike to him and proceeded, behind his back of course, to ridicule his works and to say spiteful things about his person. This, alas ! is not an uncommon occurrence among musicians.

On the whole, life in Rome was for Berlioz much the same as for the other students : apart from the routine of the Academy there were visits to the Café Greco, discussions and desultory music-making, the *soirées*, tours to Naples, Venice and Florence, a little wenching perhaps, exchanges of views with the painters and sculptors, and of course the exploration of the wonders of Rome itself. He was disgusted with the Carnival, but entranced by St. Peter's. A festal high mass in the Sistine Chapel with full orchestra and chorus was a great disappointment : the instrumentalists were either unwilling or unable to tune to the pitch of the organ, and the organist was certainly not going to be left out of the fun, so the result was distressing, to say the least. Berlioz and his companion disgraced themselves by choking with laughter when an enormous man with black whiskers sprouting liberally out of a face like that of a bloated butcher got up and sang the soprano solos. Then Berlioz had to remark for all to hear that he had never seen a bearded *castrato* before. Immediately, a woman in front of them swung round and cried indignantly : *"Castrato ! d'avvero non è castrato ! . . . Imparate . . . che quel virtuoso maraviglioso è il marito mio !"*[1]

He was amazed to find that the Italians had not the vaguest idea of what constituted a symphony : they applied the term indiscriminately to any scrap of music played in a theatre before the rise of the curtain.[2] They had scarcely heard of Beethoven or Weber. While he was in Rome he wrote the overture *Rob Roy*, the *Scène aux Champs* of the *Symphonie fantastique*, which he re-wrote almost entirely, *Le Chant de Bonheur* of the monodrama *Lélio*, and the *Méditation religieuse*, for choir and orchestra, on a prose translation of Moore's poem *Ce monde entier n'est qu'une ombre fugitive.*

The beautiful country around Rome was a constant source of delight to him, and in his correspondence he refers to having enjoyed "vagabond life amid the woods and rocks, among the good-natured

[1] "Castrato ! he certainly is not a castrato ! . . . . Let me tell you . . . . . that this marvellous virtuoso is my husband !"

[2] This old-fashioned use of the word was quite common in England as well as in Italy. The old cathedral composers applied it to organ interludes in anthems, etc.

peasants, sleeping in the daytime on the banks of a torrential river, and in the evening dancing the *saltarelle* with the men and women at the inn." He describes the scenery of Rome as "stern and majestic" and writes with great enthusiasm about the ruins of the palaces and temples in the setting sun. On the other hand, we find him complaining that in Rome everything is "fifty years behind civilization" and speculating on the changes there would be if this beautiful country were inhabited by the English. Roman society bored him to distraction : he found their conversation to be "very platitudinous, very trite, very academic, very silly", and often bewailed his obligation to stay in the Italian capital when in Paris they were performing the Choral Symphony, *Euryanthe*, and such-like.

He left Rome in the summer of 1832, and after a stay of a few months with his family, returned to Paris. Immediate arrangements were made for a concert at which his *Symphonie fantastique* and its sequel *Lélio ou le Retour à la Vie* were performed. Harriet Smithson was back in Paris again, making a conspicuously unsuccessful attempt to run the English theatre, and attended the concert, not knowing, of course, that she was the heroine of "this strange and painful drama" of autobiographical music. It was an outstanding success : a triumph witnessed by such celebrities as Paganini, Alexandre Dumas and Victor Hugo. Miss Smithson was deeply moved, and Berlioz, instead of proceeding to Germany for a year in accordance with the terms of the Prix de Rome, spent the best part of 1833 in persuading her to marry him. By March of that year she had become heavily in debt owing to the utter failure of the English theatre in Paris, but she was slow in accepting him, chiefly, it is thought, on account of his extraordinary ardour. Both families were opposed to the marriage, but it took place on October 3rd at the British Embassy.

V

AFTER the honeymoon at Vincennes, Berlioz became painfully aware that he had undertaken heavy responsibilities. It is true that he was hailed by many critics as the successor to Beethoven, but his income was hopelessly inadequate,[1] and to pay off his wife's debts, he arranged a benefit performance for her at the Théâtre-Italien on November 21st. She played the fourth act of *Hamlet*, and Madame Dorval, an eminent French actress, played an act from *Antony* (Dumas). This

1 He had to borrow three hundred francs just after the wedding.

was followed by a concert of which the principal items were the *Francs-Juges* overture, *Sardanapale*, and Weber's *Concertstück* played by the illustrious Liszt himself. The *Symphonie fantastique* was to have concluded the concert, but owing to the late hour of starting, this item was not reached until midnight. Berlioz, who was conducting, was then horrified to discover that the majority of the players whose contracts did not compel them to play after midnight, were slinking out. The audience showed no willingness to go home, in fact some of them were calling out that if they could not have the complete symphony they would at least like to hear the *Marche au supplice*. Berlioz, furious and confused, had to apologise to the audience, explaining that as only five violins had remained nothing further could be attempted. Some of the more spiteful critics took the opportunity to ridicule the unfortunate composer, telling their readers that the music had driven the musicians away.

Nevertheless, Berlioz made several thousand francs on the evening, and forthwith arranged a concert at the Conservatoire for which he engaged a superb orchestra consisting of the finest players in the capital. Girard was the conductor on this occasion, and the *Symphonie fantastique* was greeted by the greatest furore the composer had ever known.

Not long after this concert Paganini approached him and requested a solo for his wonderful Stradivari viola : he said that he had no confidence in any other composer. Berlioz sketched out something and showed it to him, but he objected that the viola was not sufficiently employed in it. "What you want, then, is a viola concerto," Berlioz remarked, "and you, surely, are the man to write it." The great virtuoso protested that he was not well enough to concentrate upon composition, and eventually his request induced Berlioz to write his "symphony with alto solo" *Harold en Italie*. It was completed in the summer of 1834, and first performed under Girard's conductorship. The success of it was impaired by the conductor's failure to observe the *accelerando* in the coda of the first movement, and one of the newspaper critics ridiculed it in an article that commenced : "Ha ! ha ! ha !, haro ! haro ! *Harold* !" This staggering wit provoked some imbecile to write a letter deploring the fact that Berlioz evidently hadn't the courage to blow his brains out.

To Berlioz it was no new experience to be butchered to make a critic's holiday, but he was then struggling to make enough money to support his wife, who, incidentally, was expecting a baby, and was intensely irritated by this silly attack. He had a means of retaliation, had he wished to use it, for he had become a regular contributor to the new musical paper the *Gazette musicale*. He was a fine writer, but evidently found little pleasure in musical journalism for in his correspondence we find that he deplored the fact that he was "compelled to scribble wretched articles which pay very badly . . ."

He had by then taken a pleasant little house at Montmartre (then only a village), where many of his friends were entertained. In a letter to his sister Adèle dated May 12th 1834 he describes a "country party" that he and his wife had given at which such celebrities as Alfred de Vigny, Antony Deschamps, Liszt, Hiller and Chopin had been present. They had discussed "art, poetry, thought, music, drama—in fact all that constitutes life" in glorious weather. Their son Louis was born on August 15th of that year.

Harold en Italie was performed twice during the following December and made a fairly good impression. Berlioz then resolved to become associated with the Opéra, in which he saw the only real opportunity of making a fair income as a composer, but found this to be far more difficult than he had imagined. In order to make a living he was obliged to join the staff of the *Journal des Débats* in January 1835. This important paper was owned by the Bertin family, who were doing their utmost to assist Berlioz in gaining an entry to the Opéra. When his opera *Benvenuto Cellini* was completed in its original form (1837) they agitated incessantly to get it accepted, but Véron, the director, objected to this pressure and persuaded Adolphe Adam to write a parody of Berlioz. This was performed as an interlude at a masked ball held at the Opéra.

The year 1835 brought the composer the final payment of his Prix de Rome, and to fulfil the conditions, he should have spent that year in Germany, but with the influence of powerful friends he managed to persuade the authorities to waive that particular stipulation. He was too concerned with the task of making a living in Paris to embark upon a period of study in Germany.

Despite the efforts of such influential people as Liszt and the Duc d'Orléans, Berlioz was excluded from the Opéra until the retirement of Véron, and with no more money to come from the Prix de Rome, he had to make a tremendous effort to pay his way. In a letter to Ferrand he said that he was working like a slave for four newspapers and consequently had little time for composition. His wife made several attempts to re-establish herself in the smaller theatres of the capital, but the callous press and public had grown tired of her, and she failed pitifully. "I took her to see Hugo recently," he said in a letter to his sister, "to get from him a rôle appropriate to her talent and in which her inability to speak French perfectly would not matter. Hugo is trying to do this. . . . He offered me an opera last month. So did Scribe, but these offers are useless because of the opposition of the directors of the Opéra and the Opéra Comique . . . To be obliged to see the best years of my life lost for dramatic music simply because three villains happen also to be imbeciles ! "

Another letter to his sister on the same subject runs : " . . . I shall have no entry so long as M. Véron is there. If he goes he will give his place to his associate, M. Duponchel, the costume designer, who imagines that he loves music, but he understands it no more than Véron. Duponchel, six months ago, gave his word to Meyerbeer and M. Bertin in my presence . . . that if he became director of the Opéra, his first action would be to engage me to compose a work for it. . . . But I know what animals these directors are : I would sell Duponchel's word for a hundred crowns. I shall never forget that Meyerbeer was able to get *Robert le Diable* produced (to which the theatre owes its entire prosperity for the last four years) only by paying sixty thousand francs of his own money to the administrators of the Opéra, who would not risk the expense."

While he was engaged in this struggle for existence, other people were busy making money out of him by "pirating" his works. He received from Germany, for instance, an arrangement for four hands of his *Francs-Juges* overture ; an abominable mutilation of the original. In a letter to the perpetrator of this abortion he declared : "It is painful to me to have to protest that I am a complete stranger to this work . . . (it) is not mine, neither can I recognize my work in what remains of the overture. Your arranger has cut my score to pieces and strung it together again so that I can see in it nothing but a ridiculous monstrosity the honour of which I beg him to retain for himself . . . "

Berlioz even had cause to regret his own publication of this work in its proper form, for incapable or indifferent conductors in other countries were giving performances of it with little regard for the composer's directions. At that time there were very few conductors who could satisfactorily direct his works—he became accustomed to conducting his own compositions for that reason—and even the

HECTOR BERLIOZ after Prinzhofer

PLATE II

Symphonie Fantastique. The Ball Scene in the De Basil Ballet Company's production

PLATE III

performance of the *Francs-Juges* overture at the Argyll Rooms, London, by our own Philharmonic Society received his sharp criticism.

Early in 1837 he managed to prevail upon the Minister of the Interior, M. de Gasparin, to give him an official commission to write a *Requiem*. The innumerable little intrigues (on the part of Berlioz and his influential friends) that led up to this need not concern us here, but the Director of Fine Arts did his utmost to frustrate the commission. In his *Mémoires*, Berlioz records an interview with "this arbiter of the destinies of art and artists" who after speaking disdainfully of all the composers with the exception of Rossini, exclaimed : "There is another . . . what is his name ? . . . A German, whose symphonies they play at the Conservatoire. You are sure to know him, M. Berlioz."

"Beethoven ? " suggested the composer.

"Ah yes, Beethoven. Now *he* was not devoid of talent."

This profound statement from the official guardian of the Fine Arts stuck in the composer's memory for the rest of his life.

But he had not yet finished with the Director. The official order included a guarantee that the *Requiem* would be performed at the expense of the Government at the annual service commemorating the victims of the Revolution of 1830. The work was completed, and rehearsals started for the first performance on the next anniversary in July 1837. Just as everything was getting into shape, Berlioz received a notice from the Fine Arts Department saying that as the ceremony was to take place without music the *Requiem* would not be required.

The feelings of the composer need not be described, nor is it necessary to record in detail all the agitations that followed. Bertin and various other friends of the composer made the Director's life a misery, so much so that the harassed official lost no time in persuading General Bernard, the Minister of War, to give orders for the *Requiem* to be performed in the Church of the Invalides at the solemn memorial service to General Damrémont and the soldiers who were killed with him in the attack on Constantine on October 14th 1837.

This satisfied Berlioz, but it infuriated Cherubini, for one of his two *Requiems* had in the past always been specified for such an occasion as this. All the friends and pupils of Cherubini therefore turned against the younger composer. However, Berlioz's *Requiem* was performed with great success, despite the fact that Berlioz was not allowed to conduct it personally. In his *Mémoires* he declares that Habeneck, who conducted the work, stopped beating at the most crucial point and calmly took a pinch of snuff, and that the work was held together only by a frantic indication from himself, but this, like one or two other little stories in his *Mémoires*, is probably the product of his extraordinary imagination. In the same book he storms about the reluctance of the Minister to pay him the agreed fee, and gives one the impression that having waited many months, he was paid only after he had grasped the wretched bureaucrat by the throat, as it were. The official records, however, state that the performance took place on December 5th, that the composer was paid one thousand francs on the 15th of that month, and four thousand on the 23rd of the ensuing month.

Berlioz always considered that it was to make amends for the "intolerable injustice" done to him on this occasion that M. de Gasparin awarded him the cross of the Legion of Honour in 1839, when Duponchel, Director of the Opéra, received a similar honour.

During the year 1838, Berlioz applied for the post of professor of harmony at the Conservatoire, made vacant by the death of Rifaut, but Cherubini disqualified him because he was unable to play the pianoforte. The Director then proceeded to appoint a man who knew even less about the keyboard than Berlioz. Early in the following year, the composer accepted the librarianship of the Conservatoire : a modest appointment carrying a salary of a hundred and eighteen francs a month. During a visit to London, some kind soul tried to deprive him even of this.

In June of the same year his opera *Benvenuto Cellini* was accepted for the Opéra, and rehearsals started immediately. The entire company seemed quite convinced from the outset that the work would be a failure, and Habeneck, the conductor, took everything—including the *saltarello*[1]—at a sluggish speed that reflected his indifference tò the opera. The first performance, on September 10th, was a failure, and so were the few subsequent productions ; then it was taken off altogether. Berlioz, who for years had struggled to become a composer for the Opéra, found its doors closed to him for the rest of his life, yet sixteen years later Liszt wrote a letter to Wilhelm Fischer, the chorus-master of the Dresden Opera declaring that with the exception of the works of Richard Wagner, *Benvenuto Cellini* was the most important and most original work of musical drama produced in the past twenty years.

This catastrophe upset Berlioz's health and brought on an attack of bronchitis. Money had still to be earned, however, and he arranged

[1] This dance formed the theme of the allegro of the famous *Carnaval romain*, which Berlioz wrote some six years later.

two concerts at the Conservatoire. The first was on November 25th, but he was too ill to leave his bed, and had to engage Habeneck to conduct ; the second, on December 16th, he directed personally and made such an impression upon Paganini with his *Symphonie fantastique* and *Harold en Italie* that the great virtuoso went up to him afterwards, fell on his knees and kissed his hand. This alone delighted the composer, but two days later he received a letter, enclosing a banker's order addressed to Baron de Rothschild instructing him to pay Berlioz twenty thousand francs. It ran : "Beethoven is dead, and only Berlioz can revive him. Having heard your divine compositions, so worthy of your genius, I beg you to accept, as a token of my homage, twenty thousand francs, which will be paid to you by the Baron de Rothschild upon presentation of the enclosed. Believe me always, your affectionate friend, Nicolo Paganini."

For making this gift, various ulterior motives were attributed to Paganini (who was not, as a rule, a generous man) by the more spiteful gossips, but there is no just cause to believe that the gift was made for any reason other than that expressed by the donor. In any case, after he had settled various debts, Berlioz spent it in the way that Paganini would have wished : he forsook his odd jobs and settled down to write what he hoped would be a masterpiece. This would undoubtedly have been an opera had he not failed to establish *Benvenuto Cellini*, but he was not prepared to risk a second humiliation, so he decided to write a dramatic symphony with chorus on the theme of *Romeo and Juliet*. He started on January 24th 1839 and finished it on the following September 8th.

The new symphony, dedicated to Paganini, was first performed at the Conservatoire on the following November 24th under the direction of the composer, and repeated, after a few slight alterations had been made, twice in the ensuing month. It was a considerable success, but Berlioz made various revisions before it was published. Unfortunately, Paganini never lived to hear it : ill health necessitated a move from Paris soon after his gift had been made, and he died at Nice about a year later. One gathers that he was not well enough to visit Paris in November or December 1839.

Gautier, describing one of the performances of *Roméo et Juliette* in the *Presse* on December 11th, declared that Berlioz had "given a soul to each instrument of the orchestra ; an expression to each note". For all that, the composer made very little money out of these concerts, and in a letter to Ferrand bemoaning his small and precarious income, he says : "Serious art is quite incapable of maintaining its disciples, and will continue to be so until the government can appreciate how unjust and hateful the situation is at present." As he grew older, Berlioz became more impatient, not only with the philistine public, but also with the diplomacy that was necessary in dealing with the Department of Fine Arts : the manoeuvring in which he excelled in his youth became utterly distasteful to him—and rightly so, for one would scarcely expect a man of his genius to have enjoyed toadying to civil servants. In another letter to Ferrand, dated January 31st 1840, he says that he is so dreadfully melancholy that he feels quite indifferent towards everything. "What is going to happen to me ? In all probability nothing."

This sudden despondency seems a little unjustified for although he had in the past been subject to fits of depression—like most highly temperamental, artistic persons—conditions could not have been anything like so black as he tried to paint them. A few months after he had written the letter above, M. de Rémusat, who had succeeded de Gasparin as Minister of the Interior, commissioned him to write a symphony for the tenth anniversary of the 1830 Revolution, when certain relics were to be transferred to the monument that had been erected in the Place de la Bastille. The sum of ten thousand francs was offered, out of which the composer had to pay the cost of copying and the expenses of the first performance.

The *Grande Symphonie funèbre et triomphale*, as it was called, was scored at first for the·massed military bands that took part in this festival on July 28th, but shortly afterwards Berlioz re-scored it adding strings and a chorus. The best performance at that time was the general rehearsal held in the Salle Vivienne : a concert manager who generally made use of that hall was present and arranged with the composer for two further performances to be given there. Both were financially successful, and at one of them the younger members of the audience were so thrilled that in order to add to the volume of their applause they began smashing the chairs against the floor : a novel method of acclamation that embittered the proprietor.

VJ

In the autumn of 1841 Berlioz became acquainted with a twenty-seven-year-old singer who called herself Marie Recio, though her proper name was Marie Geneviève Martin. Through his influence she obtained an engagement at the Opéra and made her début as Ines in *La Favorite*. Later, she played the part of the page in *Comte Ory*, and Berlioz, in his review, not only praised her but mentioned her wonderful figure. This started a scandal on the lines that this very attractive half-Spanish girl was repaying the composer for his assistance in the way that is foremost in the minds of the gossips. Whether there was any definite liaison between them at the time is doubtful, but Harriet, who had already become an extremely embittered woman, for her physical charms had declined almost as quickly as her reputation as an actress, made an appalling scene. For some months she had been drinking more than is good for a woman, and her general instability was conducive to a fury of jealousy that caused her to spy upon her husband, to intercept his correspondence, and to indulge in all the other little practices with which a suspicious wife can irritate a man. She was infuriated, too, because her husband's extraordinary passion for her had burnt itself out and had been replaced by genial companionship; she could not understand that this was a normal process. It can therefore be readily understood that Berlioz, finding his home intolerable, was obliged to separate from her. He went to live with Marie, and thus had two homes to keep.

In March 1842 Cherubini died, and Berlioz hoped to be elected to the Académie des Beaux-Arts in his place, but George Onslow was appointed : a mediocre composer now forgotten by most people. He then tried for an appointment as inspector of music in the schools, but was again passed over. These two humiliations convinced him that he would never be honoured in France until other countries had recognized him, so he went to Brussels with Marie Recio and gave two concerts there. Neither met with much success, for the receipts only just covered the expenses, so he resolved to try his fortune in Germany.

With Marie—who was later to become more of a nuisance than a companion when concerts had to be arranged—he set out from Paris early in December 1842, and proceeded by way of Brussels, Mayence and Frankfurt-on-Main to Stuttgart. At Frankfurt, by the way, he attended a performance of *Fidelio* at which barely a dozen members of the audience bothered to applaud.

His first concert in Germany was given on December 29th at Stuttgart. At the first rehearsal he was amazed to find that the orchestra there could play his *Symphonie fantastique* and *Francs-Juges* overture correctly at sight. The performance itself was rather less satisfactory owing to the absence, through illness, of several of the violins, yet it was a considerable success artistically, and although little money was made, a very favourable impression was made upon the King of Wurtemberg, who, contrary to custom, had been present with all his court.

The most important outcome of this concert was the invitation he received from the Prince of Hechingen. The fulfilment of this meant a journey into the Black Forest, but a hearty welcome awaited him in the little town from which the Prince derived his title, for there he renewed acquaintance with Täglichsbeck, the conductor of the Prince's private orchestra at the Villa Eugenia, whom he had known in Paris. The orchestra was so small that only excerpts from his works could be played, but he won the life-long affection of the Prince, who from that time did his best to arouse interest in the music of Berlioz.

The next concert was given at Mannheim, and then Berlioz went to Weimar alone, hoping to escape for a while from Marie, who, much to his embarrassment, always insisted on singing at his concerts. She had a very inferior voice, and the last thing he wanted to do was to inflict her upon the none-too-eager audiences. However, she discovered his destination and followed him. A concert was given there that was most successful in spite of Marie's three solos.

Mendelssohn heartily disliked the music of Berlioz, but he received the French composer cordially when he visited Leipzig. Arriving in the middle of the final rehearsal of Mendelssohn's latest work, the *Walpurgis Night*, Berlioz was greatly impressed by the Gewandhaus, the superb orchestra and excellent chorus. He congratulated Mendelssohn afterwards and asked him to give him his baton as a souvenir. He agreed readily—on condition that Berlioz would give him his. Berlioz sent his stick on the following day with a letter that ran: "Great Chief! We have promised to exchange tomahawks. Mine is a rough one: yours is plain. Only squaws and pale-faces like ornate weapons . . . when the Great Spirit sends us to hunt in the land of souls, may our warriors hang up our tomahawks together at the door of the council-chamber." The concert took place on February 4th (1843), the *Symphonie fantastique* and the two overtures *Francs-Juges* and *Le Roi Lear* being the principal items. The leader of the

Gewandhaus orchestra, Ferdinand David, played the violin solo
Rêverie et caprice very beautifully, and (inevitably) Marie sang very
badly. The reception was mixed, for the reactionaries had already
convinced themselves that any man who could dare to demand a larger
orchestra than that used by Beethoven must be a fraud. The
Allgemeine musikalische Zeitung commented upon the composer's love
of the macabre, adding that in comparison with the "Sabbath" of the
Symphonie fantastique, Weber's scene in the Wolf's Glen would seem
like a cradle song. Berlioz did not write to please his audience, the
paper declared ; his fantasy was a law unto itself.

A charity concert was given in Leipzig shortly afterwards, at which,
among other things, the *Offertorium* from the *Requiem* was performed.
Robert Schumann was present at the rehearsal and declared that it
"surpassed everything" ; a remark that delighted Berlioz. Marie had
to sing *Absence*.

On February 6th Berlioz went on to Dresden, where he met Richard
Wagner, who had just been appointed Kapellmeister to the Royal
Court Theatre, and who assisted him in giving his first concert in the
city. The two composers never seemed to understand each other
properly : it is significant that Wagner had a great admiration for
the French composer and his works despite Berlioz's "displeasing
character." At the concert, Lipinski played the viola part in a
memorable performance of *Harold en Italie*.

At Brunswick, Berlioz met with the full force of German musical
enthusiasm, in fact during the *Orgie des brigands* (the last movement
of *Harold en Italie*) the orchestra responded with such verve that he
thought they had gone quite mad : the brass seemed to be blaring out
an accompaniment of curses and blasphemies to the strings' diabolical
frenzy ; the oboes, clarinets and flutes ran riot in their Rabelaisian
mirth, the bassoons contributed ungentlemanly noises, while the percussion completed the pandemonium. It was perfect. Berlioz told
them afterwards that they were the most successful brigands he had
ever met. The concert was one of the greatest triumphs of his career,
and it is said that even Marie's songs drew an encore. This success
was then repeated at Hamburg at the Opera house on March 22nd.

Proceeding to Berlin towards the end of March, he discovered that
the Opera house there had one of the best orchestras of its kind he had
ever known. It had fourteen first and the same number of second
violins, eight violas, ten 'cellos, eight double-basses, four flutes, and the
same number of oboes, clarinets, bassoons, horns, trumpets and

trombones. The ensemble also had harps and a good "kitchen" of percussion instruments. The highly trained chorus of sixty was doubled for grand performances before the King of Prussia, who took a keen interest in all the arts. Berlioz gave two magnificent concerts in April in the presence of the King ; the performance of his *Requiem* was so profoundly moving that his knees were knocking together with "nerves" as he conducted it.

On the way to Hanover he was suspected of being an impostor when he registered his luggage : the officials could not believe that one who was so obviously a man of very slender means (his luggage was very shabby) could be the great French composer. Little did they realize how microscopic were (and still are) the world's rewards to its artists.

The concert at Hanover on May 6th was an artistic success, but the receipts were very poor. He then went on to Darmstadt, gave a final concert there, and returned to Paris at the end of the month.

VII

Berlioz was confident that the news of his successes in Germany, of the cordial receptions he had received, of the kindness shown to him by royalty, and of the German audiences' appreciation of his works, would turn the hearts of his fellow-countrymen, and would at least give him the status he deserved. But a bitter disappointment was waiting for him : his position was scarcely altered. Money problems continued to harass him, and there was nothing to do but to return to journalism. How he loathed it ! His brain was full of music to be written : music to lift the hearts of men out of the shadows of the dull grey world, yet he had to stifle it and attend dreary concerts so that he could write useless newspaper articles about mediocre artists. Appointments that would have removed his financial anxiety and provided him with a little leisure in which to compose were given to musical nonentities, while he, one of the few truly great musicians the world possessed at that time, was passed over.

Determined to continue the struggle, he gave a concert of his own works at the Conservatoire on November 19th, making a profit of about five hundred francs. He also spent much of his time in writing a book on orchestration[1] that was published in the following spring.

[1] *Traité d'instrumentation.*

In January 1844 he wrote a work that was later to take his name to every corner of the earth : the *Carnaval romain* overture,[1] a fascinating piece of music that never fails to delight the audiences of the present day. It was first performed at the Salle Herz on February 3rd, and was enthusiastically received, an encore being demanded.

In the summer of that year he met Johann Strauss (the elder[2]), a conductor of considerable fame in the fashionable ballrooms of Vienna, and they discussed the possibility of giving a musical festival at the close of the Industrial Exhibition then in progress. Strauss secured the permission of M. Sénac, Secretary to the Minister of Trade, and plans were made for a concert, a ball and a banquet, which might have brought them both a handsome profit, but M. Delessert, the Prefect of Police promptly squashed the project. Berlioz got his influential friend M. Bertin to appeal to the Minister of the Interior, and as a result the Prefect was instructed to permit two concerts.

It was agreed that the first should be a grand concert under Berlioz, and that the second should be a "popular" concert when Strauss and his dance orchestra would play waltzes, polkas and whatnot. Dancing was forbidden, so the promoters had to lose a considerable slice of their profits on the second concert. Berlioz, who always loved everything on a grand scale, scoured all over Paris for talent, and eventually engaged no less than one thousand and twenty-two performers. He then drew up a programme that included the Scherzo and Finale from the Beethoven Fifth Symphony, Weber's overture to *Der Freischütz*, a chorus from *Les Huguenots* (Meyerbeer), the pleasure-garden scene from Gluck's *Armide*, and a few works of his own : the *Marche au supplice* from the *Fantastique*, the Apotheosis from his *Symphonie funèbre et triomphale*, and the *Hymne à la France*, composed for the occasion.

Rehearsals had to be sectional, of course, until the final one, and we are told that in the Beethoven Scherzo the thirty-six double-basses sounded like an army of angry grunting pigs ! Those who undertake the organisation of concerts in this country will know from bitter experience what preliminary work is entailed in the arrangement of even a modest-sized musical festival. Berlioz apparently took on this

---

1 Composed as the overture to the second act of *Benvenuto Cellini*, written several years previously.

2 This Johann Strauss (1804-1849) was the father of the Johann Strauss (1825-1899) whose waltzes are still popular today. The latter had two brothers Joseph (1825-1870) and Eduard (1835-1916). Eduard had a son, Johann, born in 1866, who died in 1939. They all propagated the Viennese waltz.

gargantuan task single-handed. On the eve of the final rehearsal he was horrified to discover that the greater part of the hall was still occupied by the huge machines that had been on exhibition. Frantic efforts to secure the removal of the monsters met with no success, and he was almost at his wits' end, when Strauss, who was afraid that the agitated composer would cancel everything, undertook to have the hall cleared within twenty-four hours.

The final rehearsal took place to the accompaniment of the removal of machinery, and at the conclusion Berlioz was unanimously assured by various friends who had been listening from the body of the hall, that the orchestra had been completely drowned by the chorus. Sixty carpenters had to be called in immediately. They cut the platform into two parts, and then lowered the portion reserved for the singers.

With this last difficulty surmounted, Berlioz and Strauss made a tour of the concert agents to find out how many tickets had been sold. Rapid calculations were then made, and to their horror they found that the total sales would not defray even half of their expenses! They both felt slightly faint, for the prospect of making up the deficit out of their own pockets did not bear contemplation. Withdrawal was out of the question, and they could do nothing but indulge in a fervent hope that a substantial sum would be taken at the doors.

When the huge body of performers took their places on the following afternoon,[1] Berlioz, keyed up as usual with "concert fever", forgot all about deficits and made up his mind to enjoy a feast of fine music. Just as they were about to commence, an enormous crowd surged into the hall, filling it to capacity. The concert was one of the greatest musical triumphs the French capital had ever known: imagine the effect of twenty-four horns in the overture to Der Freischütz, and twenty-five harps in the prayer from Rossini's Moïse! The consecration of the poignards from Les 'Huguenots made a deep impression upon both performers and audience. As for Berlioz, his teeth were chattering all the way through, and he was so overcome by his emotions at the end of the chorus that he had to retire from his rostrum for a few minutes to compose himself and change his clothes.

After such a wonderful concert it was a great disappointment to discover that when all the expenses had been met, the net profit for Berlioz—the remuneration for the phenomenal amount of work he had put into it—amounted to precisely eight hundred francs![2] He

1 August 1st.
2 This is the figure he gives in his Mémoires, but there is evidence that he probably received a great deal more. When speaking of the ingratitude of the public he often minimized his receipts.

consoled himself with the thought that perhaps a grateful public would repay him in other ways, but he was doomed to disappointment. It is true that he received a beautiful porcelain vase from the Duc de Montpensier.

His intense activity at this time soon had an adverse effect upon his health. He happened to meet Dr. Amussat, the professor of anatomy he had known in his student days, and the friendly physician was deeply shocked at his appearance. He told Berlioz that he was completely exhausted and on the verge of typhoid fever. Then he bled him and sent him to Nice to recuperate, and while he was there he wrote the *Corsair* overture, which was originally entitled *La Tour de Nice*. At about the same time a selection of his articles entitled *Voyage musical en Allemagne et en Italie* was published, and a note might also be made of the start of his friendship with Gl nka, the Russian composer, who came to Paris that year. Glinka founid Berlioz to be "an eccentric character" and admired his amazing inventive power in the realm of fantasy.

Berlioz was then obliged to resign himself to a life-long struggle for money, the greater part of which had to be earned as a musical journalist. This was no doubt very galling to a man of his genius, but it had its compensations, as for instance when he was sent to Bonn in August 1845 by the *Journal des Débats* for the inauguration of the Beethoven memorial, which had been erected chiefly by the efforts of Liszt. The Festival, at which the King of Prussia, Queen Victoria and Prince Albert were present, was a great delight to him : he heard the Fifth and Ninth symphonies, the *Missa Solennis*, part of *Fidelio*, and Liszt playing the E-flat Concerto.

When he returned to Paris he was able to start making arrangements for his first tour of Austria. *La Damnation de Faust* was commenced at this time, a work based on his *Huit scènes de Faust*, which occupied him throughout the tour. Marie Recio had to accompany him of course.

He gave three concerts at Vienna during November (1845) in the fine Salle des Redoutes, conducting at the desk at which Beethoven had stood. At the conclusion of the third concert a supper-party was held in his honour, during which he was presented with a beautiful silver-gilt baton inscribed with the names of the donors and wreathed with laurel leaves bearing the titles of his principal works. The Emperor sent him a gift of over a thousand francs with a note saying that he had been "amused" by his compositions : a compliment not intended to be ambiguous. Incidentally, Berlioz met several writers there who, like himself, were labouring on the "rough and stony soil of criticism" and producing little but "thistles and nettles". Other concerts were then given in Prague, Budapest, Breslau and Brunswick, most of them quite satisfactory, but of no great importance to this biography. He returned to Paris with Marie in the last week of April 1846.

A festival was held at Lille a couple of months later to mark the opening of the French Northern Railway. For this, Berlioz wrote a cantata entitled *Le Chant des chemins de fer* (The Song of the Railways), which was performed on June 14th.

His next important task was to arrange the first performance of *The Damnation of Faust*, which he completed on October 19th. He knew it would be useless to offer it to the Opéra, and had very little money to pay for a performance himself, yet he was determined to bring this work out. With the success of his *Romeo and Juliet* in mind he was led to believe that perhaps the Parisians had at last learnt to appreciate him, and that he might at least cover his expenses if he undertook the risk himself. He booked the Opéra-Comique at the extortionate price of sixteen hundred francs, and was obliged to pay heavily for the copying of the parts. Two performances were given, one on December 6th, and the other a fortnight later. Both were a complete failure: a fall of snow evidently chilled off what little enthusiasm the notices had aroused. The poor composer was ruined. A deficit of nearly ten thousand francs swallowed up everything he possessed and put him heavily in debt. The indifference to his music was bad enough, but the terrible debt as well very nearly crushed him. For two days he cursed the Parisians vehemently in his anguish. The bitterness that from time to time had provoked his castigations of the so-called musical public now overwhelmed him.

Reflection upon the more happy incidents in this biography is apt to make one wonder whether Berlioz was unreasonable in his indignation. An artist's life is generally one of vicissitudes, if not of prolonged despair. Berlioz enjoyed many great successes, and had the advantage of wealthy, influential and sympathetic friends. Did he expect too much? His *Mémoires* contain many facts that, if true, would justify his embittered outlook. There was a Superintendent of Fine Arts, for instance, who on complimenting Cherubini on one of his masses added that it was a pity he hadn't written any operas! Considering the prestige that this composer enjoyed in his day, it was rather like telling

Bernard Shaw that he ought to try his hand at play-writing. Another assertion equally astonishing is that Habeneck used only a first violin part when conducting at the Conservatoire, and that all his successors for years were equally as contemptuous of the full score. If these facts were not mere products of Berlioz's fertile imagination, he had some justification for his acrimonious attacks upon the musical institutions and the reactionary cliques.

How was he to extricate himself from this heavy debt ? The only course open to him was to gamble upon another foreign tour : he decided to visit Russia. Various friends gave him financial assistance, and with an advance of a thousand francs from the *Journal des Débats* he left Paris on February 14th 1847. Snow was falling heavily, and it took him a fortnight to reach St. Petersburg.

His first concert in Russia was given on March 15th, a magnificent affair due chiefly to the kind co-operation of Henri Romberg, the conductor of the Italian Theatre in St. Petersburg. Berlioz need scarcely have asked the King of Prussia for an introduction to his sister, the Empress of Russia, for the court gave him a most cordial reception. The programme included the *Carnaval romain* overture, the first two parts of *Faust* and the Apotheosis from the *Symphonie funèbre et triomphale*. This new, daring music had a wonderful effect upon the audience, and their delight was reflected in the financial result : twelve thousand francs clear profit. Berlioz could scarcely believe his ears. He turned in the direction of Paris and exclaimed : "Ah, *dear* Parisians ! " Another concert ten days later brought results equally as good, and among the many tributes, a letter in the newspapers from Prince Odoïewsky, who declared : "What a joy it was to hear for a second time this music of genius ! "

A four-day journey then took him to Moscow, where he found a poor standard of musicianship among the orchestra but boundless enthusiasm in the audience. A concert on April 10th brought a profit of eight thousand francs and a report in the *Gazette de Moscou* proclaiming that this "extraordinary music" contained the germ of the unknown future of the art.

Returning to St. Petersburg he found a magnificent body of singers waiting to rehearse his *Roméo et Juliette* at the Grand Theatre. When he asked how many rehearsals he could call he was told "As many as you like" : a reply as sweet as any music to one about to conduct his own work. The concert, on April 23rd, was patronized by the *élite*. Every detail of the music was performed with such care and sympathy

33

that at the end the composer fled from his rostrum and cried with joy "like a hysterical schoolgirl" for a quarter of an hour.

Most curious is the fact that at the various concerts he gave in St. Petersburg, the *Carnaval romain* overture, which had already conquered Vienna, made very little impression. Count Wielhorski, an accomplished musician who had been extremely enthusiastic about Berlioz's music, confessed that he did not "understand" it !

Berlioz left Russia during the second week in May with something like fifteen thousand francs in hand, and instead of returning straight to Paris went to Berlin at the invitation of the King of Prussia, who wanted to hear *The Damnation of Faust*, and who had offered the Opera house and half of the gross receipts as an inducement to the composer. After a fortnight's preparation, the performance took place on June 19th, but at first neither the musicians nor the audience were in the mood for revolutionary French music wedded to the poetry of Goethe. Later, when an encore was demanded, Berlioz was too annoyed to give it. Nevertheless, the King was impressed, and entertained him afterwards like a dear old friend.

VIII

Soon after his return to Paris, Berlioz received an invitation from Louis Jullien, who had become director of London's famous Drury Lane Theatre, to accept an appointment as conductor of opera at a salary of forty thousand francs a year. He accepted it and came to London on November 5th (1847), taking apartments first at 76 Harley Street, and later at 26 Osnaburgh Street, Regent's Park.

Jullien was a musical speculator who had made quite a lot of money by giving popular concerts in London : he fancied himself as a conductor of the vulgar "showman" type, and loved conducting monster orchestras with an elaborately jewelled baton. It was generally brought to him on a silver salver by a flunkey. When he started dabbling in opera he had wildly ambitious ideas of establishing Grand English Opera at Drury Lane. He engaged a good orchestra and chorus, and passable principals, but then discovered that the building of a repertoire was not a matter to be accomplished in a couple of weeks. They opened with Donizetti's *Lucia di Lammermoor*, with John Sims Reeves as the principal tenor. It was all very extravagant and resulted in a heavy loss. This was followed by Balfe's *Maid of Honour* and another of Donizetti's operas *Linda di Chamouni*, and the finances went from bad to worse. Berlioz received his first month's salary, and nothing more. He gave a concert of his own works on February 7th 1848, playing the *Carnaval romain* overture, *Harold en Italie*, excerpts from his *Faust* and the *Requiem*, the overture to *Benvenuto Cellini*, and the Apotheosis from the *Symphonie funèbre*, but very little, if any, of the profit found its way into his own pocket. The press gave very favourable reports of it.

On February 22nd he presided at the annual dinner of the Royal Society of Musicians at the Freemasons' Hall, but on that same day his anxieties were increased by the news of the revolution that had broken out in Paris. His chances of making a reasonable income in the city he loved seemed more remote than ever. Jullien was on the verge of bankruptcy. Utterly dejected, the unfortunate composer started to write his *Mémoires*.

Jullien calmly disappeared from London in June, and in the hope of making a little money, Berlioz gave a concert on the 29th of that month at the Hanover Square Rooms, but the receipts provided little profit, though once again the critics were most enthusiastic. He returned to Paris shortly afterwards, poor and disillusioned, with four people to support : his wife, Harriet, who had become paralysed, his son, Marie Recio and her mother. There was no alternative but to return to journalism.

About a week after his arrival in Paris he heard of the death of his father, and as soon as he recovered from the blow he decided to visit the Côte-Saint-André to see his sisters. From there he went to Grenoble to see his grandfather's house at Meylan. "I was longing to see again the scene of my first passion :[1] I wanted to embrace my whole past, to intoxicate myself with memories, however sad they might be. My sisters remained at the Côte, knowing that I wished to be alone on this sacred pilgrimage, which was bound to stir in me emotions too sacred for the eyes of even my nearest and dearest. I feel my heart throbbing at the very thought of relating the history of that excursion. But I will do so, if only to prove the persistence of old feelings, seemingly so irreconcilable with the new, and the reality of their co-existence in a heart that can forget nothing."

He arrived on a serenely beautiful autumn morning and found the house empty : it had been sold to a farmer who lived in a new building nearby. The door was not locked, so he entered and went into the *salon*, where the family used to gather : it was just as he had always

[1] His infatuation for Estelle.

known it . . . there were the same pictures, the same articles of furniture. Everything was unchanged. His grandfather's chair stood in its usual place, and on the sideboard there was still the wickerwork basket that he (Berlioz) had made as a boy. It was there that he had seen his uncle waltzing with the beautiful Estelle . . .

With a heavy heart he walked out into the orchard, and found that half of it had been ploughed up. But over there was the field of maize into which he had rushed for consolation when he had tried to stifle his feverish longing for Estelle. There was the tree in whose shade he had read Cervantes. He stood in silent contemplation for a while and then turned back.

Then he tried to find the house in which Estelle had lived, but lost his way, and had to enquire of some farm labourers engaged in threshing. The men shook their heads, but the wife of one of them suddenly recalled Madame Gautier and the younger granddaughter "so pretty that people used to stop at the church door on Sundays to see her pass". She indicated the way to the house, adding that it was now the property of a Grenoble tradesman.

Berlioz followed her directions. "Soon I heard the murmur of the fountain . . . there I was . . . God! how the air intoxicated me! My head was turning! I stopped for a while to steady my throbbing heart . . . I reached the avenue gate . . . A gentleman—doubtless the prosaic owner of that sanctuary—stood there, lighting a cigar. He stared at me in astonishment. I passed on without a word."

Stopping a little higher up the slope, Berlioz turned round and meditated upon the scene " . . . the sacred house, the garden, the trees, the valley below, the winding Isère, the Alps, the snow, the glaciers— all that she saw and loved. I inhaled the blue air that she had breathed . . . A cry, that no mortal tongue could translate, is repeated by the echo of St. Eynard. The past is now before me, I can see it again and adore. I am once again a boy of twelve—life, beauty, first love, infinite poetry, these are mine! I knelt, and cried aloud to the valley, to the mountains and to the skies: 'Estelle! Estelle! Estelle! I clasped the earth in a convulsive embrace . . . a sense of indescribable desolation welled up within me. . . . "

On the following day, at Grenoble, the strange, preoccupied demeanour of Berlioz aroused the curiosity of his cousin Victor. After persistent interrogation the composer explained the purpose of his pilgrimage on the previous day, adding that the consuming love of his childhood still possessed him.

"You idiot ! " Victor laughed. "Estelle is now fifty-one : she has a son of twenty-two. I studied law with him."

"Where is she now ? " the composer demanded.

"Since the death of her husband she has been living at Vif."

"Vif ! How far is it from here ? "

"About ten miles."

"I must go and see her."

"You will make a fool of yourself."

"I will first write to her."

Berlioz did not sign the letter with his name, and it was some time before Estelle entered into the curious relationship with him that to some extent alleviated the bitterness of his closing years.

IX

HE returned to Paris in September 1848, and as his father's estate could not be realized immediately, he had to wait some time for the share that eventually removed his financial anxieties. A government threat to discontinue the subsidies of the Conservatoire was successfully countered by the eloquence of Victor Hugo and other enlightened individuals, and Berlioz was allowed to retain his post of librarian. He was of course still obliged to continue his journalism, though he found time in 1849 to compose a *Te Deum*. This was not performed until 1855.

During the year 1850 he wrote the chorus *L'Adieu des bergers* under the pseudonym "Pierre Ducré", and deceived most of the critics with an assurance that it had first been performed in the year 1677. It was later embodied into a sacred trilogy *L'Enfance du Christ*. In the same year he founded a Philharmonic Society, but it was never given adequate support, and collapsed after a while.

He was very much encouraged when during the following year, Liszt wrote asking for the score of *Benvenuto Cellini*, which he hoped to produce at Weimar. The performance did not take place until March 20th 1852, when Berlioz was on his way to London to conduct the first concert of the New Philharmonic Society (founded by Cramer and others) at Exeter Hall on the 24th. The first four parts of *Roméo et Juliette* were the chief attraction on this occasion.

Liszt sprang another pleasant surprise upon him when, following the success of *Benvenuto Cellini*, he invited him to Weimar for a "Berlioz Week" in the following November. It was like a short spell of sunshine on a wintry world. Berlioz had the joy of conducting a superb performance of *Roméo et Juliette* in its entirety, and the first two parts of his *Faust* ; but better still, perhaps, the pleasure of seeing the Grand Duke and Duchess and a distinguished audience that included many of Germany's greatest musicians fervently applauding the second production of *Benvenuto Cellini* under Liszt's able direction.

But the hopes that this week raised were soon to be dashed to the ground. The same opera was mounted at Covent Garden during the next summer, and the Londoners were misled by its title into thinking that it was a work in the traditional Italian style. Their disappointment was such that the opera had to be withdrawn on the second day.

The serious consequences of his poverty—as far as the world of art is concerned—is brought home to us by his own admission[1] that at about this time he deliberately stifled the urge to write another symphony. It is curious to note that the themes for this occurred to him in a dream, but he woke with them still quite clear in his memory. He went to his desk to write them down, but stopped and reasoned thus : "This would be a large scale work which would take three or four months to write. I should become too engrossed in it to write any articles, and therefore my income would be insufficient. I should incur a heavy debt in having the parts copied out, and a still greater one in having the work performed. My wife is an invalid and needs money . . . therefore I cannot afford to write this symphony."

On the next night he had the same dream again, and heard the symphony in even more detail than previously. He awoke, and in feverish enthusiasm went to his desk to record the themes he had heard. Then he recalled the deliberations of the day before, and checked himself. He went back to his bed, and in the morning the symphony had vanished entirely from his memory. Never again did as much as a single phrase of it enter into his consciousness. What this loss meant to Berlioz—particularly when later his circumstances improved—we shall never know, but it was yet another contributory cause to those outbursts of bitterness that became more and more frequent as his genius matured.

Towards the close of 1853 he toured Brunswick, Hanover, Bremen and Leipzig, where he conducted two concerts at the Gewandhaus in the presence of many eminent musicians, including Liszt and the twenty-year-old Johannes Brahms. While he was receiving the acclamations of the leaders of German culture, the Academicians of Paris took the opportunity of appointing a musician named Clappison

[1] In his *Mémoires.*

to the vacancy at the Académie des Beaux-Arts caused by the death of Onslow. Berlioz had again been a candidate. Oh, Jerusalem, Jerusalem . . . !

His wife, Harriet, died on March 3rd 1854, and he was overwhelmed with a sense of sorrow that her later years should have been so unhappy. This provoked another outburst in his *Mémoires* : "Shakespeare, Shakespeare ! where art thou ? He alone, of all intelligent beings, could have understood me. . . . Only he could have looked with sympathy upon two poor artists, at once loving and lacerating each other. Shakespeare, the true man, if he is still in existence, must know how to succour the distressed. He is our father in heaven—if there is a heaven. An almighty being, wrapped in infinite indifference, is an atrocious absurdity. Shakespeare alone is the good God to the soul of the artist. Receive us into thy bosom, O father, and hide us there. *De profundis ad te clamo* ! Death, annihilation, what are they ? The immortality of genius—what is it ? "

Later he goes on : "If I am not at the end of my career, I am on the last steep decline—exhausted, consumed, but ever ardent . . . I adore and venerate all forms of art. . . . But I belong to a nation that has ceased to be interested in the nobler manifestations of the mind, whose only deity is the golden calf, . . . a barbarous people. In ten rich houses you will scarcely find a single library . . . books are no longer bought. Miserable novels are hired from the circulating libraries : . . . such is the literary food of all classes of society. Similarly, people subscribe a few francs a month to the music shop in order to select from the vulgar rubbish of today some masterpiece of the type that Rabelais has characterized by a contemptuous epithet."

The year 1854 is also notable for a successful visit to Hanover and Dresden in the spring, the composition of *L'Enfance du Christ*, and on October 19th his marriage to Marie Recio.

The first performance of *L'Enfance du Christ* on December 10th was a great success, but the composer was irritated by idiotic reviews declaring that he must have "mended his ways". This work was repeated several times during the ensuing six months.

Liszt's admiration for Berlioz was shown again in the following February when he arranged a fortnight's festival of the French composer's works at Weimar. *L'Enfance du Christ, Lélio ; ou le Retour à la vie* and extracts from *Roméo et Juliette, Benvenuto Cellini* and *Faust* were given with great success, and while he was there, Berlioz made a promise to Princess Sayn-Wittgenstein to write a large-scale opera based on the second and fourth books of Virgil's *Æneid*. He began work on this, *Les Troyens*, as soon as he got back to Paris. It took three-and-a-half years to complete. Liszt was at that time trying to bring Berlioz and Wagner together, for he believed that mutual help would be a great advantage to both of them. His efforts never really succeeded, for Berlioz was not particularly impressed with Wagner's work, and doubted the sincerity of the German composer's proffered friendship. However, they met several times when they were in London during the summer of 1855 : Berlioz had been engaged to conduct some concerts for the New Philharmonic Society, and Wagner was doing likewise for the older society. After this, Wagner assured Liszt that their relationship was "cordial and profound", in which case it was a pity he didn't make a better effort to understand the French composer and his works before making stupid criticisms of the latter.

The great *Te Deum* for solo voices, chorus and orchestra, commenced in 1849, was given its first performance in the church of Saint-Eustache, Paris, on April 30th 1855, and published shortly afterwards. Another work completed at about this time was the cantata *L'Impériale* (formerly called *Le Dix Décembre*). It was given at one of the concerts held in the Palace of Industry in November 1855, but was interrupted in the middle because Napoleon III wished to make a speech, and thought the music was going on too long !

Much to his surprise, Berlioz was elected to membership of the Académie des Beaux-Arts on June 21st 1856. One could not have blamed him if he had treated this belated recognition with contempt. Actually, he accepted it quite amicably, and frankly acknowledged the pleasure it gave him to associate with the other members.

Slight improvement in his financial position allowed him to spend much of his time during the next few years on *Les Troyens*. It was completed in 1859, but not produced until 1863. On that occasion, only the second part was performed (*Les Troyens à Carthage*), at the Théâtre-Lyrique, and innumerable cuts were made on the insistence of Carvalho, the director. It ran for twenty-one nights, and although Berlioz was disappointed with the production, his royalties were considerable, and having also sold pianoforte arrangements of it to publishers in Paris and London, he found himself in a position to resign his post on the *Journal des Débats*.

His last composition was the two-act opéra-comique *Béatrice et Bénédict*, written during the years 1860 to 1863. It was commissioned by Bénazet for the opening of his new theatre at Baden, and was first performed there on August 9th 1862. This comic opera, based on Shakespeare's *Much Ado about Nothing*, was a great success, and after its translation into German by Richard Pohl, Berlioz was invited to conduct the first two performances at Weimar, where it was produced at the request of the Grand Duchess in April 1863.

X

Berlioz's second marriage lasted only eight years : Marie died in June 1862, aged forty-eight. It appears that he found consolation with another young woman—only about twenty-six years of age—named Amélie. Referring to this extraordinary affair in a letter to Ferrand, he declares that she brought her love to him unsought, and that for a while he resisted. Later, he says, his loneliness got the better of him, and the need of somebody's love became so pressing that he submitted to her tenderness. Eventually he became the more active of the two, and a "final separation" became necessary. The young lady died shortly afterwards.

One of the worst moods of depression he had ever known came upon him in the autumn of 1864, and he found himself longing to revisit the scenes of his childhood, particularly to see again that house of memories at Meylan. This he did, but whereas during his former visit he had contemplated it from afar, on this occasion he entered the garden, much to the surprise of an elderly lady he found there. He explained that he had been there as a boy forty-nine years ago, and was invited into the house. Everything was just as it had always been. "I made my escape sobbing".

He wrote to Estelle that evening from Lyons, asking if he might visit her. Somewhat reluctantly, for she was six years his senior, Madame Fornier (Estelle) received him. Despite the change wrought by nearly half a century, Berlioz recognized the woman he had loved so passionately. "My soul went out to its idol, as though she were still in her dazzling loveliness." She led him into the drawing room, but his heart was too full for speech. Conversation was extremely difficult, and Berlioz said very little, but at last he asked for her hand, and pressed it to his lips. He then begged her for permission to write to her, and to visit her occasionally.

This started a correspondence that lasted for some four or five years, and which was a great consolation to the composer. Indeed, her letters did more than anything to preserve his balance of mind during his last few years, for death struck down several of his other friends, and although occasional performances of his works were given in Paris, there was no change of heart towards him on the part of the French musical public. Shakespeare and Virgil continued to afford him great pleasure. His last visit to Estelle was on September 9th 1867.

His declining health did not prevent him from going to Vienna in December 1866 to conduct his *Faust* for the Gesellschaft der Musikfreunde. Here he was received with the honour he deserved. Likewise at Cologne, where he conducted his *Harold en Italie* and an excerpt from *Béatrice et Bénédict*.

In June 1867 another cruel blow fell upon him. His son Louis, who had spent most of his life at sea, died of yellow fever at Havana, aged only thirty-three. The young man had risen to the captaincy of a large ship, and was dearly loved by his father.

Berlioz was then suffering almost perpetually from intestinal neuralgia, yet in December of that year he went once again to Russia at the invitation of the Grand Duchess Helena. He conducted concerts in St. Petersburg and Moscow and was given a wildly enthusiastic reception in both cities. The orchestras were superb and the sound of his own music being played with such exquisite skill and understanding made him unconscious of the pain he was suffering all the while.

He returned to Paris almost exhausted, and then went to Nice and Monte Carlo. A cerebral congestion caused him to fall twice on the rocks at Monaco, and he was picked up by some workmen. After a week in bed at Nice he returned to Paris.

For a while he was able to continue his normal life in the capital, going periodically to the Académie, but was later confined to his room. His mother-in-law tended him faithfully, and some of his friends visited him regularly, but his pains grew worse, and he was obliged to take doses of opium to get relief. He became bedridden during the first few weeks of 1869, and died quietly on March 8th of that year.

Here is the epitaph he chose for himself, and with which he concluded his *Mémoires*.

> Life's but a walking shadow, a poor player
> That struts and frets his hour upon the stage,
> And then is heard no more : it is a tale
> Told by an idiot, full of sound and fury,
> Signifying nothing.
> (Macbeth)

THE MAJOR WORKS OF BERLIOZ

Although Shakespeare was the idol of Berlioz, Victor Hugo and his contemporaries were probably responsible for much of his love of wild and macabre subjects, and for the extravagant, richly-coloured and dramatic expression of his thoughts. The originality and power of his works cannot be denied, and his genius for orchestration is admitted even by those who dislike his music, but his intolerance of any sort of restraint upon his emotions allowed him to write passages here and there that, in the opinion of the more conventional, spoilt the construction of several of his most inspired and brilliant compositions. This will always be a matter for controversy. There is so much in his music that is really sublime that one finds it difficult to be patient with those critics who, though utterly unproductive themselves, pounce with glee upon some "technical fault" in the work of this genius, or hold some isolated passage up to ridicule as a "banality". Thirty or forty years ago there were critics who declared that the works of Berlioz would be forgotten within twenty-five years. Far from being forgotten, more and more of them are now being understood and appreciated, and would undoubtedly be performed more frequently if the tyranny of the box-office did not so often preclude the engagement of a very large orchestra. There are few lovers of music who cannot appreciate the colourful grandeur of Berlioz : it is a contribution to the art equally as important as the purity of Palestrina and Byrd, the delicacy of Mozart or the superb, logical "architecture" of Bach. It is really just another case of beauty being in the eye of the beholder.

The heart of Berlioz was in dramatic music, but his burning ambition to express himself through opera was frustrated by the iniquitous stupidity and jealousy of his contemporaries and by the pathetic ignorance of the bureaucracy and general public. Therefore his love of drama emerged even when he believed that he was developing the symphonic art of Beethoven. The poetic "programme" music of Berlioz is of course the very antithesis of the "pure" art of the symphony ; and we may well be thankful that it is, for his genius might have been utterly stultified if he had stifled his theatrical sense and tried to produce slavish imitations of Beethoven. Let us therefore accept his music for what it is—extravagance and all.

Symphonie fantastique

This *Épisode de la Vie d'un Artiste* is of course the best known of his greater works, and when one considers that he was only twenty-six when he wrote it, the skill displayed in it becomes all the more remarkable. It is in five movements portraying all the emotions of the artist, a scene at a ball, another in the fields, a march to the scaffold, and concluding with a wonderful scene of revelry at night. The third and fourth movements are based on material used in earlier compositions. The "story" is of an artist who finds a woman who fulfils his ideals of beauty and charm, and having long sought such a person, falls violently in love with her. To continue in the composer's own words[1]: "Curiously enough, the image of her never presents itself to his mind unless accompanied by a musical thought in which he discovers the same qualities of grace and nobility as those with which he has endowed his beloved. This double and fixed idea haunts him incessantly, and it is the reason of the constant appearance in all parts of the symphony, of the principal melody in the first *allegro* (1st movement).

"After long agitation, he discovers some grounds for hope, he believes himself beloved. He is in the country one day when he hears from afar two herdsmen singing a *ranz des vaches*, and their pastoral duet plunges him into a delightful reverie (3rd movement). The melody reappears for a moment through the themes of the *adagio*.

"Then he goes to a ball,[2] but the tumult of the fête is unable to distract him : his fixed idea still comes to disturb him, and the cherished melody makes his heart throb in the midst of a brilliant waltz (2nd movement).

"In a fit of despair, he poisons himself with opium, but instead of killing him, the narcotic produces a horrible dream, during which he imagines that he has killed his beloved, that he is condemned to death, and must witness his own execution. There is a march to the scaffold ; an immense procession of executioners, soldiers and people. At the end the melody appears once more, like a last thought of love, interrupted by the fatal blow (4th movement).

"He then sees himself surrounded by a disgusting crowd of sorcerers and devils, assembled to celebrate the night of revelry. They call him from afar. The melody, which up to this time has been one of grace, now appears as a trivial, ignoble, drunkard's song ; it is his loved one coming to the revels, to assist in the funeral *cortège* of her victim. She is now nothing but a courtesan, worthy of taking part in such an orgy. The ceremony commences : the bells toll, the infernal

---

[1] In a letter to a friend.

[2] This movement was afterwards placed before the scene in the fields.

elements prostrate themselves, a choir chants the *Dies Irae*, which is taken up by two other choirs who sing a parody of it in burlesque style ; finally, there is a whirl of revelry which mingles with the *Dies Irae* on reaching its climax, and the vision then concludes."

The opening *largo* of the first movement (*Rêveries : Passions*) is very beautiful ; a thoughtful prologue to the flood of emotions in the lively *allegro* that follows. The waltz in the second movement (*Un Bal*) has been held up as an example of the banalities one finds here and there in the music of Berlioz, but the vulgarity of it is quite justified as a contrast to the other material in the movement. The original theme (the "fixed idea" melody in the artist's mind) is cleverly woven into it, yet at the same time preserves its air of detachment.

Thoughts of love and hope, and gloomy forebodings characterize the slow third movement (*Scène aux champs*) ; it is heavily emotional, but most effective. The *Marche au supplice* of the fourth movement was adapted from material originally written for the opera *Les Francs-Juges* ; sinister and terrible, with an ugly crash as the knife of the guillotine falls.

The last movement (*Songe d'une nuit du sabbat*) is a horrible riot of clever orchestration, ugly and fantastic ; an extraordinarily successful picture in music even though the scene is not a pretty one.

Lélio ; ou le Retour à la Vie

This *mélologue* is the sequel to the *Symphonie fantastique*, but a work of greater eccentricity, indeed one writer has called it "the craziest work ever sketched out by a composer not actually insane". There is certainly a suggestion of madness in it, but there is also music in the madness, and some of it is very fine. There are six monologues spoken by Lélio, the artist who returns to life with the words "Dieu ! I still live. . . . Life, like a serpent, has crept back into my heart, to tear it afresh. . . ." These monologues are interspersed with six musical movements : (1) *Le Pêcheur*, a ballad for tenor, sung behind a curtain. The words are a translation of Goethe's *Der Fischer*. (2) *Chœur d'ombres*, sung with full orchestral accompaniment while Lélio reclines on a couch. (3) *Chanson des brigands*, a vivacious, virile song for baritone and male chorus, with orchestra. (4) *Chant de bonheur*, for tenor, harp and orchestra or strings and woodwind. A most beautiful movement. (5) *La Harpe éolienne—Souvenirs*, a strange, fascinating orchestral interlude. (6) *Fantaisie sur la 'Tempête' de Shakespeare*. This is for chorus, orchestra and four hands at the piano.

Some idea of the diversity of opinion on the value of this *mélologue* may be gained from the fact that one writer (W. J. Turner) refers to it as "this truly Berliozian masterpiece" while another (J. H. Elliot) describes it as "This incredible hotch-potch". The reader will of course form his own opinion—if he ever hears the work performed in its entirety, which is extremely unlikely in this country. The last movement is by far the finest, and is sometimes played as a separate piece. It is a perfect manifestation of the composer's profound adoration for Shakespeare.

Harold en Italie

This symphony is more mature and restrained than *Lélio*; it is a pictorial impression of what he saw in Italy and an expression of his feelings while he was there. The dramatic element in it is inevitable.

The first movement bears the title *Harold aux montagnes*: *scènes de mélancolie, de bonheur et de joie,* and opens with an extremely moving *adagio* expression of melancholy. The happiness and joy is expressed in a stimulating allegro. The whole movement is beautifully constructed, and the viola solo, when played properly, is wonderfully effective.

The second movement, *Marche des pèlerins,* incorporates a very pleasing pilgrims' evening hymn, first heard from the strings. Harold, represented by the viola, is introduced later by his own theme. The passing of the pilgrims while the two monastery bells toll in the distance makes a very realistic picture.

The third movement, *Sérénade d'un montagnard des Abruzzes à sa maîtresse,* is united to the others by the solo viola; a simple yet colourful movement with some fascinating experiments in rhythm.

The last movement, *Orgie des brigands,* is chiefly reminiscences of the previous scenes and the orgy of the brigands, during which the solo viola remains silent until almost the end of the symphony.

On the whole this is an attractive symphony, and much more use could be made of it in introducing the younger audiences of today to the works of this great composer. With the exception of the first movement, it is chiefly musical painting.

Benvenuto Cellini

The one weakness of this opera is its poor libretto. But for that it would probably have become well established in the repertoires of the leading companies of Europe and America. The splendid overture is now a favourite concert piece, and so of course is the vivid, exciting overture to the second act, *Carnaval romain*. The latter was composed at a later date—1844.

The scene of the first act is laid in the palace of Balducci, the papal treasurer, who is displeased at the favour shown by the Pope to Cellini. His young daughter Teresa, is drawn to the window by the singing of the merry-makers. Cellini is there, sends her a bouquet of flowers and later enters the room. They sing a duet, which is followed by a trio on the arrival of Fieramosca, a rival sculptor. When Balducci returns, Cellini escapes but the other artist is caught. The whole act is delightful, with gay animated music contrasting with the lovely *larghetto* cavatina sung by Teresa.

The long exhilarating second act takes us to the carnival in the Piazza Colonna. What a magnificent spectacle in music ! It is difficult to find anything more exciting than this dazzling, colourful act, yet with all its sparkling freshness there is a grace of movement that lends great charm to it as a whole.

In the third act we see Cellini's studio, where the great statue of Perseus is to be cast. Here, the rest of the drama takes place, with Cellini eventually winning the hand of Teresa, and the casting of the famous statue. The workmen in the foundry provide a chorus ; a lovely barcarolle is sung by Ascanio, a friend of Cellini ; there is a chorus sung by a religious procession which Teresa contemplates from the window, a charming, expressive duet by Cellini and Teresa, and a fine sextet. The finale, in which the cast is made, is appropriately impressive. This opera was originally in two acts, then it was divided into four when Liszt produced it at Weimar in 1852, and finally it was revised and converted into three acts. It was published as Opus 23 in 1856 and dedicated to the Grand Duchess of Weimar.

Grande Messe des morts (Requiem)

This mass is not a deeply religious work, for although the doctrine of the Catholic church stirred the composer's imagination, his personal faith was very vague. To him, death was something one thought about in melancholy despondence, and the after-life was the subject of fabulous dreams. Yet the soul of the composer as reflected in this Mass is that of a great philosopher : the whole work proclaims his genius. It is scored on such a large scale that few concert-giving organisations in this country could attempt to perform it, though it could be done very effectively under the auspices of the B.B.C. It requires a chorus of eighty sopranos and altos, sixty tenors and seventy basses, and an orchestra of fifty violins, twenty violas, twenty 'cellos, eighteen double basses, four flutes, two oboes, two cors anglais, eight bassoons, four clarinets, twelve horns, four cornets, twelve trumpets, sixteen trombones, six tubas, sixteen timpani, two bass drums, four gongs and five pairs of cymbals. The brass, with the exception of the horns, is divided into four sections.

The first movement, *Requiem et Kyrie*, is a profound, sombre piece with the voices woven in very beautifully. No one could fail to be moved by the effect of the plaintive unisons of the *Christe eleison* and *Kyrie eleison*. The *Dies Irae* is rather a curious movement that taxes the musicianship of the performers, but the *Tuba Mirum* is terribly impressive chiefly on account of the sheer weight of the artillery of brass brought into commission. The sixteen timpani provide a very realistic thunderclap. Then follows a curious little movement sung by the tenors (*Quid sum miser*) with a light accompaniment of wood-wind and strings, in which the *Dies Irae* theme still persists.

The brass comes in again for the grand *Rex tremendae* ; then we have a perfect contrast in the soft and beautiful unaccompanied six-part chorus *Quaerens me*. The *Lacrymosa* is a lament, elaborated rhythmically, which brings the brass and percussion in again.

The most pleasing part of the entire *Requiem* is perhaps the *Offertorium*, which made a great impression upon Schumann. It is chiefly an orchestral movement employing the voices in a lesser capacity, meditative in character. The *Hostias* contains some extraordinary but singularly effective experiments in orchestration, and the *Sanctus*, a graceful and uplifting movement, has an impressive fugue on the words "Hosanna in excelsis". The use made of the four solo violins, muted, is noteworthy.

Finally, the *Agnus Dei* makes use of material already introduced, but is enriched with some more remarkable orchestral effects. The work concludes with a serenely charming six-fold "Amen" accompanied by sustained chords on the wind instruments against graceful movements by the strings, with the timpani adding gentle taps to the bass.

Roméo et Juliette

This *Symphonie dramatique avec Chœurs, Solos de Chant et Prologue en récitatif choral*, as the composer called it, is nothing like a conventional symphony. It opens with a Prologue in which the combat between

Montagues and Capulets is represented, as well as the intervention of the Prince. Then follows "Romeo alone—Sadness—Concert and Ball —The Grand fête at the Capulets'." Here Berlioz excels himself in his musical portrayal of love, and it becomes progressively beautiful and passionate. We see the influence of Estelle : the loveliness he saw in her and the charm of Shakespeare's genius have combined to give us some of the most exquisite music in creation.

The *Scène d'amour* that follows is also extremely beautiful. Flutes and strings, and later the horns, play an *allegretto* introduction ; then this is followed by a distant chorus. In the love-scene itself both Romeo and Juliet are silent : their emotions being expressed solely by the instruments. Berlioz has himself explained this by saying that so many have attempted to express the lovers' feelings by duets that an effort to use a different mode of expression seemed necessary, "a tongue richer, more varied, less limited, and by its very vagueness incomparably more powerful in such circumstances". How well he has made his instruments tell of those ecstatic emotions that words can but inadequately describe ! Similarly, he has painted the serenity of night with gentle mysterious murmurs forming one of the most sublime conceptions the world of music has ever known.

Next, is the scherzo *Queen Mab, or the Dream Fairy*, a delightful contrast of the utmost delicacy glistening like a dewy spider's web in the early morning sun. Light touches of woodwind and percussion, ethereal harmonics on the strings and the contribution of the harps can give us a charming glimpse of fairyland, if played properly.

The *Convoi funèbre de Juliette* is best described in the composer's own words : "a fugal march, at first instrumental with a psalmody on a single note in the voices ; then vocal with the psalmody in the orchestra." This is more melancholy, but at the same time is strangely beautiful, being in a rather less sombre mood than that adopted by Berlioz for funereal purposes in other works. When we come to *Roméo au tombeau des Capulets*, the composer tells us "The public has no imagination. Pieces addressed to the imagination have therefore no public appeal. The following instrumental scene is in this situation, and I think it is better to suppress it . . . ninety-nine times out of a hundred." It is not particularly difficult to understand, but its scrappiness is apt to be disconcerting.

The *symphonie* concludes with a finale depicting the crowd at the cemetery, strife between Capulets and Montagues, a recitative and air by Friar Laurance and a concluding sermon of reconciliation. The last movement is on a considerable scale, but nevertheless, is a trifle disappointing after the perfection of the other movements.

Symphonie Funèbre et Triomphale

This was written originally for a large military band, with a chorus taking part only in the third (the last) movement, but strings may be added *ad libitum* except in the second movement. Like so many of his other works, it demands such a large body of performers that it is sadly neglected today, though it is a great pity that some of the musical societies in the larger cities do not attempt it. The composer specifies a chorus of eighty sopranos, sixty tenors and sixty basses ; and a band of four piccolos, five flutes, five oboes, thirty-one clarinets, two bass clarinets, twelve horns, eight bassoons, one double bassoon, eight trumpets, four cornets, eleven trombones, six tubas and a percussion department of timpani, tambourines, cymbals, bass drums, and gongs.

With outdoor performances in mind, Berlioz has concentrated upon sonority rather than subtlety. It is a work that is easily understood, full of appeal to the "ordinary" listener, yet possessing great breadth and dignity. The three movements are : *Marche funèbre*, *Oraison funèbre*, and *Apotheosis*, the latter concluding with a terrific weight of instrumental jubilation and triumph.

La Damnation de Faust

As soon as we get over the liberties that Berlioz took with Goethe's famous poem, we find in this "Dramatic Legend in Four Parts" a wealth of beauty that is difficult to describe in a few lines. The first part is not outstanding except for the popular Hungarian March, but the other three are on the whole a sheer delight. What other composer could have given us anything like the enchanting scene *Bosquets et prairies au bord de l'Elbe*, the chorus of sylphs and the lovely ballet that follows ? There is a soldiers' chorus in a most intriguing rhythm, a splendid ballad *The King of Thule*, and an exquisite Romance in the final movement. The composer's technique in the *Menuet des follets* is worthy of special observation.

One cannot help feeling that this work is not at home in the concert hall. It needs a theatre, and indeed requires very little adaptation to make it into an opera comparable with anything written by those composers acknowledged as the masters of opera. It has a few passages that do not seem to come to life properly when it is performed as a cantata. Its best performances in the past have been in opera-form.

BERLIOZ

Te Deum

This mighty work could be performed to perfection in·one of our greater English cathedrals, and would be a refreshing change from the more hackneyed oratorios that are given year after year to what is too often a dwindling audience. Three choirs are necessary, but they need not be as large as those employed at the original performance in the church of Saint-Eustache, when nine hundred singers took part. The third choir, incidentally, should be composed of children. It requires an orchestra of about a hundred and fifty and an organ. The choirs and orchestra must be placed at a considerable distance from the organ : if possible at the opposite end of the church or hall.

The chief part of the first movement is the magnificent double fugue, which concludes most effectively with long *diminuendo*. Then follows the *Tibi omnes*, introduced by the organ alone with a graceful *andantino*. Smoothly-flowing polyphony is the outstanding characteristic of this lovely movement.

The composer then provides an orchestral prelude for use when the *Te Deum* is performed on military occasions. It can be omitted without spoiling the work in any way, though it is not at all unworthy of its place.

Next, another polyphonic movement, the *Dignare*. The conclusion of this lyrical prayer is particularly fine. Then follows a hymn, *Christe, rex gloriæ*, and another prayer *Tu ergo*, before the wonderful final chorus *Judex crederis*. This is really a tremendous movement, with the organ pouring forth the main theme. In a great cathedral the effect is most thrilling.

Another military number is added at the end : a march for the presentation of the colours. Of its type, it is very good music, but it is best omitted on ordinary occasions.

L'Enfance du Christ

This oratorio, which is scored on more moderate lines than most of Berlioz's works, is in three parts : *Le Songe d'Hérode, La Fuite en Égypte,* and *L'Arrivée à Saïs.* The second part was written first, and has been used as a separate work. Apart from the orchestra and chorus, a soprano, two tenor, one baritone and three bass singers are required. Incidentally, Berlioz wrote the text himself, and it is an excellent example of his fine literary style.

The first part tells of the birth of Christ, and then depicts a street in Jerusalem with the Roman soldiers on patrol. Following this is a scene in Herod's palace and the arrival of the soothsayers, with strange if not beautiful music in the dialogue. Then we come to the stable, where the superb duet sung by Mary and Joseph is enriched by a light accompaniment for strings and wood-wind. There is a graceful lullaby followed by the arrival of a choir of angels who warn them of Herod's intentions.

The second part, the Flight into Egypt, opens with an instrumental overture for strings, two flutes, oboe and cor anglais, and includes a fine chorus of shepherds. The best part of this section is the scene depicting the Holy Family resting by the wayside : the music here is simple, beautiful and perfect in its appropriateness.

In the third section the scene of Mary and Joseph begging for shelter is deeply moving. Mary is so fatigued that she is on the verge of collapse, so they knock at the door of a Roman house. Six bass voices roar at them :

> Arrière, vils Hébreux !
> Les gens de Rome n'ont que faire
> De vagabonds et de lépreux.[1]

Eventually they are accommodated by a kindly Ishmaelite family, three of whom play an enchanting little trio for two flutes and a Theban harp. During the ensuing ensemble the Holy Family are bidden :

> Allez dormir, bon père,
> Doux enfant, tendre mère,
> Bien reposez.[2]

After a short narration, the oratorio concludes with an exquisite choral epilogue that dies gently away.

Les Troyens

The Trojans is undoubtedly one of the greatest operas we possess. It is in five acts, but in the published version it has been split into two separate works, *La Prise de Troie*, and *Les Troyens a Carthage*, of three and five acts respectively. The division was made by Berlioz himself—very reluctantly—for the Théâtre-Lyrique, but the opera should always be regarded as a whole, and performed as such whenever possible, although it takes about six hours.

A detailed analysis of this tremendous work would be impossible here, but mention should be made of the famous symphonic intermezzo in Act III scene ii, *Chasse royale et orage* which is fairly well known

---

[1] Be gone, vile Hebrews !
The people of Rome have no use
For vagabonds and lepers.

[2] Go to sleep, good father,
Sweet infant, tender mother,
Soundly repose.

agitz

HECTOR BERLIOZ, painted by Honoré Daumier   PLATE IV

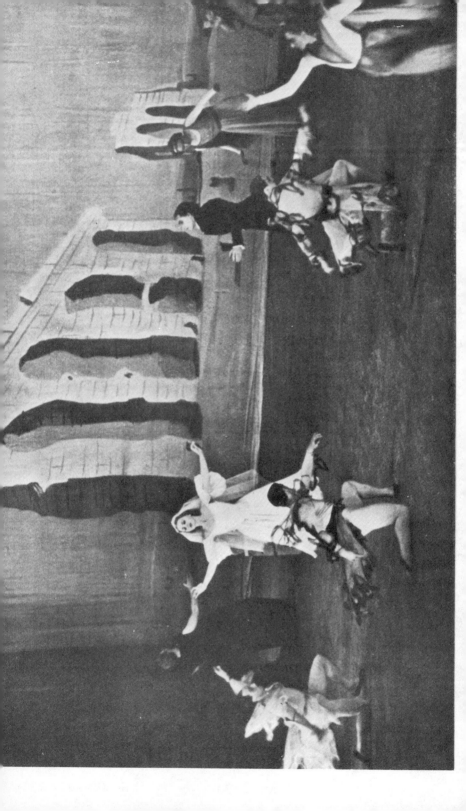

as a concert piece. In the opera it is infinitely more effective : while the orchestra is playing, water-nymphs flit about the stage and listen to the distant horns of the huntsmen. When the latter arrive, clouds gather and it pours with rain. Ascanius crosses with his huntsmen, Dido and Aeneas seek shelter from the storm in a grotto, wood-nymphs enter, fauns and satyrs appear and dance grotesquely crying "Italie ! " Suddenly a fork of lightning destroys a tree, and its branches are seized by the dancers. Then they disappear as darkness falls. The storm passes and there is an eerie silence. The curtain falls.

Another very fine passage is the death of Dido in the last scene of the last act, though the whole work becomes progressively wonderful as it reaches its final climax.

Béatrice et Bénédict

This two-act comic opera, after Shakespeare, has spoken dialogue in the French style. It contains a very amusing scene in which a *Kapellmeister* rehearses his choristers and players in a wedding song : a burlesque that gives scope for innumerable little caricatures of musician's affectations—particularly in the case of conductors. Berlioz himself indulged in several gibes at his contemporaries in this work. But there is also some very delightful music, such as the lovely duet *Nuit plaisible et sereine* (Night peaceful and serene) which is also enriched by a charming accompaniment.

To the vast majority of musicians and theatre-goers in this country this opera is unknown, yet its excellent music and Shakespearian charm would be readily appreciated by any reasonably intelligent audience. It could be produced very well at Stratford-upon-Avon.

OTHER PUBLISHED WORKS

Resurrexit
> An interesting early work from which Berlioz took material for several of his later compositions.

Le Dépit de la bergère
> A Romance with pianoforte accompaniment, written about 1825 and containing nothing of outstanding interest.

Le Maure jaloux. Toi qui l'aimas verse des pleurs.
> Two more Romances with pianoforte accompaniment, written a little later and slightly more mature.

Scène héroïque (La Révolution grecque)
> Setting of a poem by Humbert Ferrand for two soloists, chorus and orchestra, written in 1828. The finale is the only part that comes up to the standard of his later works.

Waverley. Les Francs-Juges

These two overtures are perhaps the most useful of his early works. They were written during 1827 and are both worthy of performance. The Francs-Juges is the better of the two ; typical of Berlioz in its spaciousness and dramatic sense.

Herminie

This *Scène lyrique* employs the theme used later in the *Symphonie fantastique*. It is a pleasant work with a lively finale.

Amitié, reprends ton empire

An early song, with pianoforte accompaniment, also available as a trio.

Le Montagnard exilé

Elegiac duet with pianoforte accompaniment, *circa* 1827.

Le Ballet des Ombres

For voices and pianoforte, written in 1829 ; it was withdrawn by the composer and used later in *Lélio*.

Fugues à 4 et 8 parties

Composed 1829. Not of outstanding interest.

Cléopâtre

This excellent cantata has been shamefully neglected. It is noteworthy for is originality and dramatic qualities, and is infinitely superior to most of the efforts of Berlioz's contemporaries at the time it was written—1829.

Huit scènes de 'Faust'

Originally written in 1829, but later embodied into *Le Damnation de Faust*.

Neuf Mélodies irlandaises :

1. *Le Coucher du soleil*
   Reverie for voice and pianoforte (1830).
2. *Hélène*
   A jolly little ballad with accompaniment for pianoforte or orchestra (1829).
3. *Chant guerrier*
   For male chorus and pianoforte (1829).
4. *La Belle Voyageuse*
   A most delightful little legend with accompaniment for piano or orchestra (1829).
5. *Chanson à boire*
   For male chorus and pianoforte, with effective solo passages for tenor (1829).
6. *Chant sacré*
   For full choir and pianoforte or organ ; not outstanding (1829).
7. *L'Origine du harpe*
   A curious ballad for voice and pianoforte (1830).
8. *Adieu, Bessy*
   Song with pianoforte accompaniment, composed in 1830 and re-written in 1850.
9. *Élégie*
   An unusual song for tenor voice and pianoforte (1830).

Le Pêcheur

For voice and pianoforte, embodied into *Lélio*.

Fantasie sur la 'Tempête' de Shakespeare

See *Lélio*.

Le Roi Lear

A powerful, serious overture composed in 1831.

Le Corsaire
An overture written in Nice and originally called *La Tour de Nice.*

Méditation religieuse
A solemn, philosophical work for six-part chorus and small orchestra. Words from Thomas Moore. (No. 1 of *Tristia*, Opus 18).

Rob Roy
A poor overture written in 1832.

Le Cinq mai
Cantata for chorus and orchestra ; a sombre but effective work with bass solos and an excellent finale (1832).

Coro dei Maggi
A mediocrity for chorus and small orchestra.

La Captive
Song with orchestral accompaniment after Victor Hugo. One of Berlioz's best songs : good substantial melody and charming orchestral effects.

Sara la baigneuse
For three choirs and orchestra, on the poem by Victor Hugo. A most agreeable work written in 1834.

Le Jeune Pâtre breton
For voice and pianoforte, or voice and orchestra with horn *obbligato.* Quite pleasant. (1834).

Je crois en vous
Romance for voice and pianoforte, words by Léon Guérin. (1834).

Les Nuits d'été :
1. *Villanelle*
A charming and dainty little song with pianoforte or orchestral accompaniment.
2. *Le Spectre de la rose*
An impressive but less beautiful song with pianoforte or orchestral accompaniment.
3. *Sur les lagunes*
A song similar to the above but intensely emotional.
4. *Absence*
The most beautiful song in this set.
5. *Au cimitière*
Similar to *Surles lagunes.*
6. *L'Ile inconnue*
A song of considerable breadth. Barcarolle.

Les Champs
Song with pianoforte accompaniment (1834).

Premiers transports
A contralto solo used later in *Roméo et Juliette.*

Rêverie et caprice
For violin and piano, or violin and orchestra. More conventional than most of Berlioz's other works.

Recitatives for Weber's 'Der Freischütz'
Berlioz composed these for the revival of this opera in Paris.

Hymne à la France
For chorus and orchestra, words by Auguste Barbier (1844).

Le Carnaval romain
See *Benvenuto Cellini.*

La Belle Isabeau
> For voice and pianoforte, words by Dumas (1844).

Zaïde
> Song with pianoforte or orchestral accompaniment.

Le Chasseur danois
> Ditto. Of no great importance.

Sérénade agreste à la Madone
> For harmonium or organ. Commissioned by Alexandre, the harmonium maker. Quite pretty.

Hymne pour l'Élévation
> Ditto, but polyphonic and less charming.

Toccata
> Ditto

Le Chant des Chemins de fer
> For chorus and orchestra. Written in 1846 for the French Northern Railway celebrations.

Page d'album
> Song with pianoforte accompaniment. (1847). Very poor.

La Mort d'Ophélie
> For female voices and orchestra, rather charming. [No. 2 of *Tristia*].

Marche funèbre pour la dernière scène d'Hamlet
> Mainly for orchestra with brief choral ejaculations. A most moving and impressive little work; one of the best of Berlioz's minor compositions. [No. 3 of *Tristia*].

L'Apothéose
> From *Symphonie funèbre*, for chorus and pianoforte accompaniment.

Le Chant des Bretons
> For chorus and pianoforte (1850).

Le Trébuchet
> A most unusual scherzo for soprano, alto and pianoforte (1850).

Le Matin
> A pleasant song with pianoforte accompaniment (1850).

Petit oiseau
> Another song with pianoforte accompaniment. Very graceful (1850).

La Menace des Francs
> A virile work for chorus and orchestra. With the *Hymne à la France* it was published as *Vox Populi* in 1851.

L'Imperiale
> Cantata for two choirs and orchestra. Not one of his best works (1855).

Prière du matin
> For women's and children's voices with pianoforte (1855).

Hymne pour la consécration du nouveau Tabernacle
> An excellent little work for three-part choir, written in 1859.

The Star of Liberty (Le Temple universel)
> An uninteresting work for double choir and organ, written in 1860.

Veni creator⎫
Tantum ergo⎭ Motets for female voices; useful and agreeable, but of no great merit.

César Franck

1

THE renascence of French music, for which Berlioz toiled all his life against the smug reactionaries, did not start until 1870, a year after his death, when the cataclysm brought about by the Franco-German war stimulated the musical life of France and produced a result comparable with the wonderful revival of interest in music that has taken place in Britain during the years of the Second World War. The leaders of those who carried on the work of Berlioz and who effected the regeneration of French music, were César Franck and (to a lesser degree) Saint-Saëns, and then Debussy and (again to a lesser degree) d'Indy, Ravel and Fauré. Vincent d'Indy was Franck's most devoted and brilliant pupil. Other composers who played a somewhat smaller part in the movement include Chabrier, Duparc, Dukas, de Séverac, Florent Schmitt, Roussel and so forth.

There are still many people who do not realize the significance of Franck, yet it would be difficult to over-emphasize the importance of his contribution to French musical culture. In some respects—but certainly not in all—it was neither as diffusive nor as transmutative as that made in later years by Debussy, but it did much to sustain the musical life of France when the opera was in one of its most degenerate periods. When the Parisian audiences had become sated with trash, Franck was one of the very few who were able to offer them an alternative to the dominant Wagner, whose music-dramas were stinging many a French conscience by showing up the worthlessness of much that was being produced in the opera houses. The more enlightened Parisians were looking for a French Wagner, but Berlioz—who, if he had been given the chance might even have surpassed the German master—had died almost heart-broken, and there was nobody else. So they turned to César Franck, who far from desiring glory in the opera-house, was content to spend the greater part of his life in the seclusion of his organ-loft and to lead his little group of pupils along the road that Gluck, Rameau, Bach and Beethoven had trodden. As the late

Romain Rolland once said : "He stood outside the Wagnerian movement in a serene and fecund solitude. To the attraction that he exercised by his genius, his personality and his moral greatness upon the little circle of friends who knew and respected him, must be added the authority of his scientific knowledge. In the face of the Wagnerian art he unconsciously resuscitated the spirit of John Sebastian Bach, the infinitely rich and profound spirit of the past. In this way he found himself unintentionally the head of a school, and the greatest educational force in contemporary French music." It should be noted that Debussy, whose opinions were very different from those of Franck, and whose impressionism contrasted vividly with the other's heavy romanticism, readily acknowledged the genius of Franck, and on one occasion described him as "one of the greatest of the great musicians."

Although we generally speak of César Franck as a French composer —for the greater part of his life was spent in Paris—he was actually born in Belgium, at Liège, on December 10th 1822. His ancestry is of some interest because for at least two and a half centuries the family had produced painters of considerable ability. The first of these, Jérome Franck (1540-1610) held the appointment of painter to Henry III. It is therefore not surprising to find that César Franck inherited a talent for drawing, which he cultivated during his earlier years. His father, who worked in a bank, was keenly interested in music and enjoyed the companionship of many accomplished instrumentalists. They were perhaps responsible for his decision that both of his sons should become professional musicians.

The young César Franck became so interested in music during his childhood that he needed no urging to respect his father's wish. He did extremely well at the school of music in Liège and was barely eleven when he made a tour of Belgium giving piano recitals. About a year later his father moved to Paris so that he could study at the Conservatoire. He did not actually start his course at this institution until 1837, when he was admitted to Leborne's composition class and became a pupil of Zimmermann for the piano. Within a few months he received an "honourable mention" for fugue in one of the competitions.

During the following year he came up against the obstinacy of the autocratic Cherubini, who had caused so much trouble to Berlioz. In one of the competitions, Franck did an unusual thing. After playing the set piece, Hummel's Concerto in A minor, with such remarkable skill that everybody acclaimed him as the prize-winner, he played the sight-reading test a third lower, believing that this demonstration of his unusual ability to transpose a difficult work at sight would be appreciated by the examiners. Various professors who were present expressed their amazement that a lad of little more than fifteen years could display such evidence of musicianship, but the sour old Cherubini declared that this act was a contravention of the rules, and that therefore Franck could not receive the prize. The other adjudicators objected to this sharp treatment, and at length the Director agreed to make a special award, the Grand Prix d'Honneur.

In 1839 Franck won the second prize for fugue, and in the following year took the first prize in the same examination. He had by that time started studying the organ with Benoist, and it was not long before he began to look for prizes for this instrument as well. In 1841 he entered for the organ prize and again astonished the examiners : two of the tests consisted of (a) the improvisation of a fugue on a given subject. and (b) the improvisation of a piece in sonata form on a given subject, Franck decided to combine the two in a most ingenious manner, but the subtlety of it was completely missed by the examiners, and they decided not to make an award in his case. Benoist then explained what his brilliant pupil had done and they agreed to give him the second prize, though their displeasure in being outwitted was all too obvious.

Franck then began to prepare for the Grand Prix de Rome, but in April 1842 his father suddenly resolved to take him away from the Conservatoire, so that he could start at once his career as a virtuoso. The reason for this drastic step was that the young student had been commanded to play before Leopold I, King of the Belgians, and it was presumed that after this royal honour, a large fortune could be made quite easily. The ambitious father was soon to learn that royal audiences bring only the most ephemeral glory to the musician, and very little money. For this occasion, three trios that Franck had composed at the Conservatoire were to be performed, and accordingly were dedicated to Leopold I.

II

As a virtuoso, Franck was obliged to compose pieces for the piano that would assist in the display of his prodigious technique—elaborate transcriptions, ornate, grandiose fantasias, and suchlike. Many of his earlier works are therefore of little importance, though they contain some striking innovations.

The two years following his removal from the Conservatoire were spent in Belgium, but there is extremely little accurate information concerning this period of his life. He gave various recitals and won the esteem of musicians here and there, but there is no evidence of any remarkable successes. His brother Joseph, who also trained for the musical profession, was doing even less.

The family returned to Paris in 1844 to take an apartment in the Rue La Bruyère, and it appears that the two brothers earned by far the greater part of its income by giving occasional concerts and taking pupils. César, however, devoted a fair amount of time to the composition of a variety of piano works and his Biblical eclogue *Ruth*. This was performed for the first time at the Conservatoire on January 4th 1846, and although the audience showed some appreciation, most of the critics were censorious, and called it a weak imitation of the works of Félicien David. A typical example of the criticism of those days has been quoted by Vincent d'Indy.[1] It ran : "M. César Franck is exceedingly naïve, and this simplicity, we must confess, has served him well in the composition of his Biblical oratorio *Ruth*." The same critic attended another performance of this work twenty-five years later and wrote : "It is a revelation ! This score, which recalls by its charm and melodic simplicity Méhul's *Joseph*, but with more tenderness and modern feeling, can most certainly be described as a masterpiece."

The Franck brothers derived most of their income from the lessons they gave to wealthy amateurs in Paris, but soon after the first performance of *Ruth* political disturbances caused many of them to leave the capital, and the two musicians suffered accordingly. César Franck was not the sort to worry himself unduly about money, nor, for that matter, about anything so mundane as party politics. He counted himself as one of the most fortunate and happy men on earth : he had his music, and had already won the affections of a charming young actress, Madame Desmousseaux. He had sufficient skill to provide the needs of everyday life, and some good friends. What more could a man want ? He was a devout Catholic, and had no difficulty in accepting the solution to all the problems of life provided by his faith. His family did not take kindly to his association with a member of the wicked theatrical profession, as they called it, but his determination to marry Madame Desmousseaux eventually resulted in their acquiescence. The outbreak of revolution in the early spring of 1848 did not upset his plans for their marriage. On February 22nd he went to

1 *César Franck*, by Vincent d'Indy, translated by Rosa Newmarch (John Lane, 1909).

meet his bride at the church of Notre-Dame de Lorette, of which he was the organist, only to find that the insurgents had erected a formidable barricade in its approach, and massed themselves behind it. He called to the leader, and asked for access to the church for his bride and himself and the guests. The barricade, however, could not be moved, but the insurgents—highly amused that a citizen should choose such a time to get married—helped the bride and bridegroom, and then their friends, to climb over the top of the barrier !

For a little while after the wedding the young couple lived with Franck's parents, but this arrangement was no more satisfactory than it is in these makeshift times. Moreover, Franck's father resented the loss of income so generously allowed him by his talented son in his single days. César and his wife therefore established a little home of their own. But just when they needed more money, the revolution made their conditions worse. Almost every pupil of any importance fled from Paris, and Franck was left with nothing but his very small salary as a church organist and a microscopic income from the sale of his compositions. He was obliged to take any sort of pupil he could get and to undertake some of the most menial tasks that music could offer. The man who was to compose the great D minor Symphony had to walk the streets of Paris calling here and there at the dwellings of artisans to give lessons to their children ! But the good grace with which he did this humiliating work all goes to prove his greatness.

In order to keep a couple of hours each day for study and composition he had to get up every morning at five-thirty, and he kept to this rule throughout his life. He also spent a short period each day in reading the great works of literature and philosophy that were his constant companions.

Like most French composers he felt drawn towards the opera house, and in 1851 began to write a three-act opera comique called *Le Valet de Ferme*. The libretto was supplied by Alphonse Royer and Gustave Vaes, a very mediocre pair, but popular in their day. Little did he realize what an arduous task he had undertaken. It swallowed up the precious hour or two that was set aside each day for composition and made heavy demands upon his few hours of leisure. But even that was not enough : he began working late into the night, and as one would imagine, the strain soon told upon his health. By the time the opera was finished and orchestrated in 1853 he was on the verge of a nervous breakdown.

All this effort was expended in vain, for the opera was never very successful, and in later life Franck himself thought little of it. All the same, it was a work far superior to much of that which was receiving the acclamation of the Parisian audiences of the day. A couple of years later Alphonse Royer became Director of the Opéra, but flatly refused to produce *Le Valet de Ferme*, on the pretext that it would be unfair to favour an opera that was partly his own work, and that in any case the regulations of the Opéra would not permit him to do so.

While Franck was writing this opera his friend the Abbé Dorel, the curé of Notre-Dame de Lorette, was appointed to the church of Saint-Jean-Saint-François au Marais. A benefactor had recently presented a small but excellent Cavaillé-Coll organ to this church, and when the position of organist fell vacant, Dorel immediately offered it to Franck, knowing well that nothing would please the composer more than to have access to this fine instrument. Franck accepted, but he was to stay there for only a few years.

In 1853 he undertook the additional work of choirmaster at the great church of Sainte-Clotilde, which had recently been completed. It was not long before Cavaillé-Coll was called upon to build one of his superb organs in this church as well, and in due course he erected one of the finest instruments in Paris. It was finished in 1858, a magnificent organ voiced with all the skill of this master-craftsman. There was great competition for the post of organist, but Franck, who applied solely because he wanted the privilege of playing the instrument, was successful.

The organ-loft of Sainte-Clotilde's became to him a sanctuary which he enjoyed for the rest of his life. There he worked out those masterly improvisations that were for ever a source of wonder to his pupils ; there he conceived some of his finest works, and expressed in music the great thoughts of an inspired but humble man. Here is Vincent d'Indy's description of this loft : "Ah ! we know it well, we who were his pupils, the way up to that thrice-blessed organ-loft—a way as steep and difficult as that which the Gospel tells us leads to Paradise. First, having climbed the dark, spiral staircase, lit by an occasional loophole, we came suddenly face to face with a kind of antedeluvian monster, a complicated bony structure breathing heavily and irregularly, which on closer examination proved to be the vital portion of the organ, worked by a vigorous pair of bellows. Next we had to descend a few narrow steps in pitch-darkness, a fatal ordeal to high hats, and the cause of many a slip to the uninitiated. Opening the narrow *janua cœli*, we found ourselves suspended as it were midway between the pavement and the vaulted roof of the church, and the next moment all was forgotten in the contemplation of that rapt profile, and the intellectual brow, from which seemed to flow without any effort a stream of inspired melody and subtle, exquisite harmonies, which lingered a moment among the pillars of the nave before they ascended and died away in the vaulted heights of the roof."

César Franck's genius for improvisation was unmatched in Paris, or indeed, in the whole of France. People would stand in the nave listening almost spellbound to the flood of glorious sound that his hands and feet could draw from his beautiful instrument. D'Indy says that on rare occasions one of the pupils would be called upon to play in the master's place, and that it was with "a kind of superstitious terror that we ventured to let our profane fingers caress this supernatural thing, which was accustomed to vibrate, to sing, and to lament at the will of the superior genius of whom it had become almost an integral part."

On April 3rd 1866 the ubiquitous Liszt happened to be present and heard one of Franck's masterly extemporizations. Even this renowned pianist and composer was astonished at the organist's skill, and said that there could have been nobody to equal him since the days of J. S. Bach.

III

We have now reached that period of Franck's life in which he began to write the music that was to bring him fame. He was by that time a well-known figure in Paris : a little man with an honest, kindly face ; fine forehead, bushy eye-brows and thick side-whiskers. There was nothing very striking about his appearance : he was anything but smart, and cared for no bohemian affectations. D'Indy tells us that his trousers were generally too short, and his overcoat at least one size too large. When seen in the streets of Paris he was always in a hurry, running rather than walking, for "all day long he went about on foot or by omnibus, from Auteuil to l'Ile Saint-Louis, from Vaugirard to the Faubourg Poissonnière, and returned to his quiet abode on the Boulevard Saint-Michel in time for an evening meal."

In winter as well as in summer he continued to rise at half-past five every morning. As soon as he was dressed he would go to his desk and spend two hours at composition,[1] then at seven-thirty he would

[1] D'Indy tells us that Franck called this "working for himself".

take a simple breakfast, and by eight o'clock was hurrying along the road to give his first lesson of the day. He was never free of the obligation to teach : right to the end of his days the major portion of his income was derived from his pupils, or from the colleges and schools.

After his evening meal he was invariably very tired, but there was usually plenty still to be done : a new work to orchestrate, parts to write out, or advice and help to be given to a few special pupils in whose future he was particularly interested. Those who know how strenuous a life of music can be will marvel at Franck's power of endurance.

Throughout this period his compositions consisted chiefly of organ and church music. As we have already observed, Franck was a devout Christian, and was always conscious of a desire to express his faith in music. What is commonly called "The Sermon on the Mount" had always been a great inspiration to him, indeed his very life and personal philosophy reflected his acceptance and profound understanding of Christ's teaching. For several years he had been considering the setting of "The Sermon on the Mount" to music, and one evening in 1869 he explained his desire to an old friend M. Denis, professor at the Lycée Saint-Louis. Denis was immediately impressed with the idea and persuaded Madame Colomb, the wife of a professor at the Lycée of Versailles, to write a libretto based on the *Beatitudes*.[1] Her verses were not particularly good, but were far superior to anything that the more fashionable librettists of the day could have written, and Franck, provided at last with the text of which he had so often dreamed, started the music at once.

This work was then interrupted by the outbreak of the Franco-Prussian War of 1870. Franck was too old to take an active part, and remained in the capital. Most of his pupils were involved in the conflict, and several never returned to their master. D'Indy tells us that one evening, during the interval between mounting guard at the outposts, he went to see Franck at his apartment and found him quivering with emotion at an article in the *Figaro* which extolled in poetic prose "the virile pride of our dear Paris, wounded, but resisting to the end." The composer set to work forthwith to turn this into a patriotic song, and within a few days they were singing it during the defence of the capital.[2]

1 The verses beginning "Blessed are ; . . " Matthew v. 3-11.
2 The song has not been published.

Work on the *Beatitudes* was necessarily very slow. The first two "blessings" were written during the autumn of 1870, but in the following year the plight of France distressed him to such an extent that he felt quite unable to set more of the poem. He therefore contented himself with orchestrating that which he had already written, finishing the task during the bombardment of Paris.

In 1872 something happened that neither Franck himself nor his friends could understand : he was invited to accept an appointment as Professor of the Organ at the Conservatoire. This may not seem surprising to the reader, for Franck's great skill as an organist was common knowledge, but appointments such as this were generally obtained only by endless intrigue in which the candidates courted the favour of government officials and other influential persons. The organist of Sainte-Clotilde was the last person in the country who would think of allowing anybody to "pull strings" for him, so it must be concluded that upon the retirement of Benoist, the authorities must have chosen him purely upon his fame as an organist—a singularly unusual method of selection in those days of corruption.

César Franck commenced his duties at the Conservatoire on February 1st 1872, and found himself in the midst of a staff openly hostile. He was disliked by the other professors from the very first day, chiefly because he was a "nobody", but also because he put his music before everything, and gave no thought to the acquisition of wealth and knowing the "right" people. Behind all this, of course, was professional jealousy, for the students at the Conservatoire soon became as devoted to him as his private pupils were.

Where Franck differed from other teachers was that he never taught by ready-made text-book methods. He went to great trouble to understand the problems and aspirations of every individual pupil, and guided each one accordingly. He never tried to force a syllabus of work on to them : his method was first to inspire them with his own burning love of the art, and then to teach them in a way that preserved their own individuality. No teacher could reach the heart of his pupils more easily than he. Every sincere pupil was regarded as a future trustee of his venerated art, and therefore nothing was too much trouble if it helped him to become worthy of his responsibility. No wonder they called him "Father" Franck, for his whole attitude was that of a loving and devoted parent passing on to his children a priceless heritage.

César Franck heartily disliked the feverish anxiety with which the other professors continually urged their more brilliant pupils to compete for prizes. The competitive instinct was whipped up to such an extent that students became bitter rivals, and frequently remained enemies for the rest of their lives. He considered this attitude to be utterly unworthy of the art, and did everything within his power to foster a sense of brotherhood among his pupils, so that if necessary they could help one another.

It must not be imagined that because of these gentle attributes Franck was easily pleased. His composition pupils knew only too well that no fault in their work would escape his attention : an ugly progression would cause an expression of extreme suffering to pass across his face. Similarly, a blundering or careless pupil at the organ could stir his indignation quicker than anything. For all that, he would never condemn a student's work without giving it the most careful consideration—he was too disgusted at the methods of certain critics, who would unhesitatingly proclaim a new work as worthless after a most casual first hearing, to do this.

One of the greatest joys his pupils could know was when in their compositions they wrote something quite original that happened to please him. He would play it over two or three times listening attentively to its effect, and then exclaim with a nod of approval "I like that". In those three words he could display such pleasure and approval that the pupil would feel quite thrilled with pride at his own creation. Franck's love of the beautiful in music was in itself a source of inspiration to those who studied with him. As Gustave Derepas has said,[1] "To love, to come out of ourselves, to lay aside our egotism by loving something very superior—almost unknown, perhaps—in which, however, we continue to believe . . . here is the very basis and essence of a true system such as Plato recommended to the worshippers of the celestial Venus ; such as Bossuet taught Christians to regard as the voice of moral perfection. It is the system of all great artists ; it was that of César Franck. Through it he came practically into touch with all those masters who have best depicted the ascent of the soul towards God."

Franck would never allow his pupils to pour out reams of indifferent composition merely to "get into the way of writing music", as some professors recommended. Every original piece written for him had to be composed with the heart as well as the brain. "Do not try to write

[1] *César Franck* (Fischbacher ; Paris, 1907).

too much" he would say "and what you do write must be very good."
Mere displays of clever technique made no appeal to him whatever.
He insisted upon a respect for the rules of form, but left the application
of them to the student's discretion. Tradition, too, had to be respected,
but he never allowed it to become a fetish, for he had little patience
with the reactionary attitude upheld in the Conservatoire. D'Indy
tells us that over and over again he would indicate some rather daring
novelty in a pupil's work and remark with a smile : "They would not
permit you to do that at the Conservatoire, but I like it very much."

In the same year as his appointment to the Conservatoire—1872—
Franck laid aside the *Beatitudes* for a while to compose an oratorio
called *Rédemption*, for which Edouard Blau had written a mediocre
libretto. Its first performance was given during Passion Week, 1873,
under the direction of Colonne, who was then almost unknown and
not at all experienced. Unfortunately a lengthy oratorio by another
composer was to be given on the following day, and this work took up
the greater part of the time allowed for rehearsal. Taking advantage
of Franck's good nature, the organisers of the concerts instructed
Colonne to give *Rédemption* only a quick run-through, and the result,
of course, was a very uninspired performance.

Practically the whole of the time he could spare for composition
during the next six years was given up to the *Beatitudes*. The only
other work to appear was a symphonic poem, *Les Eolides*, which was
introduced by Lamoureux in 1876 to a public that made no effort to
understand it.

The great oratorio took ten years of his life, for it was not
completed until 1879. Convinced that the Government would
appreciate the value of this monumental work, Franck arranged for
a private performance of it to be given at his own house
on a day suggested by the Minister of Fine Arts as one on which he
would be free to attend. The Directors of the Conservatoire and of
the Opéra, as well as the critics of the leading journals all promised to
attend.

With great enthusiasm Franck's pupils, who had volunteered their
assistance, all worked diligently to make the evening a success. D'Indy
was asked to play the piano part because the master himself had sprained
his wrist. Everything was ready on the appointed evening. Then
Franck received a flood of apologies : the Directors of the Conservatoire
and the Opéra had all discovered previous engagements or were detained on urgent business ; the Minister of Fine Arts, to his "profound

regret" found it impossible to attend ; and the leading critics were "compelled" to attend the first night of an operetta at one of the minor theatres.

Two or three press representatives arrived, but disappeared mysteriously about ten minutes after the performance had started. Various other guests had to leave early, and only two persons— Edouard Lalo and Victorin Joncières stayed until the end.

To one who for ten years had poured out his heart in this great work, who had toiled late into the night when he was almost overcome with weariness, this bitter humiliation was a cruel blow, yet he did his utmost not to show his feelings. His pupils saw that he was depressed for a week or so afterwards, and pointed out that it was probably the length of the work that precluded a public performance of it in its entirety. Franck therefore divided the oratorio into sections—much against his will—and offered it to the committee of the Société des Concerts du Conservatoire, who, after keeping him waiting many months, agreed to perform one of the eight parts.

It seems that the Minister of Fine Arts experienced a slight pricking of his conscience after the private performance of the *Beatitudes*, for on the retirement of Victor Massé he recommended the appointment of Franck as professor of Composition at the Conservatoire. But too many spiteful people had a say in the matter, and Ernest Guiraud was appointed. The Minister then sought another compensation for the disappointed composer, and with a singular display of tactlessness that betrayed his ignorance of Franck's genius, he caused him to be appointed an "officer" of the Academy : a minor honour given to musicians far beneath the composer's level.

Typical of Franck was his acceptance of this in good spirit, and when his infuriated pupils expressed their indignation, he would say nothing against the Minister or the members of the Académie.

IV

WE have now reached the most fruitful period of Franck's life, for the next few years were to produce many of his finest works, as we shall see in due course. These were all written during his daily period of early-morning composition or while he was on holiday from the Conservatoire. He sought neither money nor honour : composition was his principal purpose in life, and it brought him supreme happiness. D'Indy tells us how he would greet them when they

César Franck

PLATE VI

CÉSAR FRANCK at the organ

PLATE VII

CÉSAR FRANCK

Rischgitz

Lenoir's César Franck monument, Paris

PLATE VIII

PLATE IX   *Symphonic Variations.*

Scenes from the ballet to César Franck's music at Covent Garden

assembled for the autumn term. With a smiling face and beaming eyes he would say : "I have been working well these holidays :[1] I hope you will all be pleased" and then produce some masterpiece. He loved to invite all his favourite pupils to his house in the evening, to assemble them around the piano, and then to play his latest work through for their approval. He would sing any vocal parts in his queer voice, transposing, where necessary, an octave lower. Not only was he sufficiently humble to invite their criticisms, but when the more senior ones timidly offered suggestions he would welcome them, and frequently make alterations acting upon their advice.

In 1885 the Government at last awarded Franck an appropriate honour : he was created a Chevalier of the Legion of Honour by a decree dated August 4th. Even on this occasion the complete negation of tact on the part of the Minister of Fine Arts caused the award to be made not in recognition of his genius as a composer, but of his services as a professor of the organ !

Once again his pupils resented the implication, and they decided to show the Government that their master was something more than a professor of the organ by organizing a concert devoted entirely to his compositions. They collected money among themselves and their friends and as a result the "Franck Festival" took place at the Cirque d'Hiver on January 30th 1887. Jules Pasdeloup conducted the first half of the programme, which consisted of the symphonic poem *Le Chasseur Maudit*, the *Variations Symphoniques* for piano and orchestra, and the second part of the eclogue *Ruth*. Then Franck himself took charge for the second part, in which the March and *Air de Ballet* from the unpublished opera *Hulda*, and the third and eighth part of the *Beatitudes* were performed.

Alas ! the orchestra could not give sufficient time to rehearsal, and Pasdeloup made a serious blunder in the finale of the *Variations Symphoniques*. Furthermore, Franck was not an experienced conductor and the orchestra did not respond properly to his rather vague directions, so the concert was far from being a success. His pupils were bitterly disappointed in the standard of the performance.

Franck's own feelings were never expressed. He did not live to hear an adequate rendering of his *Beatitudes*. The oratorio, as a whole, was not heard publicly until the winter of 1891, a year after his death, when Colonne gave a magnificent performance of it under the auspices of the Association Artistique. It was then that people began

[1] He generally rented a little house at Quincy for the holidays.

to realize the magnitude of this work, and arrangements were made for it to be heard in the other capitals.

Throughout the years 1886 to 1888 the superb D minor symphony was taking shape, and at the same time Franck was writing his symphonic poem *Psyché* and various minor works. The symphony was played for the first time on February 17th 1889 under the auspices of the Société des Concerts du Conservatoire, although most of its influential members had been opposed to the inclusion of it. The credit for the performance must go to the conductor Jules Garcin, who with incredible obstinacy insisted on playing the new work.

Vincent D'Indy tells us that the subscribers could make neither head nor tail of it, and that he enquired of one of them, a professor at the Conservatoire and a sort of *factotum* on the Committee, what he thought of the symphony. "*That* a symphony ? " the man replied contemptuously. "But my dear sir, who ever heard of writing for the cor anglais in a symphony ? Just mention a single symphony by Haydn or Beethoven introducing the cor anglais ! There ! . . . your Franck's music may be whatever you please, but it will certainly never be a symphony ! "[1]

That such astonishing stupidity could be shown by a professor of music all goes to show what the more enlightened spirits had to endure in the year 1889. Surely, in the whole realm of music there are few symphonies more easily understood than this beautiful masterpiece of César Franck : no great knowledge of music is necessary to appreciate it, for its loveliness is as obvious as the beauty of Wells Cathedral and its precincts.[2] The soul of a great man is in this symphony.

The Sonata for violin and piano which he had completed in 1886 and dedicated to Eugène Ysaÿe was by this time getting better known, though of course Franck never lived to know the world-wide success that it would win in the hands of this brilliant violinist. The String Quartet in D, written in 1889 was surprisingly well received when it was performed at one of the concerts of the Société Nationale de Musique, which Franck had helped to found in 1871. The applause was tremendous, but the composer refused to believe that any of it was for him until the audience called persistently for the composer. He then walked very shyly on to the platform to receive the first ovation of his life—he was then sixty-eight ! When his many friends and pupils

[1] *César Franck*, translated by Rosa Newmarch.
[2] Like the architecture of Wells Cathedral, this symphony can be criticised on certain points, but both are great works of art, nevertheless.

gathered round to congratulate him on the following day, he remarked simply, but with great joy : "There, you see, the public are beginning to understand me."

The closing years of Franck's life were the most glorious. The musical world at last showed signs of giving him the recognition he deserved, and his devoted circle of pupils, more than ever aware of his genius, all regarded him as a very dear friend. D'Indy has left us a charming picture of this lovable character in his description of him at the organ "with one hand to his forehead and the other poised above his stops" preparing the instrument for one of his great improvisations. "Then he seemed to be surrounded by music as by a halo, and it was only at such moments that we were struck by the conscious will-power of mouth and chin, and the almost complete identity of the fine forehead with that of the creator of the Ninth Symphony. Then, indeed, we felt subjugated—almost awed—by the palpable presence of the genius that shone in the countenance of the highest-minded and noblest musician that the nineteenth century had produced in France."

One evening in May 1890, Franck was going to the house of one of his pupils, Paul Brand, when he was struck in the side by the pole of a horse-omnibus. In considerable pain he continued on his way, but fainted immediately after his arrival at Brand's house. He recovered sufficiently that evening to play the second piano part in the *Variations Symphoniques*, but felt very shaken and weary when he returned home.

This little accident was the start of a period of ill-health, which he did his best to ignore, for nothing would induce him to give up the work he loved. The only thing from which he abstained was personal pleasure : he had always enjoyed dining out with musical friends, but now a sense of fatigue made these pleasant social functions almost impossible. He was even obliged to refuse a cordial invitation to preside at a banquet held by the Committee of the Société Nationale, although they had arranged to perform his Quartet afterwards.

In the late summer of that year a serious attack of pleurisy developed and he was obliged to remain in bed. He was then completing his last work : the three *Chorals* for organ. On one occasion he struggled along to the church of Sainte-Clotilde, and with great difficulty climbed up to his beloved organ for the last time. There he sat, trying over the combinations of stops for the *Chorals*. It was one of his greatest wishes that this set of compositions should be finished, complete with the "registration" of stops, before his strength failed. His thoughts as he sat at his organ for the last time will never be known : he used to say to the curé of Sainte-Clotilde : "If you only knew how I love this instrument—it is so supple beneath my fingers and so obedient to all my thoughts ! "[1]

Later in the autumn Franck's condition grew worse. Complications set in and early in November he began to sink. The curé of Sainte-Clotilde brought the viaticum, and on the 8th of that month—November 1890—the great composer died. The completed *Trois Chorals* were lying on his death-bed.

The funeral service was held at Sainte-Clotilde's, and a very modest little procession then made its way to the cemetery of Montrouge. The Minister of Fine Arts did not attend, nor did he send a representative. Not a single official came from the Conservatoire : the Director, Ambroise Thomas, was conveniently indisposed, and all the other professors—Franck's colleagues for many years—made trifling excuses. But around the composer's grave gathered all who had loved him. The pall-bearers were Franck's cousin, Dr. Ferréot, Camille Saint-Saëns, Delibes and a representative of the master's organ pupils, H. Dallier. Emmanuel Chabrier delivered a short oration in the name of the Société Nationale de Musique : "Farewell, Master, . . . in you we salute one of the greatest artists of the century, and the incomparable teacher whose wonderful work has produced a whole generation of forceful musicians, believers and thinkers, armed at all points for hard-fought and prolonged conflicts. We salute, also, the honourable and just man, so humane, so distinguished, whose counsels were as sure as his words were kind. Farewell . . . "

A few years later the composer's remains were removed to the Montparnasse cemetery, and fourteen years after his death his friends erected a monument to him in the square opposite the basilica of Sainte-Clotilde. On this occasion there was plenty of ceremony, with the Director of the Institut, the Director of the Conservatoire, and all the various humbugs who wished to pay homage when it was too late. Franck's name was then world-famous, and the Conservatoire wished to lose no opportunity to claim him as one of its former professors.

[1] This remark is quoted by D'Indy from an address given by Canon Gardey on October 22nd, 1904.

The Principal Works of César Franck

Blest pair of Sirens, pledges of Heaven's joy,
  Sphere-born harmonious Sisters, Voice and Verse !
Wed your divine sounds, and mixt power employ
  Dead things with inbreathed sense able to pierce ;
And to our high-raised phantasy present
That undisturbéd Song of pure concent
Ay sung before the sapphire-colour'd throne
      To him that sits thereon,
With saintly shout and solemn jubilee ;
Where the bright Seraphim in burning row
Their loud uplifted angel-trumpets blow ;
And the Cherubic host in thousand quires
Touch their immortal harps of golden wires,
With those just Spirits that wear victorious palms,
      Hymns devout and holy psalms
      Singing everlastingly :
That we on earth, with undiscording voice
May rightly answer that melodious noise ;
As once we did, till disproportion'd sin
Jarr'd against nature's chime, and with harsh din
Broke the fair music that all creatures made
To their great Lord, whose love their motion sway'd
In perfect diapason, whilst they stood
In first obedience, and their state of good.
  O may we soon again renew that Song,
    And keep in tune with heaven, till God ere long
    To his celestial consort us unite,
  To live with him and sing in endless morn of light !
                                        J. Milton

These verses, *At a Solemn Music*, are quoted here because they indicate the spirit in which César Franck approached his art. His music is a humble, righteous man's effort to glorify his God : it reflects his utter sincerity and the warm-heartedness that endeared him to all his associates. Comparing him with Wagner, Gustave Derepas[1] has said : "César Franck's mysticism is the direct expression of the soul, and leaves him his full consciousness in his aspirations towards the divine. The human being remains intact amid the accents of love, joy

1 *César Franck*, translated by Rosa Newmarch.

or grief. This is because the God of César Franck has been revealed to him by the Gospel, and is as different from Wotan in the *Nibelungen* as midday from the pallid twilight. Franck leaves to the Germans their nebulous dreams; he clings to that part of the French temperament which, perhaps, we do not value sufficiently : good sense, clear reason, and moral equilibrium. . . . The atmosphere in which Franck moves is illuminated by a very clear light, and animated by a breath which is really that of life. His music makes us neither beast nor angel. Keeping a steady balance, as far removed from materialistic coarseness as from the hallucinations of a doubtful mysticism, it accepts humanity with all its positive joys and sorrows, and uplifts it, without dizziness, to peace and serenity, by revealing the sense of the divine. Thus it tends to contemplation rather than to ecstasy. The hearer who abandons himself with docility to its beneficent influence, will recover from the superficial agitation at the centre of the soul, and, with all that is best within himself, will return to the attraction of the supremely desirable, which is at the same time the supremely intelligible. Without ceasing to be human he will find himself nearer to God. This music, which is truly as much the sister of prayer as of poetry, does not weaken or enervate us, but rather restores to the soul, now led back to its first source, the grateful waters of emotion, of light, of impulse ; it leads back to heaven and to the city of rest."

Franck's respect for the classical tradition never made him a slave to convention. He used forms that seemed ideal for his purpose, but instead of building on their framework a slavish imitation of the masters that had gone before him, he erected a structure of his own ideas. In the light of modern knowledge we can find weaknesses in his work. He was inclined to overdo "chromatic meanderings," for instance, but this is not a very serious fault, and no man with a true love of music could fail to appreciate his better works.

In his book *Music in Western Civilization*, Paul Henry Láng of Columbia University sums up the modern musician's criticism of Franck in these words : " . . . we have movements abounding in great beauty, but the contradiction between hymnic ecstasy and symphonic flow and continuity, polyphonic-linear profile and eternally shifting chromaticism, tonal logic and hypertrophy of modulation, was too destructive to permit the emergence of an *oeuvre* that would offer both a personal and a stylistic synthesis. As in Bruckner, the organist never disappears under the cloak of the symphonist (although in Franck's case the organist wrote some of his best works for his own instrument).

On the other hand the improvisatory nature of his music, his tendency to 'pull stops' and to switch from manual to manual (the development sections in his sonata construction, notably in the symphony), and the temptation of the nineteenth-century organist, long estranged from true organ music, to permit his fingers to slide about chromatically, are always in evidence. Yet he has his supreme moments—the scherzo in the string quartet, or the organ variations in B—when the great issues are forgotten, when only the music speaks, unencumbered by theories, reminiscences and problems."

Symphony in D minor

Such a work as this cannot be analysed in a few lines. D'Indy has described it as a continual ascent towards pure gladness and life-giving light, and has referred to its themes as manifestations of ideal beauty. Its strength lies in the fine melodies and the instrumental colouring ; its weakness in its rhythmic construction, for the "aggregation of four-and two-bar phrases" tends to become monotonous. The rhythm of the various themes—lovely though they are—could have been extended in the development to give greater variety, whereas the composer has relied upon harmonic treatment and modulation to relieve monotony. We find many ingenious progressions in this work, subtleties of harmony and various innovations considered daring in their day. The middle section of the *allegretto* is exceptionally beautiful. It is interesting to note that the second theme in the first movement evidently got the composer into difficulties, but he solved the problem by moving colourful chords underneath the melody and thus giving the impression that it had changed its character.

Franck has scored this symphony for a somewhat larger orchestra than that generally employed by symphonists of his period. Mention has already been made of his use of the cors anglais, to which the beautiful melody of the slow movement is given. He also added a bass clarinet to his wood-wind, and adhered to the French theatrical tradition of using two cornets à pistons with his trumpets. The reason for their presence seems merely to swell the brass chorus.

Psyche

This symphonic poem for chorus and orchestra was composed during 1887-8. Gustave Derepas has explained :[1] "According to the old myth, Psyche, touched by love, but tempted by an indiscreet haste

1 op. cit.

for knowledge, and yielding to curiosity, falls back upon herself, powerless to rise again, and deprived for ever of the direct vision of the world beyond. Franck did not hesitate to break away from pagan tradition. His poem ends in a more optimistic mood. Psyche falls asleep, ignorant of all external sounds. The Zephyrs—her pure inspirations—bear her to the garden of Eros, the desired paradise. Her celestial spouse awaits her. But she imprudently wishes to pierce the mystery in which he has enveloped himself. The sublime vision disappears. Fallen again to earth, wandering and plaintive, Psyche breathes forth her woe. Eros forgives the legitimate ambition which he himself had inspired. Together they soar back to the light. It is the apotheosis ; the love which has no need for faith, because it sees and possesses. It is indeed a true Redemption."

There are no solos in this work, for Eros and Psyche do not express themselves in words : all their emotions are portrayed by the orchestra. The chorus is intended to be "anonymous and impersonal". It is on the whole an interesting work, very pleasantly coloured in certain sections.

Hulda

This is an opera in four acts with an epilogue, on a Scandinavian subject. The libretto, by C. Grandmougin after Bjornstierne-Björnson, is rather poor, and as Franck had little experience of the theatre, it is not surprising that this opera is now almost forgotten. It was first produced at Monte Carlo in 1894, but its excellent music did not compensate for its dramatic weakness. The pleasant ballet music is often played as a concert piece.

Ghisèle

Franck's other attempt at opera,[1] the four-act lyrical drama Ghisèle was written hurriedly not long before his death. The libretto is by Gilbert Augustin Thierry. Franck did not live to complete the orchestration of the last two acts, so this was done for him by five of his pupils : Pierre de Bréville, Ernest Chausson, Arthur Coquard, Vincent d'Indy and Samuel Rousseau. The work contains some fine music, but its dramatic value is slight, and like Hulda, is almost unknown in the opera-houses today. It was first produced at Monte Carlo on April 5th 1896.

[1] Ignoring Le valet de ferme, which was never published.

Les Béatitudes

This great oratorio for solo voices, chorus and orchestra, is in eight parts with a prologue. The best sections are the third ("Blessed are they that mourn : for they shall be comforted"), the fourth ("Blessed are they which do hunger and thirst after Righteousness : for they shall be filled"), the sixth ("Blessed are the pure in heart : for they shall see God"), and the last ("Blessed are they which are persecuted for righteousness sake : for theirs is the kingdom of heaven"). The principal weakness is in the portrayal of Satan : a fault admitted by d'Indy, who maintained that his master's character was such that he was quite unable to depict Evil in music. This explanation caused some amusement among the cynics. Nevertheless, this oratorio is a masterpiece : its lofty inspiration far outweighs its technical weaknesses, and it is worthy of a permanent place in the repertoire of those bodies who are capable of giving an adequate performance of it. The choruses, by the way, are not difficult.

The Quartet in D major

The Quartet in D major is a fine specimen of the mature Franck. Its first movement is complicated in construction ; one of the most remarkable pieces of music in the whole realm of chamber music. Two musical ideas exist concurrently in this movement, but do not become merged together. The second movement is a light and gay *scherzo* ; and the third is one of the loveliest things that Franck ever wrote—a beautiful *larghetto* that might be described as a dignified and utterly sincere prayer in music. With this, as with the first movement, the composer took endless trouble to make it perfect. The *Finale* is another complicated movement in sonata form. By introducing themes used in the previous movements Franck follows the cyclic construction used in the last movement of his Symphony. It is a very impressive movement, and brings an important work to a close with great feeling and solemnity.

Prelude, Choral and Fugue for Piano

Here is an important work, written in 1884, which is still widely appreciated at the present time. Franck's original intention was to make this a prelude and fugue in the Bach style, but he decided to link them with the choral, for this dominates the entire work. The Prelude is in classical style ; the Choral, in three parts, prepares the way for the Fugue by the use of an additional subject quite distinct from the main body ; and the Fugue itself is a masterly construction that brings the work to a brilliant conclusion.

Prelude, Aria and Finale for Piano

Written during 1886-7, this work is more in keeping with the sonata form. The dominating subject is revealed in the opening of the Prelude ; a steady, substantial tune. This reappears in the Finale, which has some marvellous passages in the bass. The work concludes very effectively by fading away to a pianissimo. This, like the preceding work, is an important contribution to the repertoire of the piano. It is not beyond the skill of the moderately-accomplished pianist, and is an excellent recital piece, satisfying to player and audience alike.

Variations Symphoniques

This work for piano and orchestra was written in 1885, and first performed on May 1st of that year at the Société Nationale de la Musique, the soloist being M. L. Diémer. Since then it has travelled all over the globe and become a favourite item with the concert-goer. It is a masterly work, yet shares with the Symphony the merit of being readily understood and appreciated. (There are some who do not consider this to be a merit, but they are not worth bothering about). As with many of Franck's works, there is a suggestion of the organist here and there, but the composer's skill in the employment of variation remains unimpaired, and there must be few to whom a sympathetic performance of this inspired music would not give pleasure.

The Piano Quintet in F minor

Another work that will help to preserve the memory of César Franck is the Quintet in F minor for piano, two violins, viola and 'cello, which was composed in 1879. It was dedicated to Camille Saint-Saëns, who ironically enough, heartily disliked it. In this, Franck has again used the system based on cyclic themes, which gives it strength and a sense of unity. The themes employed are very beautiful. The principal subject, which is announced in the opening movement, reappears in the middle of the second movement, *lento*, and is to be found again in the Finale. The brilliant, vigorous conclusion of this quintet is particularly fine. The first performance was at a concert held by the Société Nationale on January 17th 1880. Saint-Saëns was at the piano, and the other parts were played by Marsick, Rémy, Van Wœfelghem and Loys.

The Violin Sonata in A

Written in 1886 for Eugène and Théophile Ysaÿe, the Sonata in A for violin and piano is based on three quite simple themes, and is another example of cyclic construction, though in a different and rather refreshing style. It was first played in the year of its composition by Ysaÿe and Madame Bordes-Pène at a Brussels concert held in a room that contained some very valuable paintings, on account of which no artificial light was permitted. It was a winter's afternoon, and by the end of the first movement it had become so dark that the players could not read the manuscript. It was hoped that the audience would be satisfied with only the first movement but with one accord they demanded to hear the whole work. Ysaÿe exclaimed : "Let us get on with it", and the two players valiantly played the rest of the work entirely from memory ! It was an astonishing success, and Ysaÿe afterwards took the sonata on his world-wide tours.

Trois chorals

The three chorals for grand organ, Franck's last work, are of special interest. They are mature, but less vigorous than most of the composer's other organ works. All are constructed in the "great variation" form. No. 1 in E has an almost dramatic atmosphere ; No. 2 in B contains some very fine passages in the passacaglia style ; and No. 3 in A is noteworthy for its superb cantabile movement. D'Indy considered that these three chorals were the result of "the assimilation of Beethoven's heritage by a truly creative mind."

OTHER PUBLISHED WORKS

The remainder of Franck's compositions must now be listed briefly, but that does not mean that *all* the following are of minor importance. Many of the organ works, especially, are still being played in every civilized country, and are likely to remain in use long after much of our twentieth-century music is forgotten.

Trois trios concertants
> (1841)   For piano, violin and 'cello.   The first is interesting from a biographical point of view, being the work of a youth of nineteen.   Opus 1.

Quatrième trio concertant
> (1842)   For piano, violin and 'cello.   Dedicated to Liszt.   Opus 2.

Eclogue (Hirtengedicht)
> (1842)   This is a piano piece, in which the *Hirtengedicht* (Shepherd's Song) struggles for an existence amongst a good deal of elaborate writing.   Opus 3.

Duo on "God Save the King"
> (1842)   A virtuoso's duet, of little interest.   Opus 4.

Grand caprice
> (1843)   Piano solo.   Opus 5.

Andante quietoso
> (1843)   For piano and violin.   Opus 6.

Souvenir d'Aix-la-Chapelle
> (1843)   A poor piano solo.   Opus 7.

Quatre mélodies de Schubert
> (1844)   Transcribed for piano.   Opus 8.

Première fantaisie sur Gulistan
> (1844)   Piano solo.   Based on themes from Dalayrac's *Gulistan*.   Opus 11.

Deuxième fantaisie
> (1844)   Piano solo on themes from the same opera.   Opus 12.

Duo pour piano et violon concertans
> (1844)   Also on airs from the above.   Most of these early works are poor virtuoso stuff.   Opus 14.

Fantaisie pour piano
> (1845)   Based on two Polish airs.   Opus 15.

Duo à quatre mains sur Lucile
> (1846)   Duet on themes from Grétry's *Lucile*.   Opus 17.

Ruth
> (1843-6)   Biblical eclogue in three parts for soli, chorus and orchestra.   Based on the familiar story of Ruth, a work containing a number of quite interesting passages, but written when Franck was obviously under the influence of Méhul's dramatic works.

Souvenance.   Ninon.   L'émir de Bengador.   Le Sylphe.   Robin Gray
> (1842-3).   Five songs of no great importance.   *Le Sylphe* has 'cello accompaniment.

L'ange et l'enfant
: (1846) Song dedicated to Madame César Franck.

Les trois exilés
: (1852) National song for baritone and bass.

Messe solennelle
: (1858) This Mass contains some very fine music side by side with inferior passages that spoil the work as a whole. In places there is an unfortunate theatrical tendency.

Andantino
: (1858) An organ solo of no great interest.

Accompagnement d'orgue
: (1858) with an arrangement of Gregorian services for voices.

O Salutaris
: (1858) Duet for soprano and tenor.

Trois motets
: (1858) 1. *O Salutaris* for soprano and chorus.
  2. *Ave Maria* duet for soprano and bass.
  3. *Tantum ergo* for bass.

Trois antiennes
: (1859) "for grand organ".

Le Garde d'honneur
: (1859) hymn.

Messe à trois voix
: (1860) This Mass for soprano, tenor and bass, with accompaniment for organ, harp, 'cello and double-bass, was first performed in 1861, but was revised once or twice afterwards. The *Kyrie* is simple but effective; the *Gloria* has too many banalities; the symphonic form of the *Credo* spoils it; the *Sanctus* is good; the *Benedictus* is weak; the *Agnus Dei* is excellent. This work bears the Opus No. 12.

Six pièces pour grand orgue
: 1. *Fantaisie in C.*
  2. *Grande Pièce Symphonique.*
  3. *Prélude, fugue et variation.*
  4. *Pastorale.*
  5. *Prière.*
  6. *Final.*
  (1860-2) Of this collection Liszt said, "These poems have their place beside the masterpieces of Bach." No 1 has a fine canon and a beautiful *Allegretto cantando*. No. 2 is really a symphony for organ in three movements. No. 3 is noteworthy for its very fine fugue. No. 4 is quite charming. No. 5 pleasant and expressive. No. 6 is a magnificent piece, brilliant and vigorous, a great favourite with all who share the organist's traditional love of finishing with a grand splash of sound.

Quasi marcia
: (1862) A piece for the long-suffering harmonium. Opus 22. Franck abandoned the use of opus numbers after this.

Cinq pièces
: (1863) More pieces for the harmonium.

Ave Maria
: (1863) for soprano, tenor and bass.

44 petites pièces
>(1863)   Published as "Posthumous Pieces" for organ or harmonium.

Les plaintes d'une poupée
>(1865)   For piano.

Trois offertoires
>1. *Quæ est ista.*
>2. *Domine Deus in Simplicitate.*
>3. *Dextera Domini.*
>(1871)   No. 1, an excellent work for soli, chorus, organ and double-bass, is for the festival of the Virgin.   No. 2, for three voices, organ and double-bass, is for the first Sunday in the month.   No. 3, for soli, 3-part chorus, organ and double-bass, is for Easter Day.

Le mariage des roses
>(1871)   Song.   Words by E. David.

Domine non secundum
>(1871)   A Lenten offertory for soprano, tenor and bass.   Well-written and effective.

Quasi fremuerunt gentes
>(1871)   Offertory for St. Clotilde's day, for three-part chorus, organ and double- bass.

Offertoire
>(1871)   Another piece for the harmonium, based on a Breton air.

Panis angelicus
>(1872)   For tenor, organ, harp, 'cello and double-bass.   Contained in the Mass for three voices.

Rédemption
>(1871)   This is an oratorio for soprano solo, chorus and orchestra.   There are two versions.   The original was used for the first performance on April 10th 1873, at which the work suffered through the incompetence and lack of sympathy of many of the orchestra, and of the soloist.   After this, Franck re-wrote the long orchestral interlude, which has often been performed separately as a concert piece.

Passez, passez toujours
>(1872)   Song.   Words by Victor Hugo.

Roses et papillons
>(1872)   Song.   Words by Victor Hugo.

Veni creator
>(1872)   Duet for tenor and bass.

Lied
>(1873)   Song.   Words by Lucien Paté.

Prélude, fugue et variation
>(1873)   For harmonium and piano.   This is a transcription of No. 3 of the *Six pièces pour grand orgue.*

Les Eolides
>(1876)   This is a symphonic poem for orchestra, after the poem by Leconte de Lisle.   A fascinating, impressionistic work, of which there is an arrangement for piano duet made by the composer.

Trois pièces pour grand orgue
1. *Fantasia in A.*
2. *Cantabile.*
3. *Pièce heroïque.*
(1878) These organ pieces were written for the opening of the huge organ at the Trocadéro during the 1878 Exhibition. No. 2 is very beautiful and always popular. No. 3 is most impressive; a great favourite.

Le vase brisé
(1879) Song with orchestral or piano accompaniment.

Rebecca
(1881) Biblical scene for soli, chorus and orchestra. Poem by Paul Collin.

Le chasseur maudit
(1882) Symphonic poem for orchestra, (after Bürger) first performed by the Société Nationale on March 31st 1883. It is rather a poor specimen of Franck's maturity.

Nocturne
(1884) Song with orchestral or piano accompaniment.

Les Djinns
(1884) Symphonic poem for piano and orchestra (after Victor Hugo). This is not really a concerto, as the piano is treated more as one of the instruments of the orchestra.

Danse Lente
(1885) Piano solo.

Hymne
(1888) For four male voices.

La Procession
(1888) Song, originally arranged for orchestra.

Les cloches du soir
(1888) Song with orchestral accompaniment.

Psaume CL
(1888) For chorus, orchestra and organ.

Six duos
1. *L'ange gardien.*
2. *Aux petits enfants.*
3. *La vierge à la crèche.*
4. *Les danses de Lormont.*
5. *Soleil.*
6. *La chanson du vannier.*
(1888) These are part songs for equal voices. Some very beautiful writing is to be found here, especially in No. 3.

Le premier sourire de mai
(1888) This is a chorus for three female voices.

Andantino
(1889) Organ solo.

Preludes et prières de Ch. V. Alkan

(1889) Franck has arranged these in three books of organ solos. Charles Valentin Alkan (1813-1888) was a brilliant French pianist who composed a large amount of difficult and rather highly-coloured works for his instrument. Some of his music is of considerable merit.

L'Organiste

(1889-90) This collection of fifty-nine pieces for the harmonium was published after Franck's death . They are chiefly versicles for the *Magnificat*, which the composer used to improvise at Vespers.

Saint-Saëns giving his first concert at the age of 12 PLATE X

Saint-Saëns

PLATE XI

Saint-Saëns

I

Like several other French composers of his type, Camille Saint-Saëns was a brilliant musician who composed clever music, but never quite succeeded in reaching the plane of immortal genius. His works are still popular in the world's concert halls, and give considerable pleasure to all but the most sophisticated, but there are signs that some have already begun to move down that steady gradient of depreciation that has carried so many of the works of such composers as Gounod and Spohr into oblivion. However, just as the orchestral works of Mendelssohn are holding their own (and compensating for the decline of that composer's oratorios), there is still plenty of music by Saint-Saëns that even the brilliant work of some of our twentieth-century composers cannot replace.[1]

Saint-Saëns wrote music with incredible facility. He once said that compositions sprang from his pen as easily as apples grow upon a tree. He made full use of his extensive knowledge both of the classics and of the works of his contemporaries, and that explains why so much of his work is of an eclectic nature. That does not mean that it necessarily lacks originality, but one feels that if he had possessed less of that extensive knowledge of the music of others and a little more crude creative genius, he might have ranked with Berlioz in the history of French music. He thought rather too much about perfection of form and purity of style : he was more concerned with pleasing people by writing elegant music than with the unrestrained expression of his own inspiration.

He was born at No. 3 Rue du Jardinet, Paris, on October 9th, 1835, and was given the name of Charles Camille. His father, a minor official

---

[1] This sentence will perhaps cause the arching of eye-brows in some quarters, but I stand by it. There are works of both Mendelssohn and Saint-Saëns that will help to civilize the super-streamlined-atomically-energized twenty first century. My reference to our twentieth-century composers springs from my pride in the despised nation of shopkeepers that has produced such people as Elgar, Delius, Holst, Vaughan Williams, Bliss, Walton, Britten and company.

in the Department of the Interior, died about ten weeks later, and the young mother decided to send her delicate child to the care of a nurse at Corbeil for two years. It was feared that the infant possessed germs of his father's consumption, and country air was therefore a necessity.

Madame Saint-Saëns had little means of support and welcomed the opportunity of living with her aunt, Madame Charlotte Masson, who was also a widow. So when at the end of 1837 the little boy returned to Paris, he found two devoted women to care for him. Even before his third birthday he showed signs of an extraordinary sensitivity to music. Sounds of any sort aroused his interest : the striking of a clock always fascinated him ; he would sit patiently listening to the "singing" of a kettle as it approached boiling point ; and even the creak of a slowly-closing door would arrest his attention.

He was barely three when he was first placed before a piano. Instead of striking all manner of notes in the haphazard fashion beloved by most children (to the intense irritation of the people next door), he solemnly played one note at a time, listening intently to its sound as it died away. Madame Masson then "taught him his notes" and called in a tuner to put the instrument in order. While the tuning was in progress he sat in the next room, and to the astonishment of his mother and great-aunt, called out quite accurately the name of every note the tuner struck.

His first lessons at the piano were given by Le Carpentier's method, and he mastered all the rudiments within a month. So fervently did he work that his mother felt obliged to lock the instrument from time to time in case it became an obsession. He must have been an abnormally intelligent youngster, because he could read a large number of simple words when he was three.

Madame Masson was not a good teacher, but she taught him to keep his hands in the proper position, and encouraged him to employ reasonable fingering. He was not a docile pupil. Most of the easy little pieces written for children disgusted him, and he refused to play them. Those simple little melodies with a pom-tum-tum bass were learnt in about five minutes and then discarded with the scornful remark : "The bass doesn't sing". So the two women had to search through the works of the old masters—chiefly Haydn and Mozart— for suitable pieces that were not beneath his dignity. If these odd details of early childhood do not bore the reader, it would also be worth recording that while he was playing with his toys he would often hum a little tune and then go to the piano to try it out with the addition of crudely-improvised harmony.

At the age of five he could play simple sonatas accurately and with a good sense of interpretation. By that time he had already played the piano part in one of Beethoven's violin sonatas at a concert of chamber music in the drawing room of an influential friend.

He was not much older when he was taken to his first symphony concert. Up to that time he had never heard more than a single violin, and had not been very impressed with its tone, but when he heard the strings of a full symphony orchestra he was almost spellbound with delight. His pleasure was not to last long, however, because a few minutes later the brass and percussion made their entry *fortissimo*, and he burst into tears. He begged his mother to go and stop them, because he couldn't hear the music of the strings ! Eventually he made such a scene that he had to be taken from the hall.

It was not long before he was writing waltzes and galops for the piano, some of them being so difficult that a friend of the family had to play them for him. Mention should be made of the fact that even in childhood he could write music straight on to manuscript paper without trying it over first on the piano. In later years he discovered several of these childish efforts, and was very surprised to find that they all conformed to the rules of harmony, although this was a subject quite unknown to him at the time.

When he was seven, and advancing satisfactorily in his general education as well as in music, he was allowed to take piano lessons from Stamaty, one of Kalkbrenner's most brilliant pupils and a propagator of that virtuoso's method of placing a rod in front of the keyboard, upon which the forearm could rest in such a way that all muscular action but that of the hand was suppressed. In his *Musical Memories*,[1] Saint-Saëns said that this system was excellent for teaching the young pianist how to play pieces written for the harpsichord or the early piano-fortes whose keys responded to very slight pressure, but was quite useless for modern instruments and the music written for them. "It is the way one ought to begin, for it develops firmness of the fingers and suppleness of the wrist, and, by easy stages, adds the weight of the forearm and of the whole arm. But in our day it has become the practice to begin at the end. We learn the elements of the fugue from

---

1 Translated by Edwin G. Rich (John Murray ; 1921). These memoirs are from a set of essays, *École Buissonière*, published by Pierre Lafitte in 1913.

Sebastian Bach's *Wohltemperiertes Klavier*, the piano from the works of Schumann and Liszt, and harmony and instrumentation from Richard Wagner. All too often we waste our efforts, just as singers who learn rôles and rush on the stage before they know how to sing ruin their voices in a short time."

The young piano student made rapid progress with Stamaty, and was soon allowed to study harmony as well with a professor named Maleden. This teacher had studied with one Gottfried Weber[1] in Germany, who also had a "method", and it is not surprising to learn that Maleden and his brilliant young pupil were frequently engaged in heated argument.

When Saint-Saëns was ten, Stamaty decided that he should be "brought out", for a career as a child prodigy seemed to be the obvious course for the boy to adopt. He accordingly played the Beethoven C-minor Concerto and one of Mozart's concertos at a public concert in the Salle Pleyel with an Italian orchestra conducted by Tilmant. He was so successful that he was invited to play at one of the concerts of the Société des Concerts du Conservatoire, but a member of the committee was very antagonistic towards Stamaty and eventually succeeded in getting the arrangement cancelled.

Stamaty was undeterred, and insisted that after so brilliant a début the young pianist should embark immediately upon a career as an infant prodigy, but Madame Saint-Saëns was anxious about the child's health and general education, and refused to allow him to accept any more public engagements. Stamaty was very annoyed at this decision, for a child of ten that could play concertos perfectly from memory as well as the Preludes and Fugues of Bach and difficult pieces by Handel and Kalkbrenner, was not only a fine advertisement for him but a potential source of a large income. He had visions of taking the lad on tour throughout Europe, and making a handsome profit by acting as his manager. It is therefore not surprising to find that a certain coolness existed in the relations between teacher and pupil after that time.

The young pianist had already aroused the interest of several prominent people. Ingres,[2] the famous French painter, had given him a medallion bearing a profile of Mozart and inscribed : "To my young friend M. Saint-Saëns, a charming interpreter of the divine artist." This was as welcome a gift as the full score of Mozart's *Don Juan*,

---

[1] No connection with the composer of *Der Freischütz*.

[2] Jean Ingres (1780-1867), leader of the Classic painters of his day. One of his works is *La Source*, in the Louvre.

luxuriously bound in scarlet morocco, that he had received from another admirer.

At about that time he wrote a sonata, which probably inspired his mother's sharp retort to a feline woman who criticized her for allowing him to play the sonatas of Beethoven. "Whatever music will he be playing when he is twenty ? " the woman asked. "His own" came the reply.

During the next few years his mother occasionally lifted her ban upon public performances and did everything she could to encourage him, provided that music did not interfere too seriously with his ordinary education. During those years piano pieces, songs, cantatas and overtures poured from the boy's pen, but the majority were destroyed in later life.

II

WHEN he was fourteen, Camille Saint-Saëns was admitted to the Conservatoire, but first only as an "auditor," that is, he could attend classes and listen to other students doing practical work, but could not be given lessons on any instrument himself. During this probationary period he worked assiduously, concentrating at home chiefly on Bach's *Wohltemperiertes Klavier*. Stamaty had already introduced him to François Benoist, the professor of the organ at the Conservatoire. During his first few days at that institution, Saint-Saëns was given an opportunity of trying the organ during Benoist's class, but when he sat on the bench of that great instrument he suddenly felt frightened. His effort was such a nervous one that most of the students began laughing. A few weeks later, however, Benoist discovered that his ·students had been slacking and were unable to play a piece that he had set them. The young "auditor" said that he thought he could manage it, and to everyone's surprise, sat down and played perfectly. He was accepted as an ordinary pupil forthwith, and at the end of the first year won the second prize.

In his memoirs, Saint-Saëns wrote affectionately about the old Conservatoire in the Rue Bergère. ". . . I loved it deeply, as we all love the things of our youth. I loved its antiquity, the utter absence of any modern note, and its atmosphere of other days. I loved that absurd court with the wailing notes of sopranos and tenors, the rattling of pianos, the blasts of trumpets and trombones, the arpeggios of clarinets, all uniting to form that ultra-polyphone which some of our composers have tried to attain—but without success. Above all, I loved the memories of my education in music which I obtained in that ridiculous and venerable palace, long since too small for the pupils who thronged there from all parts of the world."

From the same book we learn that Benoist was a very ordinary organist, but an excellent teacher. "A veritable galaxy of talent came from his class. He had little to say, but as his taste was refined and his judgment sure, nothing he said lacked weight or authority. He collaborated in several ballets for the Opéra, and that gave him a great deal of work to do. It sounds incredible, but he always used to bring his 'work' to class and scribble away on his orchestration while his pupils played the organ. This did not prevent his listening and looking after them. He would leave his work and make appropriate comments as though he had no other thought."[1]

At the age of fifteen, Saint-Saëns entered Halévy's composition class. Unfortunately, Halévy[2] was far too engrossed in writing operas to give much attention to his class. He had won the Grand Prix de Rome in 1820, leapt to fame with the production of his so-called grand opera La Juive, and L'Eclair, an opéra-comique, and then settled down to make large sums of money by turning out inferior operas like sausages from a machine. We are told that he was a good-natured man : he was evidently one of those bland "good-natured" persons who without a scrap of compunction can take people's money and give very little, if anything, in return. He went to his class "when he had time," so more often than not his pupils taught one another whatever they could glean from text-books and from their own experiments in composition. They probably learnt far more by this method than they would have done at the feet of their master. Saint-Saëns took advantage of the professor's absences by spending a great deal of time in the extensive music library. There, he declared, he completed his education, for "the amount of music, ancient and modern, I devoured is beyond belief."

To hear the orchestral music he studied so diligently in that library he tried to gain admission to the performances of the Société des Concerts, but he found that this was "a Paradise guarded by an angel with a flaming sword, in the form of a porter named Lescot. It was his duty to prevent the profane from defiling the sanctuary." The young

---

[1] Benoist won the Grand Prix de Rome in 1815. He wrote a great deal of organ music and several mediocre operas.

[2] Jacques François Halévy (1799-1862). His real name was Lévy. Bizet was one of his pupils, and later became his son-in-law.

student soon found the way to the porter's heart, however, and to give him a chance to hear the music, this humble official went on his rounds as slowly as possible and generally managed to overlook the youth's presence altogether. Then another kind friend began giving him a place in his box : a privilege that he was to enjoy for several years. There were times when the student's enthusiasm for the music got him into trouble. He always studied the scores so thoroughly beforehand that defects in the performance, and particularly in the "interpretation" by the conductor, were all too clear to him, and he frequently incurred the displeasure of his elders by criticising in no uncertain manner. Faults that would not be tolerated in these days were passed over without comment, and it is to be feared that the venerable society rested very much upon its laurels at times.

In 1852 Saint-Saëns tried for the Grand Prix de Rome. His entry was one of considerable merit, but the adjudicators considered that as he was still only sixteen years of age, he was too young to benefit from the award, and therefore gave the prize to a mediocre young man of twenty-five. This was a great disappointment to him, but he had too much faith in himself to become despondent, and worked with all the more determination. His reward came later in the same year, when he received a prize from the Société Sainte Cécile for an ode he had written in honour of their patron saint.

Although his study of the piano and organ was continued with great enthusiasm, this prize encouraged him to attempt more ambitious forms of composition, and in the following year he completed his first symphony (No. 1 in E-flat, Opus 2) which he submitted to the same society. Fearing that the committee would not give serious consideration to a symphony from a youth of seventeen, he sent it anonymously. One can well imagine his delight when he received an official notification of its acceptance. The society performed it during the same year under the conductorship of Seghers, with great success. Berlioz and Gounod both spoke highly of it, and predicted a brilliant future for the unknown composer.

A few days later, Saint-Saëns received the following letter :

My dear Camille,

I was told officially yesterday that you are the composer of the symphony they played on Sunday. I suspected it, but now that I am sure, I must tell you at once how pleased I was with it.

You are beyond your years. Always keep on, and remember that on Sunday, December 11th, 1853, you incurred an obligation to become a great master.

Your pleased and devoted friend,

Ch. Gounod.

It was at about this time that Saint-Saëns first made the acquaintance of Liszt. Seghers frequently invited the young music student to his house, and on one memorable occasion Liszt was there, for he had given lessons to Madame Seghers, a brilliant pianist, some years previously. Saint-Saëns had been studying Liszt's works "with all the enthusiasm of my eighteen years, for I already regarded him as a genius and attributed to him, even before I saw him, almost super-human powers as a pianist." But when Liszt played a few pieces in the Seghers's drawing room, Saint-Saëns was astonished at his amazing technique. "Remarkable to relate, he surpassed even the conception I had formed. The dreams of my youthful imagination were but prose in comparison with the Bacchic hymn evoked by his supernatural fingers. No one who did not hear him at the height of his powers can have any idea of his performance."

Meanwhile, Saint-Saëns had been appointed organist[1] of the church of Saint Merry. The curé here was the Abbé Gabriel, a kindly soul deeply interested in music, and when Saint-Saëns wrote a Mass for the church and dedicated it to him, the good priest showed his appreciation by taking him to Rome to hear the famous choir of the Sistine Chapel. The young organist stayed at Saint Merry's for about five years, during which he composed another Mass (*Messe Solennelle*, Opus 4, for soli, chorus, orchestra and organ), a motet, *Tantum ergo*, another symphony (in F, unpublished), *Tarantelle* for flute and clarinet, *Fantaisie No. 1* for organ, *Six Bagatelles* for piano, *Duettino* for piano, and various minor works including songs.

His early songs require a special note, for although they are of no great importance musically, they mark a significant development in the composer's cultural life. The first one, *Guitare*, dates back to 1851, when he was only sixteen. A friend had given him the first volumes of Victor Hugo's poems. "I have forgotten who it was, but I remember what joy the vibrations of his lyre gave me. Until that time, poetry had seemed to me something cold, respectable and far away, and it was much later that the living beauty of our classics was

1 In December 1852.

revealed to me. I found myself at once stirred to the depths, and as my temperament is essentially musical in everything, I began to sing them."[1] *Guitare* was the first of Hugo's poems he set to music, and in due course it was published by Choudens.   In the same year—1851— he set Hugo's *Rêverie*, and in the following year *Le Pas d'armes du roi Jean*.   Later came *L'Attente*, *La Cloche*, and the duet *Viens*. "The older I grew the greater became my devotion to Hugo.   I waited patiently for each new work of the poet and I devoured it as soon as it appeared.   If I heard about me the spiteful criticisms of irritating critics, I was consoled by talking to Berlioz who honoured me with his friendship and whose admiration for Hugo equalled mine.   In the meantime my literary education was improving, and I made the acquaintance of the classics and found immortal beauties in them. My admiration for the classics, however, did not diminish my regard for Hugo, for I never could see why it was unfaithful to him not to despise Racine.   It was fortunate for me that this was my view, for I have seen the most fiery romanticists, like Meurice and Vacquerie, revert to Racine in their later years, and repair the links in a golden chain that should never have been broken."

When he was twenty, Saint-Saëns was introduced to Rossini, who expressed his interest in the *Tarantelle* for flute and clarinet that the young Frenchman had written in 1857, and suggested that perhaps Dorus and Leroy, two of the finest wood-wind players in Paris, would come and play the work to him at one of the musical receptions he was holding at that time.   The two artists were delighted to play before the famous composer and performed the duet exquisitely.   Rossini never had printed programmes for these social events, and everybody assumed that the *Tarantelle* was one of his latest compositions. Consequently, when the applause to the encore at last subsided, fawning admirers began telling Rossini what a masterpiece he had written.   Their superlatives poured forth in an ever-increasing *crescendo*, until finally the Italian composer cut them short with the words : "Yes, yes, I agree with you.   But the duet wasn't mine : it was written by this young man."

After that event, Saint-Saëns frequently acted as the pianist at these receptions, and as one would imagine, met a great many of the prominent figures in the world of opera.   He never ceased to regret that he was absent on the particular evening when Patti sang for Rossini for the first time.   She chose an aria from his *Barber of Seville*.

[1] *Musical Memories.*

After the thunderous applause had died down, Rossini went up, paid her a charming compliment upon her voice, and then enquired casually "By the way, who wrote that aria?" In his memoirs, Saint-Saëns tells us that he saw Rossini three days later, and that he was still boiling with rage. "I am fully aware that arias should be embellished . . . but not to leave a single note of them, even in the recitatives ! . . . that is too much ! "[1]

III

In 1858, Saint-Saëns was appointed organist of the Madeleine in succession to Lefébure Wély. This famous church was attended by the most fashionable congregation in Paris, and the post of organist carried a salary of three thousand francs a year, so there was great competition for it. Abbé Deguerry, the curé of the Madeleine, had already heard of Saint-Saëns, and was a great admirer of both his compositions and his organ-playing, so he did not hesitate to pass over all the other candidates. It was in this year, too, that Saint-Saëns completed his first piano concerto (in D, Opus 17) as well as his *Oratorio de Noël* for soli, chorus, string quintet and organ. He stayed at the Madeleine for almost twenty years.

There was in Paris at that time a musician named Abraham Niedermeyer, who had established in the capital a school for the study of church music—chiefly that of the sixteenth, seventeenth and eighteenth centuries. On the death of Neidermeyer, Saint-Saëns accepted a professorship at the school and took a class that contained several very promising young musicians including Gabriel Fauré and André Messager. He stayed there for three years and considerably enhanced his reputation as a teacher.

Of the many compositions he produced during this period of his life, mention should be made of the Third Symphony in D, which, however, was never published, the overture *Spartacus*, also unpublished, and the Orchestral Suite, Opus 49, which was completed in 1863 and eventually published fourteen years later. The first violin concerto, in A, was written in 1859, but remained in manuscript until Hamelle published it in 1868.

What made Saint-Saëns compete again for the Grand Prix de Rome in 1864 is a matter for conjecture, but it is probable that he was so

[1] Realizing that Rossini would be a dangerous enemy, Patti went to him later "for advice". She was sensible enough to take to heart all that he said, and soon became a great friend of the composer.

keen to devote the whole of his life to composition, that he would have relinquished his remunerative post at the Madeleine had he been given the opportunity of going to Rome under the conditions of the award. It seems almost incredible, but on this occasion the jury again rejected him. He was twenty-eight years old, they said, and had already established himself so well as a composer that he was in no need of the benefits of the Grand Prix. The award therefore went once again to a person of very limited talent : a young musician named Victor Sieg, who did nothing more than obtain an organistship and a school-inspectorship in later life. One cannot help wondering whether the art of Saint-Saëns would have developed on different lines had he been successful and taken up the prescribed period of residence in Italy and Germany. There can be no doubt that at this impressionable stage in his career he would have derived great benefit from the privileges of the award, all the more so because his art was essentially eclectic : entirely different from that of Debussy, for instance, who was intensely individualistic, and, as we shall see later in this book, was neither interested in, nor disposed to make use of, the privileges of the Grand Prix.

Proof of the pre-eminence of Saint-Saëns among the younger French composers at that time[1] came when he competed with over a hundred other musicians in the composition of a prize cantata for the International Exhibition of 1867. His setting of *Les Noces de Prométhée* was easily the best, for Berlioz, who was one of the adjudicators, wrote to his friend Ferrand : "I was writing these few lines to you from the Conservatoire, where the jury . . . for the competition in musical composition at the Exhibition had to assemble. . . . On the preceding day we heard a hundred and four cantatas, and I had the pleasure of witnessing the crowning (unanimous) of my young friend Camille Saint-Saëns, one of the greatest musicians of the present day. . . . How happy Saint-Saëns will be ! I went straight to his house to tell him of his success."

The prize-winner must have esteemed it a great honour to be a "young friend" of the great Berlioz—though he little realized at that time the full extent of Berlioz's greatness, for not until many years after the death of this wonderful character did the world acknowledge his genius. Berlioz had always taken a keen interest in the career of Saint-Saëns ever since the latter, as a young man of barely twenty, had made a brilliant transcription of the mélologue *Lélio* for piano and voice

[1] Berlioz was then over sixty, César Franck was forty-five.

for the publisher Richault in 1855. It is one of the finest transcriptions of Berlioz we possess : one of the few that show proper understanding of that composer's technique.

Saint-Saëns had already become very interested in opera, and it was chiefly in connection with this that the two composers frequently came together. For instance, in January 1866 Berlioz was supervising the production of Gluck's *Armide* at the Théâtre-Lyrique, and we find him writing to Ferrand thus : "Madame Charton-Demeur, who plays the trying part of *Armide*, comes every day to rehearse with M. Saint-Saëns, a great pianist, a great musician, who knows his Gluck almost as well as I do. It was curious to witness her gradual enlightenment. This morning, in the "Hatred" scene, Saint-Saëns and I shook hands. We were speechless. Never did any other man discover such accents. And to think there are people who blaspheme this masterpiece . . ."

In his admiration for Berlioz, Saint-Saëns was never gushing : he could appreciate most of the great man's qualities, but was not afraid to criticize what he believed to be his faults. The somewhat ruthless treatment of the singers' voices in some of Berlioz's choral works, for instance, frequently drew complaints from the younger composer. In his memoirs he says : " . . . it must be admitted that Berlioz treated the voices in an unfortunate way. Like Beethoven, he made no distinction between a part for a voice and an instrument. While except for a few rare passages it does not fall as low as the atrocities which disfigure the grandiose *Mass in D*, the vocal part of the *Requiem* is awkwardly written. Singers are ill at ease in it, for the timbre and regularity of the voice resent such treatment. The tenor's part is so written that he is to be congratulated on getting through it without any accident, and nothing more can be expected of him." Saint-Saëns then goes on : "What a pity it was that Berlioz did not fall in love with an Italian singer instead of an English tragedienne ! Cupid might have wrought a miracle. The author of the *Requiem* would have lost none of his good qualities, but he might have gained what, for lack of a better phrase, is called the fingering of the voice, the art of handling it intelligently and making it give without an effort the best effect of which it is capable." Summing up he says that Berlioz was a genius, but that the word genius accounted for the fact that he wrote badly for voices and sometimes permitted himself the strangest of freaks. "Nevertheless, he is one of the commanding figures of musical art. His great works remind us of the Alps with their forests, glaciers, sunlight, waterfalls and chasms. There are people who do not like the Alps. So much the worse for them."

Saint-Saëns also enjoyed the friendship of Wagner, whom he had first met in 1861 when he was acting as pianist at the Paris Opéra, for in that year the great German composer came to Paris to be present at a production of *Tannhäuser*. Wagner was amazed to find a young pianist who could play his complicated scores with ease and at the same time show such understanding in his interpretation. Some years later, Wagner was at a banquet in Bayreuth when he toasted Saint-Saëns as "the greatest living French composer."

Early in 1868 Saint-Saëns conducted a series of concerts in Paris at which the great pianist-composer Anton Rubinstein appeared as the soloist. They had become friends rapidly, and during a conversation after the eighth concert, Rubinstein happened to say that he had never yet conducted a concert in Paris. Saint-Saëns immediately suggested that he should do so, and arrangements were made for him to appear in this rôle about three weeks later. The young French composer then decided to write a pianoforte concerto for the occasion, and laying aside various other tasks, set to work at full speed. Thus the famous Concerto No. 2 in G-minor came into existence. He finished it only a few days before the concert and arranged with Rubinstein to play it himself. As one might expect, with the composer at the piano and the able Russian composer wielding the baton, the concerto was an outstanding success, though Saint-Saëns said himself that he did not play well owing to fatigue. News of the concerto spread quickly in musical circles, and many of the leading virtuosi of the day included it in their repertoire. In due course it became known all over the world. That such a work as this could have been written and scored so quickly, is proof of the remarkable creative ability and capacity for hard work that enabled this composer to produce such an extensive range of compositions in his lifetime. Needless to say, it was the delightful Scherzo that won the favour of the audience at the *première*.

In the same year, the prestige that he had won in musical circles was officially recognized, for he was made a Chevalier of the Legion of Honour.

IV

AT about the same time, Saint-Saëns was trying to get a footing in the world of opera, but he encountered much the same difficulties as those that had made Berlioz so embittered. The fact that he had already distinguished himself as a symphonic composer, pianist and organist had not the slightest effect upon the management of the Opéra and the Opéra-Comique, indeed his accomplishments merely increased their prejudices against him. Likewise, Delibes, Bizet and Massenet were also trying to establish themselves in opera, with as little success.

Through the influence of Auber, Saint-Saëns had received from Leon Carvalho, the director of the Théâtre-Lyrique, a libretto that several other composers had refused to touch, *Le Timbre d'Argent*, but it must be confessed that this had been given chiefly to keep the enthusiastic young composer quiet, for there was little possibility of the opera being produced. Saint-Saëns, however, had taken it seriously, discovered the serious faults in it, and persuaded Barbier and Carré to make several important amendments to the script. Then he had retired to the heights of Louveciennes for two months and worked diligently on the score. Carvalho had been singularly uninterested in the composer's announcement that the score was ready, and for two years would not even consent to hear it. Finally, wearied by Saint-Saëns's persistence, he invited him to dinner one evening in 1867 and allowed him to play the score through on the piano afterwards. The evening started in an atmosphere of cool politeness that was merely a cloak for the impatience of Carvalho and his talented wife ; but it concluded with both of them showing marked enthusiasm for the opera. It was a masterpiece, they thought, but to ensure its success, Madame Carvalho would have to sing the principal part herself. This, however, was subordinate to that of the leading dancer, so Carvalho insisted that it should be developed considerably. Furthermore, the eminent director had a mania for collaborating in some way in the works he produced, and through the years 1868 and 1869, the opera was subjected to endless minor revisions.

In his *Musical Memories* the composer tells us : "He tormented us for a long time to make the dancer into a singer on his wife's account. Later he wanted to introduce a second dancer. With the exception of the prologue and epilogue, the action of the piece takes place in a dream, and he took upon himself the invention of the most bizarre combinations. He even proposed to me one day to introduce wild animals.

Another time he wanted to cut out all the music with the exception of the choruses and the dancer's part, and have the rest played by a dramatic company. Later, as they were rehearsing *Hamlet* at the Opera and it was rumoured that Mlle Milsson was going to play a water scene, he wanted Madame Carvalho to go to the bottom of a pool to find the fatal bell. Foolishness of this kind took up two years. Finally, we gave up the idea of Mme Carvalho's co-operation. The part of Hélène was given to beautiful Mlle Schroeder, and the rehearsals began."

Saint-Saëns had been longing to see this opera produced, but another disappointment was soon to come. While the rehearsals were in progress, the Théâtre-Lyrique collapsed financially, and everything was abandoned.

A few weeks later hope was revived when Perrin, the manager of the Opéra, offered to take over *Le Timbre d'Argent*. Further adaptations of the opera had to be made to make it suitable for the larger stage, and Perrin took the opportunity to demand various revisions in the cast. During the course of these there was a great deal of disagreement on all sides, and it soon became evident that Perrin had lost interest in the whole thing.

However, his nephew du Locle then took charge of the Opéra-Comique and said he would like to stage the opera there. This meant further adaptations, and although Saint-Saëns was willing to do anything he could to oblige du Locle, the joint authors of the libretto were less eager. To make matters worse, they fell out between themselves. One lived in Paris and the other in the country, and it fell to the long-suffering composer to travel incessantly backwards and forwards in an endeavour to get them to agree. At last all seemed settled, and then the Franco-German war broke out! The production had to be postponed.

Throughout the siege of Paris the composer served in the National Guard, and during a lull in the fighting wrote the familiar *Marche Héroïque*, which he dedicated to the memory of his friend Henri Regnault, the painter, who was killed in a battle on the outskirts of the city. It was in these difficult days that Saint-Saëns and a few other leading French musicians founded the Société Nationale de Musique, but it had scarcely begun to function when civil war broke out in Paris. The evacuation of the German troops from the capital led to the (second) Commune of Paris, who ruled the city ruthlessly in the spring of 1871 until they were suppressed by the troops of the National

Assembly of France. During that terrible spring, Saint-Saëns sought refuge in London, where he found Gounod and various other fellow-countrymen. His début in this country was made at a concert held by the Musical Union during this short sojourn, and the cordial welcome he received was no doubt responsible for the many return visits he made in later years. He also gave several recitals on the Albert Hall organ.

Back again in Paris, where order reigned once again, Saint-Saëns settled down to the composition of some of the greatest works that bear his name. He had always been deeply impressed by the symphonic poems of Liszt, and immediately after his return he decided to write a symphonic work to illustrate a given subject himself. In the same year—1871—he completed the first of the symphonic poems that have done so much to keep his name in the concert programmes during the past thirty or forty years : *Le Rouet d'Omphale*. It was a great success, and was published in the following year.

His début in the world of opera was made at about this time, not with *Le Timbre d'Argent* after all, but with a one-act opéra-comique *La Princesse Jaune*, which du Locle had asked him to write in lieu of the abandoned opera. Most of the critics were blatantly hostile. In these days of atonality, it seems incredible that a famous critic of the 'seventies could have written : "It is impossible to tell in what key or what time the overture is written" about such a harmless little work. What would this gentleman have said about an evening of Schönberg ?

All the same, arrangements for the production of *Le Timbre d'Argent* were resumed, and a brilliant Italian dancer, whose services had been sought two years previously, was re-engaged. It really looked as if the opera would be staged after all. Then Amédé Achard, the principal tenor, withdrew because he said the part was too heavy for him. Then du Locle began to lose interest . . . then the Opéra-Comique closed for financial reasons !

The indomitable composer tucked the score underneath his arm and went out once again to find someone to produce it. He found that Vizentini, who had just re-opened the Théâtre-Lyrique, was feeling very pleased with himself after the most successful production of his first play *Paul et Virginie*. Saint-Saëns offered him the opera and at the same time induced some of his friends at the Ministry of Fine Arts to promise the manager a small subsidy if he would produce it. He agreed, and then the troubles started all over again. The leading tenor proved difficult, Vizentini wanted to make cuts that the composer would not approve, the stage manager and the ballet master were rudely impatient, the mediocre orchestra said the music was unplayable, and so forth. But as the final rehearsal drew near, Vizentini realized that the opera might easily become a great success, and became more amenable. On the opening night there was no doubt about it : the opera was a triumph despite the incoherence of the libretto and the denunciation of the critics. It should be added that Vizentini eventually became one of the composer's greatest friends.

Saint-Saëns visited London again in July 1874 when he was invited to play one of his concertos at a Royal Philharmonic concert. It is not at all clear which one he took, but it was probably the Second Concerto in G-minor. This was considered to be very modern in those days, and the composer told the Society's directors that if they felt alarmed by it, he would gladly substitute a Beethoven concerto. The records of the Society bear silent witness to the mentality of the board in those unenterprising days : Saint-Saëns played the Beethoven Concerto in G. Five years later, however, they invited him to play his Second Concerto during another visit to this country.

It was during one of these many visits to England that the French composer sustained injuries that for a time proved quite serious. He had arranged to take part in one of Sir Julius Benedict's concerts, and just before he had to appear on the platform he fell through a trap-doorway that had carelessly been left open. He recovered sufficiently to play the items of the advertised programme, but when he went to acknowledge the applause he discovered that he could not bend his back at all. It troubled him for some months but he was well enough to visit Russia and Austria in 1875.

The year 1877 stands out prominently in the life of this composer, for it was then that he completed his famous opera *Samson and Delilah*. All his associates in Paris thought he was quite mad in attempting to write an opera based on a Biblical story, and even his closest friends, to whom he played the second act one evening at his house, told him that it would be useless to continue with the work. Only one solitary person showed any interest in it—Liszt, that wonderful musician who was always the first to perceive the genius of his contemporaries and who rarely refused to lend them his assistance. He told Saint-Saëns to have the opera ready for production at Weimar at the end of that year. To the end of his days, the French composer acknowledged that but for the encouragement of Liszt, this opera (which was originally known as *Dalila*) would never have been completed. Liszt's production of it was a complete success, and it was not long before it was repeated at Cologne, Hamburg, Prague and Dresden, to mention only the greater of the German cities that acclaimed it.

Saint-Saëns naturally presumed that after this incontestable proof of its merit, he would be invited to submit the opera for production in Paris. He waited, but nothing happened. He then sought out two impresarios, Halanzier and Vaucorbeil, and offered them the opera, but both refused it. For twelve years it was unknown in France! When at last his native land recognized this masterpiece, it was first produced not in Paris but at Rouen. The Parisians heard it first in the autumn of 1890 at the Eden Theatre, and some time later it was included in the repertoire of the Opéra—but not until it had been produced in a dozen French provincial cities, in Switzerland, Italy and elsewhere on the Continent.

In Great Britain it was banned on account of the Lord Chamberlain's rule against operas based on Biblical subjects, and no stage performance was heard until it was mounted at Covent Garden in 1909. An "oratorio" performance was given in 1893 under Sir Frederick Cowen at a Covent Garden promenade concert, and it was afterwards given in that form at the Queen's Hall with great success.

Among the many major works written by Saint-Saëns during the 'seventies, we find another opera Étienne Marcel, the oratorio Le Déluge, the cantata La Lyre et la Harpe, the three other symphonic poems Phaéton, Danse Macabre, and La Jeunesse d'Hercule, the Symphony No. 2 in A-minor, the Piano Concerto No. 4 in C-minor, the Quartet for piano, violin, viola and 'cello, and the Messe de Requiem.

V

TURNING for a moment to the composer's private life, we find that there is not much of importance that has any bearing upon his musical career. He married Marie-Laure Truffot on February 3rd 1875, had one son at the end of that year and another in 1878. The latter was a fateful year, for just after he had completed the Requiem mentioned above (in the month of May) his elder son fell from a fourth floor window and was killed. Another tragedy came soon afterwards with the death of the younger son at the age of seven months.

In the summer of 1879 he was in England again for the Birmingham Festival, at which his cantata La Lyre et la Harpe was sung. His delight in the musical life of our great midland city was later expressed in his book *Harmonie et Mélodie* :[1] "I wish those who believe the English to be devoid of feeling for music could hear the Birmingham singers. Accuracy, precision in time and rhythm, delicacy in light and shade, charm in sonority,—this wonderful choir combines everything."

During one of the many visits to England at this time he was presented to Queen Victoria by the Baroness de Caters at Windsor Castle. He had been warned that the Queen's great dignity often gave the impression of coldness, and was therefore surprised when Her Majesty came into the room with both hands extended to greet him. "Her Majesty wanted to hear me play the organ . . . and then the piano. Finally, I had the honour of accompanying the Princess[2] as she sang an aria from *Étienne Marcel*. Her Royal Highness sang with great clearness and distinctness, but it was the first time she had sung before her august mother, and she was frightened almost to death. The Queen was so delighted that some days later, without my being told of it, she summoned to Windsor Madame Gye, wife of the manager of Covent Garden—the famous singer Albani—to ask to have *Étienne Marcel* staged at her own theatre. The Queen's wish was not granted."

The composer's great interest in England induced him to base his next opera on a chapter in the history of Britain. He asked Léonce Détroyat and Armand Sylvestre to prepare a libretto, and in due course set to work on the four-act opera *Henry VIII*. His friendship with the music librarian at Buckingham Palace enabled him to make a study of a great deal of our national music. In a collection of seventeenth century manuscripts of music for the harpsichord he found a very fine theme which he employed to good effect in the opera.[3]

While he was at work on this opera he was elected a member of the Institut (Académie des Beaux-Arts), and at the same time was composing various other works, making concert tours, and carrying out all the other engagements that took up so much time in his very full life. Rehearsals for *Henry VIII* began in the autumn of 1882, and by the time it was ready for the opening night, March 5th 1883, Saint-Saëns felt utterly exhausted and was obliged to take a complete rest, first at Algiers and then at Cauterets. He returned to Paris in the following October to find *Henry VIII* established in the repertoire of the Opéra.

[1] Published by C. Lévy, Paris, 1885.   [2] Princess Beatrice.

[3] This theme was also used many years later in the march he wrote for the Coronation of King Edward VII.

His next major task was the composition of the magnificent Third Symphony in C-minor for our own Royal Philharmonic Society. It was finished early in 1886, and the composer came to London to direct its first performance on May 19th. This great symphony, which uses an organ and four-hand piano as well as a full orchestra, was afterwards dedicated to the memory of his good friend Franz Liszt, who died in the same year.

The operatic stage then claimed his attention once again, for in the following year he wrote the lyrical drama *Proserpine*, which was produced almost immediately at the Opéra-Comique, with great success.

It was probably during this period of his life that he wrote that ever-popular zoological fantasy *Carnaval des animaux*. This amusing work was not published until after his death, for he would never allow it to be played during his lifetime, probably because he feared that musical jocularity with animal imitations would impair his reputation. It was from this work that the tremendously popular melody *Le Cygne* (The Swan) for 'cello and piano was taken. It was published separately while he was alive.

The life of Benvenuto Cellini (1500-1571), the famous Italian sculptor, had always fascinated Saint-Saëns, so he decided to write an opera on this subject. It had to be called *Ascanio*, for Berlioz had already used the sculptor's name for the title of an opera on the same theme. The Opéra accepted *Ascanio*, and started rehearsals late in 1889. The opening night was fixed for March 31st 1890, and then to everybody's surprise, the composer disappeared. Enquiries at his home brought only the information that he had left Paris for an unknown destination. Weeks went by, and the musical world grew extremely uneasy at the absence of news of his whereabouts. The first night of the opera passed, the whole of April went by, and still he was not to be found.

Eventually he was discovered in the Canary Islands. He had been enjoying a complete rest incognito. As soon as his identity was discovered admirers swarmed around him, and there was nothing to do but to return to Paris. But this holiday stirred in him a great desire to travel, and in the ensuing years he was frequently journeying to foreign parts. In the winter of 1891, for instance, he went as far afield as Ceylon, and while he was there revised his opera *Proserpine*. Returning through Egypt he found Cairo to be a very pleasant place for a lengthy sojourn, and wrote a musical picture of it : *Africa*, a fantasia for piano and orchestra.

During the 'nineties he was frequently in England. In June 1893 he went to Cambridge to receive an honorary degree of Doctor of Music in the company of Tchaikovsky, who died later that year, Max Bruch and Arrigo Boito. But one of his most pleasant recollections of the last decade of the nineteenth century was his second visit to Windsor Castle, where the great Queen once again received him. In his memoirs he writes : "Dinner was over, and princes in full uniform and princesses in elaborate evening dress stood about, waiting for her Majesty's appearance. I was heartbroken when I saw her enter, for she was almost carried by her Indian servant and obviously could not walk alone. But once seated at a small table, she was just as she had been before, with her wonderful charm, her simple manner and her musical voice. Only her white hair bore witness to the years that had passed. She asked me about *Henry VIII*, which was being given for the second time at Covent Garden, and I explained to her that in my desire to give the piece the local colour of its times I had been searching in the royal library at Buckingham Palace. . . . The Queen was much interested in music, and she appeared to be especially pleased in this discussion."

Before we leave the nineteenth century, passing mention must be made of the composer's visit to the Far East in 1895, when he toured through parts of China, and of the Jubilee concert given in his honour at the Salle Pleyel in Paris in 1896 to celebrate the fiftieth anniversary of his first public appearance. Of special interest, too, is the music he wrote for *Déjanire*, a tragedy by Louis Gallet, which was to be presented at the open-air performances in a huge arena at Béziers, in southern France. Two performances of this work were given there during August 1898 before an audience of ten thousand. Saint-Saëns assembled an enormous orchestra and chorus for the occasion, and conducted himself.

Then he accepted an invitation sent by the Argentine government, and visited Buenos Ayres to give concerts of chamber music. We next find him in Brussels appearing at concerts with Eugène Ysaÿe, to whom he had dedicated a String Quartet.

VI

WE might at this juncture consider one or two impressions of Saint-Saëns received by his contemporaries at about this time. In the reminiscences of Francesco Berger,[1] that eminent musical nonagenarian who died in 1933, we find the composer described as "a man of middle stature, square-set, with a finely chiselled nose, and a wonderful pair of alert, penetrating eyes. He has a remarkable speaking voice, loud and very shrill, and he utters so rapidly that it is difficult to follow him—his words flash from him like sparks from an anvil."

His encyclopædic knowledge of many other subjects besides music[2] and his remarkable wit made him a wonderful conversationalist, yet he was neither pompous nor affected. He invariably seemed to be bright and cheerful, and the impression of some that he was "cold" in the concert hall was derived erroneously from his very calm and collected attitude on the platform. His literary works include poetry, various books on music and musical matters generally, and even a few plays.

His interest in everything around him is exemplified in his first work of the twentieth century : Le feu Céleste, a cantata in praise of electricity, which was produced at the first official concert at the Paris Exhibition in May 1900.

The next major work to come from his pen was the opera Les Barbares, which he wrote to a libretto by Victorien Sardou and Gheusi for open air performance in the arena at the town of Orange. It was never produced out of doors, however, and after various revisions was staged at the Paris Opéra. It was well received at the time, but in later years lost its popularity.

In 1904 he wrote both the words and music of a one-act opera Hélène. This was first produced not in Paris but at Monte Carlo in the following February. In the same year it was brought to London and staged at Covent Garden with Melba in the title rôle.

Two years later another opera, L'Ancêtre, was also given its première at Monte Carlo, then in the autumn the composer visited the United States. Unfortunately on the way over he was taken ill, and was in poor health all the time he was in America. All the same, he insisted

1 Reminiscences, Impressions and Anecdotes (Sampson Low, Marston & Co.)

2 It is said that he had a "profound knowledge" of philosophy and astronomy.

upon fulfilling his engagements, and appeared at Washington, Philadelphia and Chicago, receiving a great and cordial welcome on each occasion.

He recovered soon after his return to Paris and in a spirit of thanksgiving wrote a magnificent setting of the hundred-and-fiftieth psalm *Praise ye the Lord* for double chorus, orchestra and organ. Then he went to Cairo and wrote the incidental music to Eugène Brieux's drama *La Foi*.

In 1907 the town of Dieppe honoured him by the erection of a statue, and he was present at the unveiling ceremony. In the same town a museum was built in his name : an institution of great value to the musical historian.

During a visit to London at about this time, the composer had the honour of playing with Josef Hollman, the violinist, before Queen Alexandra at Buckingham Palace. He was presented to the Queen who appeared to be in poor health, but who received him with the utmost cordiality. "She spoke to me about her mother, whom I had seen at Copenhagen with her sisters, the Empress Dowager of Russia and the Princess of Hanover. . . . I do not know how it happened but I remained speechless at this lead from the Queen. . . . After M. Hollman and I had played a duet, she expressed a desire to hear me play alone. As I attempted to lift the lid of the piano, she stepped forward to help me raise it before the maids of honour could intervene. After this slight concert she delivered to each of us, in her own name and in that of the absent king, a gold medal commemorative of artistic merit, and she offered us a cup of tea which she poured with her royal and imperial hands."[1]

We must now pass over various minor works written during the early part of the present century, and come to his last opera *Déjanire*. The libretto was prepared from Louis Gallet's tragedy of that name, and the composer used most of the music he had written during the 'nineties for the dramatic production in the arena at Béziers. The opera was written on a large scale, and when it was first produced at Monte Carlo on March 14th 1911 it was very well received. Equally successful was the production at the Paris Opéra in the following November, but soon afterwards its popularity waned, and there was never any great enthusiasm for it in later years.

---

[1] Saint-Saëns played before various royal personages all over Europe from time to time, but to record details of all these solemn receptions and ceremonies would, I think, make this biography very tedious.

Saint-Saëns was in London again in June 1913 to be present at a Jubilee Festival at the Queen's Hall to mark his seventy-five years of music from the first piano lesson he received from Madame Masson before his third birthday. With the exception of a Mozart Concerto, the entire programme was devoted to his own works, including the fine C-minor Symphony. He received an album containing the signatures of a large number of British musical personalities, and an address was read by Sir Alexander Mackenzie, Principal of the Royal Academy of Music, which included this tribute : "Amid the varied developments of modern music, you have worthily upheld the highest traditions of your national art ; you have been the champion of its cause and carried its classic banner from triumph to triumph. With 'progress' for your watchword and with unique versatility, you led the advance of French music in every branch, and you are justly acknowledged today to be its most gifted and exalted representative."

In the same year Saint-Saëns completed an oratorio called *The Promised Land*. This was sung at the Gloucester Musical Festival that autumn in the composer's presence. Incidentally, he had just been raised to the rank of Commandeur of the Legion of Honour.

The Great War did little to restrict his activity, for he wrote an *Elégie* for violin and piano, and a *Cavatina* for tenor trombone and piano in 1915; and in the following year went as representative of France to the Panama-Pacific Exposition at San Francisco, writing a cantata, *Hail California*, for chorus and orchestra, to mark the occasion. After that he toured South America.

When peace returned, most people imagined that this octogenarian would retire and make no further effort to write music during his last few years. On the contrary, the end of the war seemed to inspire him to fresh creative effort : at the age of eighty-three he wrote his second String Quartet, *Morceau de concert* for harp, a *Marche interalliée*, *Cypres et Lauriers* for organ and orchestra and various minor works !

During 1920 he composed a second *Elégie* for violin and piano (Opus 160), Six Fugues for the piano, and an *Odelette* for flute and orchestra ; and on October 9th he celebrated his eighty-fifth birthday in Paris by appearing as composer and executant at a concert held at the Trocadero.

The last year of his life was equally eventful, though most of it was spent at Algiers. There he wrote a Sonata for oboe and piano, a similar work for clarinet and piano, and another for bassoon and piano. His last *opus* was numbered 169 : *Feuillet d'album* for pianoforte. Right up to the last few months of his life he retained his skill at the keyboard, and even appeared at a concert in Algiers just before his death, which took place in the salubrious climate of that Mediterranean seaport on December 16th 1921.

THE GREATER WORKS OF SAINT-SAËNS

Gounod once described the extraordinary versatility of Saint-Saëns by saying that he could write at will a work in the style of Rossini, Verdi, Schumann or of Wagner, but the French composer was too good a musician to imitate any of the masters of whose works he possessed such an amazing knowledge. If we examine his music we find little that is not the original Saint-Saëns. As the late Romain Rolland once said : "One seems to be passing through scenery that one has seen before, and that one loves, but one can never find direct resemblances ; nowhere, perhaps, are reminiscences more rare than with this master, who carries in his memory all the ancient masters. It is by the spirit itself that he resembles them."

The same critic's analyses of his works were shrewd and rather harsh, because he over-emphasized their weaknesses. "The most individual feature of his moral physiognomy seems to me to be a melancholy languor that has its source in a somewhat bitter sentiment of the nothingness of things, with fits of lassitude of a slightly sickly nature, succeeded by fits of a rather fantastic humour, of nervous gaiety, of a capricious taste for parody, burlesque, and the comical." Rolland was apt to overlook the wealth of fine stimulating music ; the colourful, happy melodies and the delightful harmonies that this composer produced. True, his music is rarely very deep, but his meditative passages have a peaceful charm of their own, and something, surely, must be said for his lucidity and sense of balance.

His chief weakness is revealed in one of his own statements : "The artist that does not feel completely satisfied by elegant lines, by harmonious colours and by a beautiful succession of chords, does not understand the art of music."

Samson and Delilah

The following is a synopsis of the opera, to which there is no overture :

ACT I : The scene is a square in Gaza, Palestine, where the Israelites (first behind the curtain) bewail the Philistine tyranny. Samson (Tenor) enters and revives their spirits with his heartening prophecy of deliverance. Here the music becomes more and more dramatic until the entry of the satrap of Gaza, Abimelech (Bass) who in a curious solo taunts the captives, jeering at their prayers and their God. Samson attacks and slays him, and leads the revolt of the Israelites, who then rush off the stage.

The High Priest of Dagon (Baritone) enters and in a furious monologue demands vengeance. A Messenger (Tenor) brings the news that Samson is leading his people to destroy the harvested grain. With the other Philistines present they leave, and are succeeded by aged Hebrews, one of whom (Bass) sings a psalm of deliverance.

The Hebrews are in turn replaced by Delilah, with Philistine girls, and in a very charming scene the temptress addresses Samson, eventually ensnaring him in an alluring scene while an old Hebrew utters words of warning. Samson is too much under her spell to listen to the aged Hebrew. The priestesses of Dagon then try to entice the Hebrew warriors by doing an extremely voluptuous dance to fascinating music.

ACT II : The scene is Delilah's house in the valley of Soreck. It is night, and flashes of lightning may be seen in the sky. While Delilah waits for Samson, the High Priest of Dagon urges her to lure him into revealing the secret of his colossal strength. She has made three attempts already, but without success. The priest departs and Samson enters, having made up his mind to bid her farewell. But he cannot resist her, despite the thundering heavens from which he hears the voice of God in yet another warning. The seduction scene is remarkably beautiful. After the events recorded in the Biblical story,[1] Delilah cries "'Tis done ! ", and the Philistine soldiers rush into the house and overpower the hero.

ACT III : The first scene is the Prison of Gaza, where the shorn Samson, blind and in chains, is turning a hand-mill and appealing in anguish to heaven for pity. Outside, the Hebrews (behind the stage) lament their betrayal.

The second scene is the interior of the Temple of Dagon. Samson is brought in and taunted by Delilah, who cruelly reminds him of her caresses, and sings snatches of the melodies used during the second

---

[1] Delilah finally surrenders herself only on condition that he reveals his secret. He tells her that his strength is due to the fact that never in his life has his hair been cut. Later, when he is asleep on her bosom, she cuts off all his hair.

act. The Philistines rejoice in bacchanalian dances, and there is a striking orgiac hymn to Dagon, the whole working up to a marvellous climax. This is suddenly interrupted by the voice of Samson praying for one final mercy : the restoration, for but a moment, of his former strength. A child leads him to the great pillars of the temple, and standing between two of them he takes one in each arm, and with the granting of his supplication, pulls the vast structure down in ruins upon all within it, bringing the work to a close with one tumultuous climax.

As one would imagine, this vivid and intensely dramatic opera can be wonderfully effective if adequately produced. The composer has caught the spirit of this grand story and used all his skill to enhance it with singularly appropriate music. The solo as well as the chorus work is rich in fine melodies, the characterization is well defined, and the orchestration provides just the brilliant splashes of colour required to portray the pagan atmosphere in contrast with the Hebrew sobriety.

Le Timbre D'Argent

This opera, which a critic once described as "a nightmare in four acts which lasts five hours" is rarely heard today. The story tells of a young painter, Conrad, who receives from the evil Doctor Spiridion a magic call-bell, which at each stroke will give him anything he desires at the expense of the death of a friend. Conrad is anxious to win the love of Fiametta, a beautiful dancer, and for that reason is urgently in need of wealth. He decides to make use of the bell, and obtains great riches, but one of his friends dies in consequence. But the luxury that he now enjoys is not sufficient to attract Fiametta, and ultimately he resorts once again to the bell in order to get her. He strikes it, and his dear friend Benedict dies. Filled with horror, he smashes the bell—and then wakes up to find that the whole thing has been a dream.

Many people blamed the fantastic libretto for the failure of this opera, but it is no worse than several others that are still in use. The music is rather immature, but there is plenty of good writing in it. The best part is undoubtedly the splendid overture, which might be heard more as a concert piece.

Étienne Marcel

All that seems to be known of this opera today is the pleasant ballet music. The story is of Étienne Marcel, provost of the merchants, who led the revolt of the Parisians against the Dauphin Charles during the regency in the middle of the fourteenth century. The provost loses his popularity and agrees to open the gates of Paris to the troops of Charles the Bad, King of Navarre. His daughter, Beatrice, is in love with Robert de Lorris, the Dauphin's equerry. Maillart, an agitator, assassinates Marcel for his treachery, and there is a poignant scene when Beatrice throws herself upon her father's body while her lover entreats her to fly with him. The opera ends with the triumphant entry of the Dauphin, and general exultation.

The most successful part of this work is the portrayal of the mob : the scenes of disorder and violence convey an excellent impression of the mentality of the Parisian rabble of the fourteenth century. It is a pity that this opera is being allowed to pass into oblivion. But who knows ? The wonderful renascence of music in Britain today may result in the regular performance of such works as this when our cities acquire new theatres. At the present time, it is the lack of accommodation that retards the efforts of those who are trying to revive opera in this country.

Henry VIII

The libretto of this opera is such a travesty of historical fact that few would swallow it today, so as far as we are concerned this work is a waste of good music. Briefly, the story tells of Henry's suspicions that his recently-acquired Anne Boleyn is "carrying on" with Don Gomez, the Spanish ambassador. The banished Katharine of Aragon is lying ill at Kimbolton, and is in possession of a compromising letter from Anne to the Spaniard. The King travels to Kimbolton with Gomez, and arrives to find Anne there also trying to obtain the dangerous document. In the hope of stirring bitterness in Katharine's heart, he displays passionate affection for Anne, but Katharine is not sufficiently spiteful to harm her successor. She becomes weaker, and after throwing the letter into the fire, dies without divulging the secret. The opera closes with the frustrated and still-suspicious Henry reminding Anne that any further deception will cost her her head.

The librettists spared nothing to make the King appear the dirty dog that he was, but in their anxiety to do this they got rather a wrong conception of his general character. They missed a splendid opportunity to excel at characterization. To comply with the traditions of the Paris Opéra, Saint-Saëns had to introduce a ballet, and by providing a series of Scottish dances to be performed before the Papal legate at Richmond, he gave us the Suite that for years has been popular in the concert hall. The ballet was omitted at both of the productions of this opera at Covent Garden.

Proserpine

The libretto of this opera was revised some years after its original production. The scene is Italy during the sixteenth century. Proserpine, a courtesan, is madly in love with a young nobleman named Sabatino, who is engaged to Angiola. The story is of her efforts to prevent the marriage. Even with the assistance of a bandit she fails to eliminate Angiola, and finally she confronts the couple, tells Sabatino of her love for him, and drawing a stiletto tries to kill her rival. He stops her, and she then plunges the weapon into her own breast and dies. In the original version she actually strikes Angiola, and Sabatino then wrenches the stiletto from her hand and kills her with it.

Some people consider this to be one of the best of Saint-Saëns' operas, but nobody seems to have had sufficient confidence to revive it in recent years.

Ascanio

Louis Gallet's libretto was based upon the drama *Benvenuto Cellini* by Paul Meurice. The story is rather complicated. Colombe, the lovely daughter of the Provost of Paris is greatly admired by Benvenuto Cellini, and deeply loved by his favourite pupil Ascanio. Scozzone, a girl in love with Cellini, and the Duchesse d'Etamps, who desires Ascanio, are plotting against Colombe. Cellini discovers that Ascanio and Colombe are in love and gallantly withdraws his own suit. He suggests that to protect the girl from the Duchess, she should be sent in a reliquary to a convent. This is agreed, but the Duchess hears of the plan, and makes arrangements for the reliquary to be taken to her house and detained sufficiently long for Colombe to be suffocated. Scozzone refuses to be a party to this horrible crime, and in remorse for her previous efforts to injure Colombe, sacrifices her own life by taking Colombe's place in the receptacle. Cellini then asks the King to consent to the marriage of Colombe and Ascanio. The Duchess is horrified to discover that she has murdered Scozzone, of whom she was very fond, and Cellini is heartbroken.

Despite the weak libretto, this opera is worthy of an occasional revival. One cannot analyse the score in a few lines, because there are so many details that attract the attention. On the whole, it is a good specimen of a well conceived opera of its period ; the composer was evidently very attracted by the subject, and spared no effort to maintain in the music its dramatic interest right through to the end. In this opera, too, there is some pleasant ballet music.

Phryné

In this highly-amusing little two-act opéra-comique, Phryné, a very beautiful young courtesan, is in love with Nicias, who has an uncle, an elderly magistrate. The latter strongly disapproves of her, but also finds her quite irresistible. Her play with this old gentleman all goes to make the work most entertaining, though one wonders whether our English magistrates—particularly the ones over ninety-five—would appreciate all the good fun in this admittedly risqué opera.

Is it too much to hope that some day one of our enterprising "little" theatres might produce this ? Various modifications could be made for economy's sake without spoiling it in any way.

Les Barbares

This lyrical tragedy was written for open-air performance at Orange, and was never very satisfactory in the opera house. The story tells of the invasion of the town of Orange by the Teutons, who are about to sack it when their chief, Marcomir, discovers there the beautiful Floria, the priestess of Vesta. He offers to spare the town and its inhabitants if she will give herself to him. She agrees after a while, and is rewarded when Livia, widow of Euryalus, the Roman consul, discovers that Marcomir was the murderer of her husband, and stabs him to death with a piece of the weapon that she has extracted from her husband's body.

The opera is not likely to be revived, unless the BBC would care to make a broadcast version of it, but its lengthy overture is occasionally heard as a concert piece.

Hélène

Saint-Saëns wrote his own libretto for this, which is a lyrical poem in one long act divided into seven scenes. Hélène, wife of the Doric King, is consumed with love for Pâris, son of Priam, who is their guest. She is in anguish, and prays to the gods to be delivered of this illicit love. Her prayers are not answered, and she decides to throw herself into the sea, but Aphrodite appears, surrounded by nymphs, and urges her to obey the call of love. Pâris comes on the scene, and is

more ardent than ever, but she still resists, and prays to her father Zeus
for help. Pallas, his messenger, comes during a storm, and warns the
lovers that terrible things will happen if they unite. They see a vision
of Troy in flames with Pâris and all his family being slain. But love
wins, and Pâris declares himself prepared to meet anything, even
death, rather than lose Hélène. She, too, makes a similar declaration,
and they sail off in a ship to Troy, with arms entwined.

The chief fault with this opera is that the composer has written
music altogether too genteel to convey a good impression of the
burning, overwhelming passion experienced by the two lovers. For
this, a heavily emotional style, in which Saint-Saëns did not excel, is
required.

L'Ancêtre

The libretto of this three act opera resembles Romeo and Juliet·
Raphael, the hermit, tries to reconcile the families of Fabiani and Nera,
between whom there has been a feud for many years. Tebaldo Nera
is in love with Margarita, foster-sister of Vanina Fabiani, who also
loves him. Vanina's brother is brought in dead, having been shot by
Tebaldo, and Nunciata, the ancestress of the Fabiani family, persuades
the jealous Vanina to shoot Tebaldo at an opportune moment. Meanwhile, Tebaldo and Margarita meet, and after the former's explanation
that he killed Vanina's brother in self-defence, the hermit blesses
their union. Nunciata gives Vanina a gun, but the latter drops it, for
she is unable to commit the murder after all. The incensed Nunciata
thereupon goes out to kill Tebaldo herself, with Vanina following.
There are two shots, but Vanina flings herself in front of the man she
loves and saves his life at the cost of her own.

The characterization here is good, and the composer's great skill
has added much to the dramatic intensity of the story. The love scene
in which Tebaldo meets Margarita while she is cutting roses is
delightful ; and the characterization of the horrible old ancestress is
very well done. Even in these days of pepped-up technicolour-
musicals from Hollywood, this opera would probably stand revival.

Le Rouet d'Omphale

This, the first of the symphonic poems, is Saint-Saëns at his best.
It was inspired by the old legend of Hercules, after the murder of
Iphitus, serving as a slave to Omphale, for whose charms he has fallen.

The composer explains on the score that he has tried to illustrate "feminine seduction ; the triumphant struggle of weakness over strength." He has done so quite beautifully. Very well drawn is the impression of Hercules who has to work at the spinning wheel with Omphale's women : it depicts the beaten hero in a very subdued, humble frame of mind, longing for the mocking woman who now wears his lion's skin. The poem concludes with a most impressive *diminuendo* in which all but the first violins fade out.

Phaeton

The second symphonic poem also takes its subject from mythology. Phaeton, son of Phoebus,[1] begs his father for permission to drive the chariot of the sun, but in time betrays his incapacity, for the horses diverge from their proper course, and threaten the earth with conflagration. Jupiter sees the danger and hurls a thunderbolt at Phaeton, who falls into the river Eridanus. The composer's musical description of the drive through space is a brilliant accomplishment. The brass despicts the burning orb ; strings and wood-wind portray the galloping horses. As the latter get more and more out of hand the poem works up to the great climax : the thunderbolt crashes with all the resources of the full orchestra, a great blow on the gong adding to the shattering effect produced by the more usual equipment of the percussion department. The poem ends with Sun's theme reiterated in the form of a lament for the death of Phaeton.

Danse Macabre

A gruesome poem by Henri Cazalis inspired the third symphonic poem. In this weird graveyard waltz we hear the clattering of bones (produced by a xylophone) and all manner of spectral horrors mixed up with a parody of *Dies Iræ* until the crowing of a cock heralds the dawn, when the grisly assortment of skeletons and spooks subside to the vaults. The popularity of this work suggests that there are plenty who like this sort of thing.

La Jeunesse d'Hercule

In this, the last of the symphonic poems, it seems that the composer did not adhere too strictly to the mythological tale, but it follows more or less the incident of the Choice of Hercules, wherein he sits in a lonely place trying to decide his future mode of life. Virtue and

1 The sun.

SAINT-SAËNS from the painting by Benjamin Constant

PLATE XII

Rischgit

SAINT-SAËNS, bronze by Dubois

PLATE XIII

Pleasure appear before him, the one offering a life of toil and glory, the other a life of pleasure and ease. He chooses the former. Saint-Saëns allows him to take part first in the wild bacchanalian orgy of the nymphs and satyrs—portrayed by exciting voluptuous music— before he realizes the folly of unrestricted licentiousness. However, this is a masterly, colourful work, with a fine, strong, central theme and well-executed elaboration.

Symphony in C-minor

This great achievement is generally called his Third Symphony, though actually it is his fifth. Although it is in. the traditional four movements, it is made to appear in two parts only, because the first movement leads straight into the Andante, and the Scherzo is followed by the Finale without a break. The Allegro opens, after a very brief introduction, with the violins giving out the principal theme *staccato*, in a restless anxious mood. Later, a second theme is introduced, calm and beautiful, which changes the atmosphere entirely in due course. In a most unusual manner, the Andante is brought in, with the organ accompanying the lovely serene melody given to the strings. In the second half, the Scherzo is rather weird, with grotesque treatment of the main theme. Here, the piano is employed to contribute striking arpeggios. The Finale is suggestive of triumphant accomplishment, and the symphony concludes in a brilliant fashion.

The use of the organ in this fine symphony is fully justified, and its effect is impressive, but the presence of the piano is rather unnecessary : the composer might have done better by scoring the arpeggios for the harp. It has been suggested, however, that as the symphony was dedicated to Liszt, the splashes for the piano were intended as a reminder of that composer's prodigious skill as a virtuoso.

Piano Concerto No. 2 in G-minor

The great popularity of this work can be readily understood ; it is one of the best concertos we possess. The serious first movement has plenty of feeling, and holds the attention from the outset. This is followed by the jolly Allegro Scherzando, merrily expressing the high spirits of youth and full of irresistible charm. The concluding Presto uses a vigorous Tarantella that brings just the right atmosphere at the end.

Piano Concerto No. 4 in C-minor

This concerto is equally as good and is probably even more popular. It is in two sections, and makes use of two principal themes which are treated in various ways to depict a succession of emotions. The transformations are done very well, and the whole work is a model of good construction and lucidity. Restlessness and doubt in the first movement give way to confident energy in the imaginative second, and the work concludes in a very happy mood of achievement.

Piano Concerto No. 5 in F

Not so well known, but full of interest is the last piano concerto. It is quite different from the others, for it reflects many of the composer's impressions of Egypt and the Far East. The Andante movement has a definite Oriental atmosphere, and includes a song that the composer heard the boatmen singing on the Nile. Here and there we get a fine impression of the ancient serenity of Egypt beneath cloudless blue skies, and in the Finale we find a very realistic description of the voyage across the Mediterranean : there is a suggestion of the ship's screw cutting through the water, and a short storm.

Violin Concerto No. 3 in B-minor

This concerto has for years occupied an important place in the repertoire of violinists all over the world. It is rather superficially brilliant in the style beloved by the less intelligent type of virtuoso, but it does not entirely lack interest for the more serious student of music. The second of the three movements is a very pleasant barcarolle affording good opportunity for the effective use of harmonics at the end.

'Cello Concerto in A-minor

There are not many concertos for the 'cello that appeal so readily to the concert-goer as this pleasant work. It is in one movement only, but this is divided into three sections ; the second being the delightful little minuet that Joseph Hollman popularized as a solo. This concerto is unusually original, and its compactness makes it all the more attractive to those who like plenty of variety in concert programmes. It was composed in 1872 and has held its own for over seventy years.

Other Works

Owing to the very limited amount of space available in this book, the remainder of Saint-Saëns' compositions must be listed briefly. During his long life he wrote an enormous amount of music, and it is only to be expected that various items have now become obscure. The following list does not include the seventy odd songs, nor the dozens of hymn tunes, minor motets, etc., and is not absolutely complete as far as unpublished works are concerned. Its length precludes more than occasional annotations.

OPERAS

La Princesse Jaune
   (1872) Opéra-comique in one act. Opus 30.

Frédégonde
   (1895) This five act opera was left unfinished by Ernest Guiraud, and completed by Saint-Saëns. It was a failure.

Déjanire
   (1911) Four-act tragédie lyrique. An interesting opera, well constructed, and successful during the years preceding the Great War. Déjanire (Deianira), wife of Hercules, tries to stop his philandering with other women by giving him the garment of Nessus, which was supposed to have the power to reclaim a husband's affection. It still contains poison from the arrow with which Hercules killed Nessus, and causes the husband's death.

BALLET

Javotte
   (1896) Ballet in one act ; three tableaux.

CHORAL WORKS
(including songs with orchestral accompaniment)

Ode à Sainte Cécile
   (1852) MS.

Messe Solennelle
   (1856) Mass for soli, chorus, orchestra and organ. Opus 4.

Tantum Ergo
   (1856) Motet for chorus and organ. Opus 5.

Oratorio de Noël
   (1858) A Christmas oratorio for soli and chorus accompanied by string quintet and organ. Opus 12. A simple but very beautiful work ; graceful and full of pleasing melodies.

Scène d'Horace
   (1860) For soprano, baritone and orchestra. Opus 10.

Cœli enarrant (Psalm XVIII)
   (1865) Motet for soli, chorus and orchestra. Opus 42.

Cantate
> (1868) Written for the centenary of the birth of Hoche. This has not been published.

Le Déluge
> (1875) This oratorio for soli, chorus and orchestra contains some very fine writing, and is considered by some to be one of the composer's best works yet it is very rarely performed. The words of this "Biblical poem" are by Louis Gallet. The very fine Prelude is well-known as a concert piece.

Messe de Requiem
> (1878) It is said that Saint-Saëns wrote this requiem mass in eight days, but it is by no means insignificant. The *Agnus Dei* is perhaps the best part. The whole work is scored for orchestra. Opus 54.

La Lyre et la Harpe
> (1879) This is a fine setting of Victor Hugo's *Ode*. Liszt spoke very highly of it, and it should certainly be performed more frequently. It is scored for soli, chorus and orchestra. Opus 57.

La Fiancée du Timbalier
> (1887) Setting of Victor Hugo's ballade for mezzo-soprano and orchestra. Opus 82.

Nuit Persane
> (1891) Cantata for soli, chorus and orchestra based on the set of songs known as *Mélodies Persanes*. Words by Armand Renaud.

Pallas Athéné
> (1894) For soprano and orchestra. Words by J. L. Croze.

Lever de soleil sur le Nil
> (1898) Setting for contralto and orchestra of the composer's own description of this scene.

Panis Angelicus
> (1898) For tenor solo accompanied by string quintet or organ.

Offertoire pour la Toussaint
> (1898) For four voices with organ.

La Nuit
> (1900) Soprano solo, female chorus and orchestra. Words by G. Audigier. Opus 114.

Le Feu céleste
> (1900) For soprano, chorus, orchestra, organ and orator. Words by Armand Sivestre. Opus 115.

Lola
> (1900) Scène dramatique for two characters. Opus 116. Words by Stephan Bordèse.

La Gloire de Corneille
> (1906) Cantata for soli, chorus and orchestra. Words by S. C. Lecomte. Opus 126.

Praise ye the Lord (Psalm CL)
> (1908) Cantata for double chorus with organ and orchestra. Opus 127. Very impressive.

The Promised Land
> (1913) Short oratorio for soli, chorus and orchestra. Opus 140.

Hail California
> (1915) Cantata for chorus and orchestra.

UNACCOMPANIED CHORAL WORKS

Sérénade d'hiver
Les soldats de Gédéon
Saltarelle
Les Guerriers
Madrigal
Chants d'automne   All these choral works are for male voices.
A la France
Ode d'Horace
Le Matin
La Gloire
Les Marins de Kermor
Les Titans
Chanson de Grand père   (for two female voices).
Chanson d'ancêtre   (for baritone solo and male chorus).
Calme des nuits
Les Fleurs et les Arbres
La Nuit   (soprano solo and female voices).
Romance du Soir
Laudate Dominum

ORCHESTRAL WORKS

Symphony No. 1 in E-flat
     (1853). Opus 2.
Symphony in F
     (1856) Not published.
Symphony in D
     (1859) Not published.
Symphony No. 2 in A-minor
     (1859) Scored for small orchestra without trombones. Very pleasant Scherzo, but otherwise not outstanding. Opus 55.
Suite for Orchestra
     (1863) Consists of Prelude, Sarabande, Gavotte, Romance and Finale; in classical style. Opus 49.
Spartacus
     (1863) An unpublished overture.
Rapsodie Bretonne
     (1866) Based on an early work for organ, using Breton hymn tunes.
Marche Héroïque
     (1871) This has been very popular for years. Opus 34.
Une nuit à Lisbonne
     (1880) A graceful barcarolle. Opus 63.

La Jota Aragonese
> (1880) Opus 64.

Suite Algérienne
> (1881) An attractive suite inspired by the composer's sojourns in Algeria consisting of Prelude, Rhapsody, Mauresque, *Rêverie du soir*, and *Marche militaire française*. Opus 60.

Hymne à Victor Hugo
> (1881) Chorus may be used *ad lib.* Opus 69.

Le Carnaval des animaux
> (date of composition uncertain). See the biography for further details of this fantasia, which includes the favourite melody *Le Cygne.*

Sarabande et Rigaudon
> (1892) Opus 93.

Coronation March for King Edward VII
> (1902) Opus 117.

Ouverture de Fête
> (1909) Opus 133.

Marche interalliée
> (1919).

PIANOFORTE AND ORCHESTRA

Concerto No. 1 in D
> (1858) Interesting since it shows the composer's early development. Opus 17.

Concerto No. 3 in E-flat
> (1869) An excellent concerto, for whose neglect it is difficult to suggest a reason. The Andante, in which a fine melody is played on muted strings is very agreeable, and the Finale is excitingly energetic.

Allegro Appassionato
> (1884) Opus 70

Rapsodie d'Auvergne
> (1884) Opus 73.

Africa
> (1891) This attractive fantasia is based on tunes sung by the natives while the composer was in Africa ; a very colourful work. Opus 89.

VIOLIN AND ORCHESTRA

Concerto No. 1 in A
> (1859) Opus 20. Not of great interest.

Concerto No. 2 in C
> (1859) Opus 58. Ditto

Introduction et Rondo Capriccioso
> (1863) Very pleasant and popular with violinists all over the world. Opus 28.

Concert piece
> (1880) Quite an attractive little work. Opus 62.

Havanaise
> (1887) Another travel picture in music. Opus 83.

Caprice Andalous
> (1904) Ditto. Opus 122.

La Muse et le Poète
> (1909) For violin, 'cello and orchestra. Opus 132.

VIOLONCELLO AND ORCHESTRA

Concerto No: 2 in D-minor
> (1902) Quite an interesting concerto, but for some reason unpopular. Opus 119.

CHAMBER MUSIC

Quintet for Piano and Strings
> (1855) Rather immature, with a mixture of banalities and quite brilliant ideas. Opus 14.

Suite for 'Cello and Piano
> (1862) A youthful but well-written work. The pensive serenade makes good use of the sombre lower register of the 'cello.

Trio No. 1 in F
> (1863) For piano, violin and 'cello. Notable are the very successful cross-rhythms in the *scherzo* and the amusing *pizzicato* effects. The andante is a gentle, ballad-like movement.

Sonata No. 1 for 'Cello and Piano
> (1872) Mature and vigorous; the three movements are linked by interrelated themes. The fine second movement, *andante*, originated in an organ improvisation. Opus 32.

Quartet for Piano and Strings
> (1875) For piano, violin, viola and 'cello. Quite ingenious with an extraordinary variety of minor devices. Opus 41.

Trumpet Septet
> (1881) An unusual work for trumpet, piano, two violins, viola, 'cello and double bass. Opinions differ considerably about the value of this work. The trumpet seems a trifle embarrassed, especially in the rather naive passage where it plays a French regimental call. Opus 65.

Sonata No. 1 for Violin and Piano
> (1885) Genteel and very well constructed, with an excellent Finale. Opus 75.

String Quartet No. 1
> (1889) Rather dry, but relieved by the interesting *allegro quasi presto* and the *molto adagio*. Opus 112.

Trio No. 2 in E-minor
> (1892) For piano, violin and 'cello. A large-scale scholarly work in five movements, too detailed to be described briefly. Worthy of attention. Opus 92.

Sonata No. 2 for Violin and Piano
> (1896) Of this the best part is the *allegretto scherzando*, an enchanting movement of great delicacy.

Sonata No. 2 for 'Cello and Piano
> (1905) Simple and graceful, but spoilt by its weak finale. Opus 123.

String Quartet No. 2
> (1919) Pseudo-Mozart in parts. Uninteresting but for the delightful *andantino* interlude and the gay *allegretto*. Opus 153.

Sonata for Oboe and Piano
>   (1921)   Quite a useful little work.   Opus 166.

Sonata for Clarinet and Piano
>   (1921)   Of no great interest.   Opus 167.

Sonata for Bassoon and Piano
>   (1921)   A useful addition to the very small repertoire of this instrument. Opus 168.

ORGAN

Fantaisie No. 1
>   (1856)

Bénédiction Nuptiale
>   (1859)   Opus 9.

Trois Rapsodies sur des cantiques Bretons
>   (1866)   Opus 7.

Trois Préludes et Fugues (first book)
>   (1894)   Opus 99.

Fantaisie No. 2
>   (1895)   Opus 101.

Marche religieuse
>   (1897)   Opus 107.

Trois Préludes et Fugues (second book)
>   (1898)   Opus 109.

Sept improvisations pour grand orgue
>   (date uncertain)   Opus 140.

Fantaisie No. 3
>   (probably 1910)   Opus 137.

Cyprès et Lauriers
>   (1919)   Organ and orchestra.   Opus 156.

MILITARY BAND

Orient et Occident
>   (1869)   A march.   Opus 25.

Hymne Franco-Espagnol
>   (1900)

Sur les bords du Nil
>   (1908) Another march, not particularly descriptive of the banks of the Nile. Opus 125.

PIANO SOLO

Six Bagatelles
>   (1855)   Opus 3.

First Mazurka
>   (1868)   Opus 21.

Gavotte
>   (1871)   Opus 23.

Second Mazurka
(1871) Opus 24.
Romance sans paroles
(1871)
Six Etudes (Set 1)
(1877) Opus 52.
Menuet et Valse
(1878) Opus 56.
Third Mazurka
(1882) Opus 66.
Album
(1884) Opus 72. Contains: Prelude, Carillon, Toccata, Valse. *Chanson Napolitaine*, Finale.
Souvenir d'Italie
(1887) Opus 80.
Les Cloches du Soir
(1889) Opus 85.
Valse Canariote
(1890) Opus 88.
Suite
(1892) Consists of: Prelude and Fugue, Minuet, Gavotte and Gigue. Opus 90.
Thème varié
(1894) Opus 97.
Souvenir d'Ismalaïa
(1895) Opus 100.
Valse Mignonne
(1896) Opus 104.
Valse Nonchalante
(1898) Opus 110.
Six Etudes (Set 2)
(1899) Opus 111.
Valse langoureuse
(1903) Opus 120.
Six Fugues for Piano
(1920) Opus 161.
Feuillet d'album
(1921) Opus 169.

PIANO: FOUR HANDS

Duettino
(1855) Opus 11.
Koenig Harald Harfagar
(1880) Opus 59. After Heine's Ballade.

Feuillet d'Album
>   (1887)   Opus 81.
Pas redoublé
>   (1887)   Opus 86.
Berceuse
>   (1896)   Opus 105.

TWO PIANOS

Variations sur un thème de Beethoven
>   (1874)   Opus 35.
Polonaise
>   (1886)   Opus 77.
Scherzo
>   (1889)   Opus 87.
Caprice Arabe
>   (1894)   Opus 96.
Caprice Heroïque
>   (1898)

MISCELLANEOUS

Tarantelle
>   (1857)   Flute, clarinet and orchestra.   Opus 6.
Sérénade
>   (1866)   Piano, organ, violin, viola (or 'cello).   Opus 15.
Romance
>   (1868)   Piano, organ and violin.   Opus 27.
Berceuse in B-flat
>   (1871)   Piano and violin.   Opus 38.
Romance in D-flat
>   (1871)   Flute and orchestra.   Opus 37.
Romance in C
>   (1874)   Violin and piano.   Opus 48.
Romance in F
>   (1874)   Horn and orchestra.   Opus 36.
Allegro appassionato
>   (1875)   'Cello with piano or orchestra.
Romance in D
>   (1877)   'Cello and piano.   Opus 51.
Wedding Cake
>   (1885)   Caprice valse for piano and strings.   Opus 76.
Caprice sur des airs Danois et Russes
>   (1887)   Flute, oboe, clarinet and piano.   Opus 79.
Le Cygne
>   (1887)   From the Carnival of Animals.   'Cello and piano.
Morceau de concert
>   (1887)   Horn and piano.   Opus 94.

Chant Saphique
(1892) 'Cello and piano. Opus 91.

Fantaisie
(1893) Opus 95.

Barcarolle
(1898) Violin, 'cello, harmonium and piano. Opus 108.

Fantaisie
(1907) Violin and harp. Opus 123.

Elégie (No. 1)
(1915) Violin and piano. Opus 143.

Cavatina
(1915) Tenor trombone and piano. Opus 144.

Morceau de concert
(1919) Harp and orchestra. Opus 154.

Odelette
(1920) Flute and orchestra. Opus 162.

Prière
(date uncertain). 'Cello and organ. Opus 158.

Elégie (No. 2)
(1920) Violin and piano. Opus 160.

MUSIC TO THE FOLLOWING PLAYS:

Déjanire
(Louis Gallet).

Parysatis
(Jane Dieulafoy).

Antigone
(Paul Meurice and A. Vacquerie).

Andromaque
(Racine).

L'Assassinat du Duc de Guise
(Henri Lavedan).

La fille du tourneur d'ivoire
(Mme Henri Ferrare). Music not published.

La Foi
(Eugène Brieux).

Debussy

I

A<small>T</small> an exhibition held at the famous Salon des Refusés, Paris, during the year 1863, there appeared a picture entitled *Sunrise : an Impression*. The artist, Claude Monet (1840-1926) little realized, at the time, that his appropriate choice of a title would give the name to a movement that would have a profound effect not only upon the world of pictorial art, but upon music, and, in a lesser degree, upon poetry also. Monet was one of that brilliant group of French artists who rebelled against the ideas of the old academic painters : they refused to assemble on large canvases masses of minute details that could be perceived only by circuitous inspection. They believed that the eye must be able to apprehend at one glance the complete picture, including of course its "atmosphere" and something of the emotions stirred within the artist by the particular scene portrayed. To do this, they maintained that the eye should not be compelled to rove about the canvas looking at individual details, which they believed to be merely complementary to the principal idea. Thus in looking at an impressionist picture we tend to admire the complete scene and its "atmosphere" rather than realistic details of the rabbit in the right-hand corner. We "feel" the picture with a sense of vague satisfaction.

Monet, by the way, must not be regarded as the rock upon which impressionism was built, indeed like Pissarro (1830-1903) and Sisley (1839-1899) he was more of a Luminarist. His impressionistic creed was first expounded by Manet (1832-1883) and Whistler (1834-1903), and also taken up by such artists as Degas (1834-1917) and Renoir (1841-1919).

Turning to poetry, we find that the same movement was at work in the symbolist school of thought, which revolted against realistic and "photographic" forms of expression. Verlaine (1844-1896), Baudelaire (1821-1867) and Mallarmé (1842-1898), for instance, reacted against the Romanticism of such poets as Victor Hugo (1802-1885) and his contemporaries, and we shall see in this biography how they influenced Claude Debussy, who became acknowledged as the founder of the impressionist "school" in music. It will be observed that the movement affected music later than the other arts.

It is interesting to note that the impressionist painters were in their turn severely criticized by the "modern" school, who concentrated more upon form, rhythmic design and so forth. These moderns include the Cubists and the so-called Futurists. Then came "expressionism" —another modernistic development. in which the artist concerns himself not with the representation of objects, but with the expression of his "inner experiences" and other abstractions—which has also been reflected in music. The foremost expressionist in music is Schönberg ;[1] his music is subjective rather than objective, but whether or not this is synonymous with "progressive" is a matter of opinion.[2]

Even to those who detest modernist tendencies in the arts, the part played by these movements in the general *evolution* of art is of considerable importance ; and surely, when we realize how painting, architecture, literature, drama and music are related, we cannot trace these influences without wondering what the future has in store for us. It is a fascinating subject, but not one that can be discussed in this biography.

Achille-Claude Debussy[3] was born in a modest dwelling over a china shop at 38 Rue au Pain, Saint-Germain-en-Laye (not far from Paris) on August 22nd 1862, son of a clerk who having tried his hand at most things, had taken the little business immediately after his marriage on November 30th of the previous year. A daughter, Adèle, was born within the next two years, and as the shop did not prosper, the little family moved first to Clichy and then to Paris, where they settled in the Rue Pigalle. Three more children arrived in due course, but with Adèle, they were all put in the care of an aunt. Only Achille was brought up at home by his parents.

Debussy's father was a man of humble origin, but he appears to have made the most of the very small amount of education he received, and took an interest in cultural pursuits. He eventually found employment as a book-keeper with the Compagnie Fives-Lille of Paris, and scarcely deserved the nickname bestowed on him by his son : "the old vagabond". Madame Debussy, a devoted, sentimental woman, was passionately fond of her musical son, and was responsible for his

[1] A biographical sketch of Schönberg and a survey of his work will be found in my *Composers' Gallery.*

[2] Some people see in this expressionist music just an unpleasant phase of "advanced" Romanticism !

[3] In later years Debussy reversed the order of his Christian names.

early education. Unfortunately, she was anything but qualified to do this, and in early manhood Debussy made the unhappy discovery that his spelling differed substantially from that of his more cultured friends. It is not surprising, then, to find that he was always very reticent about his childhood.

It is interesting to note how a man's frustrated ambitions can come out in his children. Debussy's father longed to be a connoisseur of music, art and poetry, but never possessed sufficient intelligence. His son, on the other hand, was so gifted that even in childhood he seemed to possess those powers of discrimination that his father strove for years to acquire. He was a curious little fellow : reserved and pensive, disliking both lessons and games, but instantly attracted by anything beautiful. Brightly-coloured butterfles, for instance, were a source of constant delight to him ; he was fascinated by little ornaments, engravings, paintings and jewellery. Delicacy in anything, particularly in pictures, never ceased to charm him : he would spend hours admiring a miniature. Even with his food he was fastidious : at parties he would consume some dainty little pastry while all his friends were stuffing themselves with more substantial fare. Bulk never appealed to him in any way. People were astonished that so poor a boy from a very ordinary home could possess such aristocratic taste.

The only time he cared to join in the play of other children was when they sang "rounds". Even the most simple tunes and harmonies enchanted him, and an opportunity to hear a band in one of the public gardens was never missed. Imagine, therefore, the tremendous impression made upon him when his father took him to the opera. *Il Trovatore* was to him a colossal experience : he was overwhelmed with the wealth of music and drama. It was a glimpse of a new wonderland of music and colour.

When he was seven, he made the first of several visits to Cannes, and was deeply impressed by the beauty of the shore and sea. While he was there his aunt, Mme Roustan suggested that he should learn to play the piano, and sent him to an elderly Italian teacher named Cerutti. There is little reliable information concerning his first year or two at music. It seems that the teacher was not particularly interested in his little pupil, and found no evidence of unusual talent. Debussy was inclined to waste time playing by ear various little tunes that he had heard, and which had fascinated him, or by trying over various chords that struck him as being unusually beautiful.

It had already been decided that Debussy was to be prepared for a naval career when Mme Mauté de Fleurville,[1] a pianist who had been one of Chopin's pupils, happened to hear him play and declared that he undoubtedly possessed talent for music. She offered to teach him herself gratuitously, and Debussy's father (who fancied himself as the father of a great virtuoso) not only agreed but used all his influence to make the boy work with great diligence. Actually, no urging was necessary, for Mme Mauté was an excellent teacher and inspired him with her own great love of music—and for the works of Chopin in particular—so that when at the age of eleven he sat for the entrance examination at the Paris Conservatoire, he passed quite easily. There was then no doubt about music being the career for him, and his father, anxious to see him earning money at the earliest possible moment, insisted upon his practising for anything up to eight hours a day.

II

In October 1873, the students of the Conservatoire were mildly surprised to find in their midst a stumpy little boy, obviously of the working-class, who looked decidedly ill-at-ease. Having had very few opportunities of mixing with better-class children, he felt extremely embarrassed and awkward ; a rather pathetic and bewildered little figure wearing a sailor's hat that had been acquired at Cannes.

But Albert Lavignac, the professor in charge of the *solfège* class, soon discovered that this odd little boy possessed a remarkable ear for music : sight-reading and transposition presented no great difficulties to him, complex rhythms did not worry him in the least, and he seemed to understand even the most involved harmonic progressions. More than that, he displayed remarkably refined taste in music. Lavignac was very proud of the high and rigorous standard maintained in his class, and took a great interest in Debussy ; an interest that helped to remove the boy's dislike of the rules of harmony. After the other students had gone home, the professor and his favourite pupil would stay behind discussing technicalities and modern trends in music, and even confess to each other their sympathies with those musical revolutionaries whose ideas were so abhorrent to the more stale types of academician. It was Lavignac who introduced Debussy to the music of Wagner by playing to him the overture to *Tannhäuser*. Debussy

[1] The mother of Mathilde Mauté, who for a little while was the wife of Paul Verlaine.

stayed in his class for four years, and won the third prize for *solfège* in 1874, the second prize in the following year, and the first prize in 1876.

In the autumn of 1873 he was admitted to the advanced piano class, but the elderly Professor Marmontel, who had been teaching there for thirty years, was a pedantic man possessing little patience with revolutionary youngsters who would not concentrate upon his uninspiring technical exercises. To such a man, students of the Debussy type were a source of irritation ; besides, they propagated those heresies that made all his laboriously-acquired erudition look horribly obsolete, and therefore they were a menace to his security. It must be admitted, however, that this brilliant youngster was not an ideal pupil : he seemed too restless to work studiously at the prescribed subjects, and frequently neglected his work to explore the greater works of the classical and romantic composers for his own edification. He loved to play Bach, to arrange the quartets of Mozart for the piano, and to bask in the music of Chopin and Schumann. He would improvise queer little preludes that would puzzle, amuse or exasperate Marmontel, according to his mood. The old pundit eventually decided that Debussy loved *music* but disliked the piano ; which all goes to show that he never really understood his brilliant pupil, although he could see that he was unusually gifted.

One of Debussy's contemporaries has recorded that in the piano class this odd little student used to astonish them all by his weird playing. Awkwardness or timidity was perhaps responsible for the way he used to throw himself at the keyboard and exaggerate all his effects. He always seemed to be in a violent temper with the instrument, and throughout the more difficult passages would breathe noisily. Later, we are told, these faults diminished, and he amazed everybody by the wonderfully delicate effects he could get in the softer passages.

Ambroise Thomas, the Director of the Conservatoire at the time, was extremely impatient with Debussy and treated his efforts ruthlessly in the examinations. At the competition held at the Conservatoire in 1875, Debussy distinguished himself by his playing of Chopin's second *Ballade*, and it looked as if he would become a virtuoso. In the following year, however, the test piece was a Beethoven sonata, and he was less successful. He received the second prize in 1877 with his interpretation of the first movement of the Schumann Sonata in G-minor, and one of the musical journals prophesied a brilliant future for him as an executant, but that was the last of his successes at the Conservatoire, much to the disappointment of his father.

Debussy's professor of harmony was Émile Durand, a second-rate musician of the most uninspired variety, and he also proved anything but helpful in the development of the young composer. He took a delight in condemning as "unorthodox" every spark of originality shown by the lad, so Debussy decided to play him up by deliberately writing his exercises in such a way as to include the greatest possible number of consecutive fifths and other "ungrammatical horrors". His efforts were little else but a riot of barbaric colours. Then he would often sit at the piano when the lesson was over and while Durand was trying to clear up outstanding questions raised by other pupils, would play incredible successions of grotesque chords as if they came naturally to him and were necessary to his spiritual welfare. The professor was at first quite distracted by this extraordinary student, but in time realised that many of the youth's eccentricities were put on for his special benefit, and became a little more amicably disposed towards him. On one occasion he even admitted that Debussy's efforts were "ingenious".

César Franck was at the Conservatoire at that time, teaching the organ and improvisation, so Debussy went to him for a while to get some knowledge of the "king" of instruments. He liked Franck, and as there is evidence of that distinguished composer's influence in his work, we might reasonably conclude that he studied diligently with him taking improvisation as well. He did not always agree with Franck, of course, and in later life became less enthusiastic about his compositions.

By the rules of the Conservatoire, he was unable to enter a composition class without having first obtained a "recommendation" in harmony, and as he had obtained no such award from Durand, he found himself in something of a predicament. Fortunately, he solved his difficulty by winning the first prize in the score-reading class run by Auguste Bazille, for this was accepted in lieu of the prescribed recommendation.

During the summer of 1878, he had enjoyed a pleasant diversion in the form of a visit to London with some friends of his family, and had heard a performance of Sullivan's *H.M.S. Pinafore*. Another opportunity even more exciting came in the summer of 1880, when Mme Nadejda von Meck, the patroness of Tchaikovsky, required a pianist for the trio she kept at Chenonceau castle. Marmontel recommended Debussy, who was accepted. So the young student had the pleasure of playing a great deal of Tchaikovsky's music and also of improvising to the distinguished lady. She was very pleased with him, and took him on a tour to Florence, Venice and Vienna. Little is known about his activities during this tour, though he heard *Tristan and Isolde* at Vienna, met Wagner in Venice and wrote a *Danse bohémienne* which Mme von Meck sent to Tchaikovsky for criticism. The famous Russian composer considered that it was a pleasant little piece but much too short, and pointed out that not a single thought had been developed to the end.

Returning to the Conservatoire in the autumn, Debussy entered Ernest Guiraud's composition class. Guiraud, who had known Berlioz, was an excellent and enlightened musician who shared many of Debussy's ideas on art generally, and he became a personal friend to the student. The other members of the class regarded Debussy as an eccentric, and the majority of the staff looked upon him as a trouble-making nuisance. He would sit at the piano producing strings of fantastic chords, and when his fellow students looked on in horror, he would jeer at them.

In the following spring he approached Mme von Meck again in the hope of getting another engagement for the summer. She was then in Russia and had a pianist on her staff, but hadn't the heart to refuse him, and he therefore journeyed to Moscow during July 1881. There is not much information to be found concerning his visit to Russia, and though he must certainly have extended his knowledge of the works of the Russian composers, we are told that all he brought back to Paris was "an old opera by Rimsky-Korsakov and some songs of Borodin". It might be added that he fell violently in love with Madame von Meck's exquisite fourteen-year-old daughter Sonia, and calmly asked his employer for permission to marry the girl. That an unknown, penniless musician of such humble parentage should have the audacity to ask for the hand of this mere child, daughter of one of the richest and most aristocratic women in Russia, seemed almost incredible. Many years later, when Debussy had found fame, he had more than one opportunity of visiting Sonia, who was then married to a nobleman, but steadfastly refused.

Back at the Conservatoire again, he started to work diligently for the coveted Grand Prix de Rome and at the same time tried to augment his slender allowance by acting as the accompanist to a singing-class held by Madame Moreau-Sainti, to whom he dedicated his first song

Nuit d'étoiles in 1882. Then he accepted a similar appointment with the Concordia Choral Society, whose conductor was Charles Gounod, then at the height of his fame as a composer.

Incidentally, at Madame Moreau-Sainti's class he met Madame Vasnier, the beautiful young wife of an elderly architect. She invited Debussy to her flat very frequently, ostensibly to discuss literature and art with him. The young student loved the cultural atmosphere of her home, and it is quite true that they did discuss those subjects, but they discovered other mutual pleasures as well, for she became his mistress. Curiously enough, the husband believed his wife to be indulging in nothing but a mild and innocent infatuation for the youth, and did nothing to interfere ; in fact, he and Debussy remained on terms of cordial friendship. Apart from that, however, Madame Vasnier played an important part in his life by introducing him to the poetry of Verlaine and Mallarmé. To Debussy, who was striving to educate himself, the works of such poets as these were a great inspiration. It was at about this time that he wrote *Fantoches*, one of the *Fêtes galantes* on the poems of Verlaine.

An article written later by Madame Vasnier's daughter Marguerite, to whom he gave music lessons, tells us that at that time Debussy was a big, beardless youth with well marked features and thick, black curly hair which he wore flat upon his forehead. His hair would get untidy by the evening, and suit him much better. The Vasniers thought that he looked like a type of medieval Florentine. He had a most interesting face, with penetrating eyes. His hands were strong and bony ; his fingers "square".

It appears that he asked them if he could work at their home because he was getting little support from his family and could not afford adequate apartments of his own. Madame Vasnier was quick to seize this opportunity of having him always near at hand, and for five years most of his work was done in their flat on the fifth floor of a house in the Rue de Constantinople. He composed either at an old Blondel piano, or walking about the room. Mlle Vasnier says that he would improvise for a long time, then walk up and down the room humming with a cigarette in his mouth, and finally would commit his thoughts to paper when he was quite sure of them. He made few corrections afterwards, but was rarely satisfied with his efforts.

Of his general manner, Mlle Vasnier says that he was very quick to take offence and was most sensitive. The most trifling remark would put him in a good humour or make him sullen or angry. He was extremely unsociable, and was apt to be rude to any of the family's friends who happened to call when he was there. If he met anybody he liked, he would play or sing Wagner to them, or entertain with imitations of some contemporary composer.

At the Conservatoire he continued to be a recalcitrant student, and on one occasion when his fellow-students were standing aghast at the fantastic harmonies he was producing at the piano, he suggested that they should go and tell the Director that he was ruining their ears. One or two of them probably took him at his word, for the registrar was instructed to keep an eye upon this "dangerous" young man. This official found Debussy at the piano one day and asked him what rules he followed, since he believed that dissonant chords need not be resolved. The student retorted that he followed his own pleasure in such matters. The registrar departed pale with indignation.

Due chiefly to the sympathetic restraint exercised upon him by Guiraud, Debussy gained the second prize in the competition for the Grand Prix de Rome in 1883—he was just beaten by Paul Vidal— and in the following year, at the age of twenty-two won the coveted Grand Prix itself with his cantata *L'Enfant prodigue*. The feelings of the adjudicators were to some extent swayed by the enthusiasm of Gounod, who had not the slightest doubt about the young student's genius. Twenty-two of the twenty-eight academicians voted in favour of Debussy's entry, but one or two of the critics considered it inferior to the work submitted by Charles René. Charles Darcours, writing in *Figaro* declared: "The competition this year has brought to our notice a young musician of talent; a student who does not, perhaps, surpass his colleagues in actual attainments, but who proves in the very first bars of his composition that he is not one of the common herd. This is worth something in an age when everybody has talent and no one individuality. . . . M. Debussy . . . is a musician who is destined to meet with a great deal of praise . . . and plenty of abuse. At any rate, he is the most *alive* of the candidates this year and for many years past. Even the opening bars of his score reveal a courageous nature and an outstanding personality. . . . M. Debussy's cantata is an exceedingly interesting work because of its colouring, the expressive quality of the occasionally over-emphasized declamation, and above all, the exuberant individuality it portrays. . . . It is now the duty of this young musician to find his own path amidst the enthusiasms and the antagonisms he is sure to arouse."

Although he wished to partake of the material advantages of the Prix de Rome, Debussy was full of contempt for the manner in which the competition was held, and for the mentality of the adjudicators. His entry was written in a spirit of temporary and insincere acquiescence to their stupidities, and he afterwards criticized it as "a hybrid form partaking clumsily of all that is trite in opera and choral symphony. It is indeed an invention of the Institut : one of whose authorship no one need boast." He was equally outspoken about the conditions under which the contest was held. "They expect you to be full of ideas and inspiration at one particular time of the year. If you are not in form that month, so much the worse for you. It is a purely arbitrary affair, with no significance for the future." The candidates, he declared, were trained like horses for a race. "The umpires are the members of the Institut . . . whether the games are played in music, painting, sculpture, architecture or engraving. It has not yet occurred to anybody to include a dancer on the committee, though this would be logical, for Terpsichore was not the least among the nine Muses."

His reception of the result of the competition has also been described in his own words : "I was on the Pont des Arts awaiting the result . . . and watching with delight the scurrying of the little Seine steamers. I was quite calm . . . so seductive was the charm of the gay sunshine playing on the ripples ; a charm that keeps those picturesque loiterers who are the envy of Europe, hour after hour on the bridges. Suddenly, someone tapped me on the shoulder and said breathlessly 'You've won the prize ! ' Believe it or not, I can assure you that all my pleasure vanished ! I saw in a flash the boredom and vexations inevitably incident to the slightest official recognition. Besides, I felt I was no longer free."

What really worried Debussy was the thought of separation from Madame Vasnier and her charming home, for the conditions of the Grand Prix stipulated that he should proceed in due course to Rome for a further period of study.

III

ONE would have thought that the prospect of three years' sojourn at the Villa Medici in the company of the music prize-winners of former years and those studying painting, sculpture, architecture and engraving, would have pleased him, but he went there ready to take offence at the slightest encroachment upon his liberty. He described it as a cosmopolitan hotel, "a compulsory civilian barracks." Roman society, he said, was "aloof and inhospitable" and he complained bitterly about the food provided for the students, affirming that they narrowly escaped poisoning and protesting that dyspepsia was not a necessary addition to the aesthetic equipment of an artist. Writing to Madame Vasnier he said : "Here I am in this abominable villa . . . the artistic atmosphere and *camaraderie* that we are told about seem to me very exaggerated. . . . This is not the life for me : their happiness isn't mine. . . ." and he complained that the other students had lost the good-hearted friendly ways of their Parisian days : they seemed stiff and impressed with a sense of their own importance—"too much Prix de Rome about them."

He continued work upon a setting of Théodore de Banville's comedy *Diane au bois* which he had begun in Paris and which Guiraud had told him to keep dark until after he had secured the Grand Prix, in case it turned all the academicians against him. "The Institut[1] will not approve, for of course only their way is the right one. But I cannot help it. I am too fond of my freedom, and of my own ideas. This is the only kind of music that I can write."

Diane au bois was eventually abandoned, and he seems to have been perpetually concerned about the small amount of progress he was making artistically, even though he enjoyed the stimulating company of many other talented musicians, including Paul Vidal, with whom he read through scores of every type. Moreover, he was given many opportunities to travel and to get inspiration from the other arts. He met Boito at Milan, and got from him an introduction to Verdi, whom he found at Sant' Agata busy in his shirt-sleeves planting vegetables. The great composer refused to discuss contemporary musicians because he felt that he had made enough enemies already ; indeed he seemed far more interested in his garden than in music. At Sgambati's house Debussy met Liszt, who joined with his host in playing the Saint-Saëns Variations for two pianos on a theme of Beethoven. This, incidentally, was the last time Liszt played in Rome.

Debussy also spent much of his time in the art galleries, and was particularly attracted by the works of the pre-Raphaelites. He became a great admirer of Whistler, and a friend of such people as Gaston Redon, the architect, Lombard, the sculptor, and Marcel Baschet, the painter. The last-named, by the way, painted a very fine portrait of

1 Académie des Beaux-Arts.

him. His reading at that time was chiefly of the works of Baudelaire, Verlaine, Spinoza and Shakespeare. He discovered the poems of D. G. Rossetti at about the same time as he realized the beauty of the pure music of Palestrina and Orlando di Lasso. Above all, he was then a violently passionate Wagnerian, and like most of the other young music students, regarded Bayreuth as his spiritual home. We need not, then, be surprised to find Wagnerian tinges in many of his earlier works.

An article in the *Revue des Arts Français*[1] by Xavier Leroux, one of his contemporaries, gives us this useful sketch of him at that time : "Those who knew him only superficially might have considered him a fantastic, whimsical creature. On the contrary, he was strong-willed, and knew his own mind : he was capable of faithful and devoted friendship, was very sensitive and emotional, gay and full of vitality. He was quite incapable of deceit : his face reflected all his feelings, his joys and even the slightest sorrow. He could not keep his troubles to himself : it was absolutely necessary for him to have a friend in whom he could confide. In his extravagance he could rarely resist any desire or temptation. His moods were very variable : he had caressing feline ways, and was prone to sudden outbursts of temper. In everything, he took a delight in all that was refined, delicate, complicated and unusual. This refinement was evident in his dress, the perfumes he affected, the ornaments with which he surrounded himself, and the bindings of his favourite books. The latter, like his favourite musical compositions, were works that appealed especially to his love of the exquisite and the complex. In the matter of food he was equally extreme : he either lived on fried eggs and tea (his favourite beverage, in the making of which he was particularly adept) or indulged in highly *recherché* dishes and famous vintage wines. He detested pomposity in any of the arts. What made the strongest appeal to him was the expression of intimate feelings. Human productions planned on a grand scale astonished him, and aroused neither admiration nor enthusiasm."

When he submitted to the Académie his *Zuléïma*, a work for chorus and orchestra on a text from Heine's *Almanzor*, which he later destroyed, he was severely censured. The *Journal officiel* declared : "The work that earned for M. Debussy the first prize for musical composition in 1884 gave the Académie reason to expect that this exceptionally talented young artist would provide further evidence of the melodic

1 1918.

and dramatic qualities that he exhibited in the competition piece. The Académie must record with regret that on the contrary, M. Debussy seems at present to be afflicted with a desire to write music that is bizarre, incomprehensible, and impossible to execute. With the exception of a few passages that show individuality, the vocal part of his work is uninteresting, both as regards the melody and the declamation. The Académie hopes that time and experience will bring salutary modifications to M. Debussy's ideas and compositions."

Massenet considered that Debussy was "an enigma", but would probably have criticised him in sharper terms if he had known how the young student was openly boasting that his primary desire was to forget everything that he had been taught at the Conservatoire.

It should be recorded that during the early part of the year 1886 Debussy became so restless at Rome that on one occasion he packed up and returned to Paris. Madame Vasnier probably convinced him of the foolishness of this flight, and he went back to the Villa Medici in a slightly better frame of mind, though it was not long before he was writing letters declaring that he was longing to see some Manet and to hear some Offenbach : a paradox that he attributed to the air of Rome, which "puts the most ridiculous ideas into one's head."

In the latter part of 1886 and during the first month or two of the following year he was able to concentrate upon a new work, *Printemps*, which was inspired by Botticelli's *Primavera*. This symphonic suite in two parts for chorus and orchestra seems to have taxed his skill and patience to the utmost, for in a letter written at the time to Émile Baron he admitted that it was giving him a lot of trouble and that he was leading a life much harder than that of a convict. He explained that he was trying to compose "a work in a very special colour which would cover a great range of emotions. It is to be called *Printemps*. It will not be a descriptive *Printemps*, but a human one. I should like to express the slow and miserable birth of beings and things in nature, their gradual blossoming, and finally the joy of being born into some new life. All this without a programme, for I despise all music that has to follow some literary text. . . . So you will understand how very suggestive the music will have to be. I am doubtful if I shall be able to do it as I wish."

This work formed his second *envoi* to the Académie, and was given a slightly better, if somewhat mixed, reception. The official verdict in the *Journal officiel* included these remarks : "Certainly, M. Debussy does not transgress through dullness or triteness. On the contrary, he shows a rather over-emphasized taste for the unusual. His feeling for colour in music is so strong that he is inclined to overlook the importance of accuracy of line and form. He should beware of this vague impressionism, which is one of the most dangerous enemies of artistic truth. The first movement of M. Debussy's symphonic work is a sort of prelude—an *adagio*. Its dreamy atmosphere and its studied effects result in confusion. The second movement is a bizarre, incoherent transformation of the first, but the rhythmical combinations make it somewhat clearer and more comprehensible. The Académie awaits and expects something better from such a gifted musician as M. Debussy."

While he was still in Rome he first made the acquaintance of the Symbolist publications : two magazines, *La Revue indépendante* and *Vogue*, which were sent to him by Émile Baron. These and the recently published works of Jean Moréas, together with Rabbe's translations of Shelley, gave him the notion that music was not reflecting the new spirit in art that it should : the other arts were progressing, he felt, and music was not. This made him all the more restless in Rome, and in the spring of 1887 he decided to ignore the regulations of the Grand Prix and return to Paris

IV

Of his next five years in the French capital there is not a great deal of reliable information, but what there is of it is significant because this was an important period in the composer's life. His friendship with the Vasniers did not last long, and his principal confidant seems to have been the poet Pierre Louÿs, for although he was acquainted with such people as Mallermé, Whistler, Verlaine, Jules Laforgue and Henri de Régnier, he rarely sought their company because he was sensitive of his lack of education. In those days the cultural life of Paris was being affected by the cult of Wagner.

The outstanding event in 1887 was Debussy's visit to Vienna to meet Brahms. According to André de Ternant,[1] he first wrote to Brahms, but received no reply ; so he called twice at the great composer's house, but "the lion of Vienna" was not on view. Eventually, he got in touch with a secretary at the French embassy whose wife had been a pupil of Brahms and this lady arranged a luncheon at which only Brahms, Debussy and herself were present.

[1] The London-born French music critic and journalist.

While the lion was feeding he uttered not a word, but after he had consumed several glasses of French champagne he quoted a singularly tactless extract from Goethe's *Faust*, and then delivered an uninspiring monologue which need not be recorded here. Finally he expressed his great admiration for Bizet and invited Debussy to lunch with him in the town and to accompany him to a performance of *Carmen* afterwards. It seems that the great composer took a fatherly interest in the young Frenchman and showed him everything of interest in Vienna before he departed.

Another important journey that year was his visit to London to meet Franz Hueffer, music critic to *The Times* and director of the *Musical World*, who tried—unsuccessfully—to help Debussy to get some of his manuscripts published in this country. The London publishers were not prepared to take any risk upon the work of a young Frenchman unknown in England.

On his return to Paris he settled down to work on his third *envoi* for the Prix de Rome, *La Damoiselle élue*, a cantata for solo voices, chorus and orchestra on Gabriel Sarrazin's translation of Rossetti's *Blessed Damozel*. It was completed in 1888, and drew the following criticism from the academicians : "The text chosen by M. Debussy is in prose, and rather obscure, but the music that he has adapted to it is deficient neither in poetry nor charm, although it still shows signs of that systematic tendency towards vagueness of expression and form of which the Académie has already complained. In the present instance, however, these propensities and processes are much less noticeable and seem to some extent justified by the very nature of the subject and its indefinite character."

It was customary for the Académie to hold a concert each year for the performance of the *envois* of the holder of the Grand Prix who in that year was returning from his prescribed period of residence in Rome. In 1889 the works of Paul Vidal, Debussy's predecessor, were performed, and in the following year there should have been a "Debussy Festival", as the recalcitrant prize-winner cynically called it. The academicians, however, informed Debussy that they could not agree to the performance of his *Printemps*, and the young composer was so infuriated that he said he would rather forgo the concert altogether than submit to the exclusion of this work. Another narrative tells us that he lost the concert by refusing to provide an overture for the prize-distribution. Which of these two versions is true does not really matter ; the more important fact being that *La Damoiselle élue* was not performed until 1893, when it was given by the Société Nationale, and *Printemps* was not heard until 1913 !

Something of a mystery surrounds Debussy's *Fantaisie* for piano and orchestra. This work was written during 1889 and 1890 as one of the *envois de Rome*, but was never sent to the Institut. It was dedicated to the pianist René Chansarel, and was to have been played at one of the concerts of the Société Nationale in April 1890 under the direction of Vincent d'Indy, who had spent a great deal of time with the orchestra in rehearsing it. After the last rehearsal but one, Debussy removed the parts from the stands and without a word to anyone took them away. Vincent d'Indy then received a letter from him saying that he had decided to withdraw it.

One explanation is that Debussy took a dislike to the "heaviness" of the orchestration of this work, though one of its outstanding features is the excellence of its instrumentation. The more likely reason for his action is that he took a dislike to the Finale ; in any case he refused to allow the work to be performed during his lifetime.

At this stage we must pause for a moment to consider some of the influences that were brought to bear upon Debussy's artistic career during these early years in Paris. First, there were the impressionist artists and symbolist poets who generally gathered around Stéphane Mallarmé, and Edmond Bailly, the publisher, who encouraged the young composer by publishing several of his earlier works.

These artists and poets, he discovered, held views very much in accordance with his own, and he was fascinated by their dream of a fusion of all the arts. Paul Dukas, one of Debussy's contemporaries, once declared that Verlaine, Mallarmé and Laforgue provided them with "new sounds and sonorities. They threw light upon words such as had never been seen before. They used methods that were unknown to the poets that had preceded them : they made their verbal material yield subtle and powerful effects hitherto undreamt of. Above all, they conceived their poetry or prose like musicians and, like musicians, they sought to express their ideas in corresponding sound values."

Thus it was the writers and the artists—Degas, Berthe Morisot, Renoir and Monet—and not the musicians who influenced Debussy. "Impressionism, symbolism and poetic realism" Dukas wrote, "were united in one great contest of enthusiasm, curiosity and intellectual emotion. All these painters, poets and sculptors were concerned in analysing matter : they bent over it, scrutinized it, altered it, and remade it to suit their taste. Their one endeavour was to make words, sounds, colours and lines express new shades of emotion."

The stupid and unimaginative criticism they had to face tended to unite them, indeed it also brought into their ranks the more extreme Wagnerians, whose views were quite different. We shall see in a moment how Debussy passed through the Wagnerian phase. He mixed with comparatively few musicians, who were rarely able to see far beyond the sphere of music, and preferred to broaden his mind with the other muses. With Pierre Louÿs he would spend hours in the art galleries concentrating with an almost religious devotion upon his favourite paintings : a slothful figure with a muddy complexion, a bulging forehead with his hair combed down over it, dark eyes and a mere sketch of a beard. Jacques-Émile Blanche found him :[1] "a material-minded fellow, always very taciturn unless he wanted a good address for procuring caviar, of which he was inordinately fond ; a sleepy, heavy creature, always on the look out for music publishers, whom Louys was constantly extricating from straitened circumstances ; a Prix de Rome who suggested an old-fashioned model for an historical painting."

Debussy made two "pilgrimages" to Bayreuth for the *Bühnenfestspiel*, one in 1888 and the other in 1889. On the former occasion he went as a solemn and passionate Wagnerian : the religious atmosphere in the theatre affected him profoundly, and he was shocked and irritated when during the prolonged intervals between the acts of *Parsifal* his friends indulged in flirtations with the young female attendants and waitresses : their coarse banter seemed like sacrilege. On his second visit, he heard *Parsifal* and the *Mastersingers*, as before, and *Tristan und Isolde*, but this time felt very disillusioned : he found that he disliked Wagner's aestheticism and indulgence in heavy dramatic effects, but still liked his music.

Little is known about his private life at this time, which, perhaps, is just as well, for his extreme love of sensual pleasure and appalling extravagance, and above all, his weakness in the face of temptation, suggest that he did not spare the oats. It was somewhere around the year 1888 that he met a girl who was nicknamed Gaby[2]: an attractive blonde with exceptional green eyes who became his mistress. He lived with her for about ten years, first in the Rue de Londres, and then in the Rue Gustave-Doré, but even during this period he indulged in

1 This is quoted from an article on Pierre Louÿs in *Nouvelles Littéraires*, June 13th 1925.
2 Gabrielle Dupont was her proper name.

extremely passionate affairs with various other women, including a young singer and a fairly well known society woman.

In 1889 he often went with Paul Dukas and Robert Godet to the Exposition Universelle to meet musicians of other nations and to hear their works. He heard Chinese, Spanish, Hungarian, Algerian and Javanese orchestras and was impressed at the vivid contrast their music made to the conventional harmonies and rhythms that had been used in his own musical education. What appealed to him most of all was the curious Javanese orchestra which accompanied the Bedayas, those lithe and fascinating dancers. Their use of the Oriental pentatonic scale, of intoxicating rhythms and unusual harmonies gave him a new vision in music altogether.

At the same time he discovered the music of such Russian composers as Glazounov, Mussorgsky, Rimsky-Korsakov, Borodin, Balakirev and Glinka, for in the past he had heard little Russian music apart from that of Tchaikovsky and Rubinstein. Mussorgsky, especially, had a considerable influence upon him, chiefly as an antidote to the Wagnerian tendencies that he had consciously or unconsciously assimilated. In Mussorgsky's music he found evidence of one who, like himself, had rebelled against the petty rules beloved by the reactionary academicians.

Some small part in Debussy's musical development was perhaps played by Erik Satie (1866-1925), that eccentric French composer who tried so hard to be funny but so rarely succeeded. Beloved, in later years, by those who dabbled in atonality, he wrote bits of things with unresolved ninths in an attempt—not altogether unsuccessful—to be original, and then gave them silly titles, such as *Pieces in the Shape of a Pear.* Debussy was associated with him for many years, and rather liked his crazy whimsicality, but it is unlikely that he took much notice of his work, except, perhaps to get an odd idea here and there with which to succeed where Satie failed.

The music of Chopin and Grieg made a considerable impression upon Debussy, and he admired much of Gabriel Fauré's work. The influence of César Franck is not difficult to trace in many of Debussy's compositions, and it is also probable that the young composer drew some benefit from his frequent conversations with Gounod.

V

As far as the general musical public was concerned, Debussy was quite unknown as a composer until he was thirty-one. Then, on April 8th 1893 the Société Nationale gave a concert at the Salle Érard at which *La Damoiselle élue* was performed with the works of various other contemporary composers. This cantata was published at about the same time by Bailly, but Debussy was so diffident about its reception that he had only a hundred and sixty copies printed. Like most of his published works, it was beautifully produced with a coloured cover by Maurice Denis. In the concert hall, however, *La Damoiselle élue* made a great impression upon the advanced section of musical thought. Charles Darcours, writing in *Figaro*, said that there was more life in it than in all the other items on the programme put together. "It is very insinuating and extremely modern. After listening a few days ago with deep admiration to the lofty beauty of Palestrina's music, we felt an almost guilty delight on hearing this composition, for it is very sensual and decadent, rather corrupt in fact, but it has pages of exquisite, sparkling beauty. How refreshing is a touch of youth! We understand that M. Debussy was admitted to the Société Nationale quite by accident, yet new blood like his is just what that venerable institution needs. This sub-cutaneous injection may perhaps produce dangerous eruptions in the young musicians of the near future, but after all, such an incident would be less serious for the Société Nationale than death."

Shortly after this concert he came to an important decision. Early one evening during the previous summer he had been walking along the Boulevard des Italiens and had seen a recently-published copy of Maurice Maeterlinck's drama *Pelléas et Mélisande*. He had bought it and had been so charmed with it that he had written some incidental music to a number of its scenes. On May 17th 1893 he saw this drama produced at the Théâtre des Bouffes-Parisiens, and although the literary critics of Paris denounced it, he made up his mind to use it as a libretto for an opera.

He went to Ghent to see Maeterlinck forthwith. His interview, in which he sought the Belgian dramatist's permission to turn the work into an opera, has been described in his own words in a letter to Ernest Chausson : "I saw Maeterlinck and spent a day with him in Ghent. At first he behaved like a girl meeting an eligible young man. Then he thawed and became charming. He talked about the theatre as only a very remarkable man could. As regards *Pelléas*, he has given me full permission to make any cuts I desire, and has even indicated some very important and advisable ones. He says that he knows nothing whatever about music : when he goes to hear a Beethoven symphony he is like a blind man in a museum. But he is really very good, and talks with a delightful simplicity of the wonderful things he discovers. When I thanked him for entrusting *Pelléas* to me, he did his utmost to prove that it was he who was indebted to me for so kindly writing music to it ! "

We have seen that Debussy had become disillusioned in Wagner. To quote his own words : "I am not inclined to imitate what I admire in Wagner. My conception of dramatic art is different : according to mine, music begins where speech fails. Music is intended to convey that which is inexpressible in words : I should like her to appear as if emerging from the shadowy regions to which she would from time to time retire. I would have her always discreet."

In seeking a libretto, he wanted to find a poet "who would only hint at things, and would thus enable me to graft my thought upon his ; one who would create characters whose history and abode belong to no particular time or place ; one who would not despotically impose scenes upon me, but who would allow me, now and then, to outdo him in artistry and to perfect his work."

The opera was revised so many times that it took nine years to complete in its final form, and then it was finished only just in time for its first production. There were times when he felt very dissatisfied with what he had written, and when he felt doubtful about the whole project. We find him writing to his friend Ernest Chausson early in 1894 saying : "The colour of my soul is iron-grey, and dismal bats wheel about the steeple of my dreams. My only hope is in *Pelléas et Mélisande*, and God only knows if that won't end in smoke."

Debussy's income in those days was most precarious, and he was obliged to give lessons and to make transcriptions for publishers in order to live. This of course was most distasteful to him, for in his elegant and grandiose way he hated people to look upon him as a mere working musician. Chausson persuaded him to accept engagements to play Wagner, for he was an excellent pianist, but one can well imagine how he disliked doing this when one considers that he was trying to dissociate himself from Wagnerian influences in the writing of *Pelléas et Mélisande*.

отhèque de l'Opéra, Paris

DEBUSSY, painted by his friend Marcel Bachet   PLATE XIV

PLATE XV   Scenes from Debussy's opera

PLATE XVI   *Pelléas et Mélisande*

He finished the opera in the spring of 1895—only to discover the need for innumerable revisions. Eugène Ysaÿe, the eminent violinist, who greatly admired Debussy and his work, tried to get it produced at the Théâtre de la Monnaie, Brussels, but did not succeed, and suggested a concert performance of certain parts of it. Debussy was deeply grateful to the virtuoso for his kind interest, but would not consent for the following reasons (which he set out in a letter to Ysaÿe) : "First, if this work has any merit, it is in the connection between the drama and the music. It is obvious that at a concert performance this connection would disappear, and no one could be blamed for seeing nothing in those eloquent 'silences' with which this work is starred. Furthermore, it is only on the stage that the simplicity of this work gains significance. At a concert performance they would throw in my face the American wealth of Wagner, and I should be like some poor fellow that couldn't afford to pay for 'contra-bass tubas' ! In my opinion, Pelléas and Mélisande must be given as they are, and then it will be a case of taking them or leaving them, and if we have to fight, it will be worth while."

The remodelled opera was finished in 1897. Then on going through it, Debussy again expressed dissatisfaction, and but for the timely intervention of his friend Pierre Louÿs, he would have destroyed the entire work. In that year it was accepted by Albert Carré for production at the Opéra-Comique, but this did not take place until five years later.

Meanwhile, Debussy's String Quartet was performed by the Ysaÿe Quartet at another concert held by the Société Nationale on December 29th 1893. The select audience—which consisted of the musical *élite*, the connoisseurs, snobs and other precious individuals—were scandalized by the composer's audacity in trying to invade the hallowed realm of chamber music with his queer harmonies, complex rhythms, unusual colours and rich embroidery. Guy Ropartz, writing in the *Guide musical* described it as "A very interesting work in which the predominant influence is that of young Russia, with poetical themes and rare tone-colouring. The first two movements are especially noteworthy." It is significant that this quartet was played several times during the ensuing years.

Some mention should be made here of the introduction of Debussy's works to the people of Brussels by the Libre Esthétique. A concert devoted to his works was given under the auspices of this society on March 1st 1894 by the Ysaÿe Quartet, a symphony orchestra and a choir of about thirty female voices. The programme consisted of the

String Quartet, *La Damoiselle élue,* and two *Proses Lyriques,* which had been recently completed. It is interesting to note the criticisms of Maurice Kufferath in the report he wrote for the *Guide musical.* The Quartet is described thus : " . . . Bounding rhythms, violent harmonic jerks alternating with languid melodies on the violin, viola and 'cello, which bring to mind the chromatics of oriental melodies ; *pizzicato* effects suggesting guitars and mandolines ; copious floods of rich, sustained harmonies that are reminiscent of the *Gamelang.* . . . It is neither banal nor commonplace. On the contrary, it is very distinguished, but one does not know how to seize upon it. It is more like a hallucination than a dream. Is it a work ? One hardly knows. Is it music ? Perhaps so, in the sense that the canvases of the neo-Japanese of Montmartre and its Belgian suburb may be called paintings." Of *La Damoiselle élue* he said that there was a vagueness of expression caused by the constant changes of rhythm; there were unexpected modulations; the accumulation of superimposed themes, subjects and patterns ; and a straining after rare and unforeseen combinations. The *Proses Lyriques,* he said, reminded him of the occasion when Rubini and Lablache sang the duet from *I Puritani* at the interval of a second instead of a third : " . . . At times, the result was pure cacophony. If this was not done for a wager, one must seriously conclude that it points to a defect of the auditory sense, similar to the defect of sight that is responsible for the distorted vision of certain painters." Kufferath did, however, pay tribute to many fine qualities in Debussy's work and added : "Our grandchildren will be better able to judge, and perhaps they will call us old fogies for not understanding Debussy, just as we did in the case of our predecessors who did not appreciate Wagner." How many times remarks like that were to be made in the next fifty years !

The item that was to conclude that concert at Brussels was omitted because the composer had not finished revising it—*Prélude, Interlude et Paraphrase finale pour L'Après-midi d'un faune.* During 1894 Debussy revised this work, which was inspired by Mallarmé's eclogue, and reduced it to the form of a Prelude only. This was performed at a Société Nationale concert on December 22nd of that year ; a purely orchestral work that was in time to be recognized as one of the composer's finest efforts. Stéphane Mallarmé had heard it played on the piano before the concert and had told the composer "This music prolongs the emotion of my poem and fixes the scene far more vividly than colour could have done." With this delightful specimen of musical impressionism, Debussy established for all time his own idiom in music. The concert was a success, and the *Prélude à l'Après-midi d'un faune*[1] was repeated several times soon afterwards, but the tone-poem made little impression upon the critics : a few made brief, feeble criticisms, but the rest evidently thought it was worth no more than a vague, passing reference. All the more advanced musicians, however, and particularly the younger ones, acknowledged Debussy as a master and pioneer. For all that, his income remained inadequate, because although the pleasant *Petite Suite* and the *Arabesques* had been published, his works were still virtually unknown to the masses. He came to London again in 1895, met Saint-Saëns on the way over, and Sir Hubert Parry at the Royal College of Music, but apparently nobody seemed sufficiently interested in him to help in the introduction of his music to the British people.

When Debussy refused to permit a concert performance of excerpts from *Pelléas et Mélisande* he offered Eugène Ysaÿe three *Nocturnes* for violin and orchestra. In 1897 these were re-arranged as a symphonic "triptych" for orchestra and female voices, but it was not heard until the end of the century.

Meanwhile he had met a young dressmaker named Rosalie Texier at an informal gathering of his friends. She was a good-looking and rather charming girl with dark brown hair, but at first he took little notice of her : he thought she was pretty but peevish. Then, observing some of her little mannerisms, he began to imitate her for the amusement of his other friends, and as she took this in a good spirit, they became better acquainted. A few years later, on October 19th 1899, they were married. Her intellectual inferiority did not, apparently, worry the composer, and he seems to have admired her very simple taste in dress as well as in most other things. In this he was fortunate, for his income was still very small, in fact on his wedding morning he had to give a piano lesson in order to pay for the wedding breakfast at the Brasserie Pousset.

Debussy was by this time beginning to look more middle-aged and mature : he was slightly stouter, but retained his languid manner. A contemporary described him thus : "His beard was soft and silky, his hair thick and rather curly. His features were full, his cheeks plump, and he had a bantering manner beneath which there was a subtle shrewdness. He was an ironic and sensual figure, melancholy and voluptuous ; his complexion was of a warm amber brown. He was highly strung ; master of his nerves, but not of his emotions, which must

[1] *Prelude to 'The Afternoon of a Faun'.*

have affected him deeply, especially as he tried to conceal them. In love's retreat and night's inveigling sweetness he must have known some passionate hours. Irony was part of his nature, as was also his love of pleasure. He had a mischievous sense of humour and an acknowledged love of good living. His tongue could be barbed, and he had a certain carelessness of speech. His gestures were rather affected, his enthusiasms were well controlled, and his taste was un-failing. Although his appearance suggested the contrary, he was very simple-hearted. Debussy was as much a bohemian of Montmartre as he was a man of the world. In his reclusion there was something feline."

He always needed the companionship of his friends, and was inclined to lean heavily upon them at times. He often admitted to them that he felt lonely and helpless without their support. According to his friend René Peter, he was superstitious : "He would not go to bed without first thoroughly blowing his nose and then placing his slippers so that the toes pointed outwards. (Not to do this was to tempt Providence.)" Yet religion and all its attendant superstitions made no appeal to him whatever. "His atheism was sensual and instinctive" Jean Lépine has said. "To find support for his lack of belief there was no question of making any serious study as Voltaire, Renan and Anatole France did. Nor did he seek any philosophic system to defend himself : he simply experienced no desire for religion." It might be added that he was very fond of cats, and that green was his favourite colour.

VI

THE first two parts of the triptych *Nocturnes* were performed at the Concerts Lamoureux in December 1900, the year in which Debussy also won general recognition at the official concerts at the Universal Exhibition with his Quartet, *La Damoiselle élue*, and the three excellent *Chansons de Bilitis*, which he had written in 1897.

The *Nocturnes* in their entirety were first heard in October 1901 at one of the Concerts Lamoureux, and were a great success, so much so that many of the academicians who had ridiculed Debussy in the past—and would have liked to continue doing so—scrutinized this work in a desperate attempt to prove that its more normal attributes, its form and so forth, differed very little, if at all, from those of the more conventional music with which they were familiar. They suddenly realized that something new in art had "arrived" and that by ridiculing it they could no longer cover their obsolescence. Jean d'Udine of the *Courrier musical*, like most of the critics, was generous in his praise : "One cannot imagine a more delightful impressionist symphony. It is made up entirely of splashes of sound. It does not trace the sinuous outlines of definite melodic curves, but its treatment of timbres and chords—its harmony, as the painters would say—maintains a certain strict homogeneity that replaces the beauty of line by the equally plastic beauty of a skilfully distributed and logically sustained sonority."

Shortly afterwards Debussy accepted an appointment as music critic on the staff of the *Revue Blanche*, and for six months expounded his aesthetic doctrine to the advanced literary and artistic circles that supported this modern journal.

At the beginning of January 1902, *Pélleas et Mélisande* was finished, and rehearsals started at the Opéra-Comique on the 13th of that month. Even then, Debussy was making last-minute revisions, and the progress of the opera was also impeded by various other disturbances. The worst of these was the quarrel that broke out between Debussy and Maeterlinck. The latter had recently married Georgette Leblanc, and Debussy agreed that she should play the part of *Mélisande*. She threw herself into the work with great enthusiasm, but after a few rehearsals Maeterlinck was amazed to read in a newspaper that Debussy had allowed the management to engage another woman for the part. The enraged dramatist considered that Debussy had betrayed him, and taking his stick he went round to the composer's apartment seeking vengeance. Madame Debussy evidently kept them apart, for no violence was done,, but Maeterlinck wrote an embittered letter to *Figaro* roundly condemning the whole production. "Arbitrary and absurd cuts have made it incomprehensible" he declared. "They have retained certain passages that I wished to delete or improve as I did in the libretto that has just appeared, and from which it will be observed how far the text adopted by the Opéra-Comique differs from the authentic version. In short, the *Pelléas* in question is a work that is strange and almost hostile to me ; and as I am deprived of all control over my work, I can wish only for its immediate and utter failure."

André Messager, the director of music and principal conductor at the Opéra-Comique, invited all the principals to his house, where Debussy played through the score at the piano and at the same time sang through all the solo parts, transposing, where necessary, an octave lower. Messager tells us that "The impression produced by his music that day was, I think, a unique experience. At first, there was an atmosphere of diffidence and antagonism ; then gradually the attention of the listeners was caught and held ; little by little emotion overcame them ; and the last notes of Mélisande's death-scene fell amidst silence and tears. At the end, they were all quite carried away, and eager to set to work as soon as possible."

Mary Garden, a Scottish-American actress, played the part of Mélisande and her pronunciation of certain words with an English accent started disturbances in the audience during the public dress rehearsal. Efforts to ridicule the plot amused irresponsible elements in the house, and the Under-Secretary of State for Fine Arts insisted upon certain cuts being made—one of these was a reference to the bed in Mélisande's chamber.

Among the critics, opinion was sharply divided concerning the value of this opera as a work of art. Louis de Fourcaud, in the *Gaulois*, declared : "By indulging in cerebral subtleties and an unwholesome craving for novelty, the composer has arrived at a doctrine of complete negation. He renounces melody and its development ; he renounces the symphony and its deductive resources. . . . I do not deny that M. Debussy often achieves rare and even beautiful effects. . . . This nihilistic art, which curtails everything, which throws off the bonds of tonality and liberates itself from rhythm, may provide a diversion for ears that are *blasé*, but it cannot arouse any deep emotion in our hearts. . . . What we aspire to is a really deep human art, not continual effects of titillation which are fundamentally morbid. One cannot serve ideals without ideas. One cannot quench the thirst of souls with doubtful pharmaceutical beverages."

Another critic assured his readers that he heard nothing but a series of harmonized sounds which succeeded one another without interruption, "without a single phrase, a single *motif*, accent, form or outline. And to this accompaniment, unnecessary singers droned out words, nothing but words : a sort of prolonged monotonous recitative, unbearable and moribund."

On the other hand, Pierre Lalo, in *Le Temps*, maintained that the music "has that utter refinement which betrays no sign of effort and which seems inborn and instinctive with M. Debussy ; so much so that one fancies he could not write otherwise." He then goes on to say that "A lively, subtle and almost intangible rhythm animates it with an undulating, quivering life. Its brief, delicate, melodic ideas are expressed in the most individual manner, in the most persuasive accents and the most suggestive idiom. Finally, it has the virtue of being always *musical*, a very characteristic and felicitous quality . . . "

Gaston Garraud, in *La Liberté*, was full of praise : "In order to satisfy the noblest and most courageous of artistic ideals, M. Debussy has created a music of his own. His work overflows with it : everything in it is music. The words form a framework that sustains but never dominates. Significant expression seems to be the only object, yet it remains a means. The music exists for the sake of its own beauty, its own delight. M. Debussy takes his place, more definitely even than Wagner, among the sensualists in music, of whom Mozart was the greatest." Romain Rolland, in the German *Morgen*, described the opera as one of the three or four outstanding achievements in French musical history.

By a public accustomed to Wagner, *Pelléas et Mélisande* was not easily understood, yet within a little while it became a great success. It is worthy of note that Théodore Dubois, the Director of the Conservatoire, was so disturbed by the impressionist opera that he forbad the students in the composition classes to go to it.

After the fourth performance, Messager had to come to London to fulfil an engagement at Covent Garden, and Henri Büsser, his deputy and chorus master, took his place. Nevertheless, the opera continued to prosper, and we find Debussy writing to Messager and reporting : " . . . Friday : a splendid house, including M. Jean de Reszke. An attentive audience . . . " At the seventh performance, people were being turned away. Later in the year, Jules Combarieu, who was then connected with the Ministry of Education, was instrumental in getting an official honour for Debussy : the Croix d'Honneur. The composer accepted it chiefly for the joy it would bring to his parents, and his friends congratulated him for bestowing an honour upon the French Government by allowing them to decorate him !

This great success brought him the allegiance of thousands of young dilettanti desperately anxious to be in the new fashion, but public life did not appeal to Debussy, and he retired as soon as possible to the home of his wife's parents at Bichain. Nevertheless, people began to talk of the Debussyists and Debussyism, and the composer's ideas were made the basis of a new cult.

For several months during 1903 Debussy acted as the music critic for the paper *Gil Blas*, and in April came to London to report on the production of the *Ring* at Covent Garden. While he was here he wrote only two articles, and these were chiefly amusing satires on Wagner's music. On his return to Paris he went to a performance of the compositions submitted by the holder of the Prix de Rome for that year, and was appalled at the drivel that had won the academicians' approval. "It might have been written by a pork butcher" he declared.

VII

THE year 1904 brought a complete change to Debussy's life. For some years he had been friendly with Madame Sigismond (Emma) Bardac, a wealthy Jewess who was the wife of a financier, and who had been Gabriel Fauré's mistress. Fauré, incidentally, had dedicated his *Bonne Chanson* to her, and she had sung it in public. This woman had for some time been a great temptation to Debussy, and the suspicions harboured by Rosalie (generally called Lily), his first wife, had led to strained relations between husband and wife. . Madame Bardac was well known in the world of music, for she had an excellent voice which she could use with great artistry, and her son, who had studied at the Conservatoire, dabbled in composition and was a zealous Debussyist. This brilliant, cultured woman contrasted vividly with the homely Rosalie, who was ingenuous to the point of naïvety. It is to be feared, however, that her wealth was the greatest attraction to the composer, for recognition of his genius had done little to improve his financial position.

The climax came in June when Debussy deserted his wife and persuaded Madame Bardac to elope with him. The consequences were catastrophic. His wife tried to shoot herself, and was taken to a hospital with severe injuries in the breast. Divorce proceedings were instituted. Because of the Bardacs' high social position the whole of Paris bubbled with scandal. The artists, musicians and poets, who would countenance and even delight in promiscuity, were disgusted at the thought of a composer selling himself to a rich woman and at the same time breaking the heart of a faithful wife. Most of his friends turned against him, and he came to England to stay for a while at Eastbourne until their indignation had burnt itself out.

There is little to be said in defence of Debussy, who had always been envious of those who led a life of luxury, except that his financial position had certainly become grave. He had sold outright the copyright of *Pelléas et Mélisande*—much against his will—and had become weary of poverty, even though it was shared willingly by his wife. His new alliance brought him new troubles, however, for he became involved in complications that worried him for the rest of his life.

A daughter was born to his second wife in the autumn of 1905 She was named Claude-Emma, but always known as Chou-chou. The parents were married some time afterwards. They took a house in what is now the Avenue Foch, and it was here that Debussy spent the rest of his days. His daughter was a source of great delight to him, "the fulfilment of one of his most cherished hopes" according to Louis Laloy, the critic. To her he dedicated a small collection of piano pieces called *Children's Corner*, but she was not a brilliant child as far as music was concerned. She died at the age of fourteen.

While he was at Eastbourne he put the finishing touches to his three symphonic sketches called *La Mer*, and in due course they were performed in Paris by Chevillard at one of the Concerts Lamoureux. A public still smouldering with resentment expected these pieces to be something on the lines of the pleasant sea-music in the second act of *Pelléas*, and their disappointment made them more than ever inclined to disparage him. Several of the critics seemed to be more concerned with reflecting the feelings of the people than in forming a responsible opinion of the sketches for themselves. Pierre Lalo, writing in *Le Temps*, concluded that Debussy desired to feel rather than actually felt, a deep and natural emotion. "For the first time in listening to a descriptive work by Debussy, I have the impression of beholding not nature, but a reproduction of nature ; marvellously subtle, ingenious and skilful, no doubt, but a reproduction all the same. . . . I neither hear, nor see, nor feel the sea."

M. D. Calvocoressi, however, considered that *La Mer* marked a new phase in Debussy's evolution. "One gains the impression that M. Debussy, having diligently explored the domain of sonorous possibilities, has in this work considerably condensed and clarified the result of his discoveries, and his music tends to acquire the absolute eurythmic quality that characterizes all masterpieces. . . ."

From that time until the outbreak of the Great War the work of Debussy was the subject of exasperating controversies that at times spread far beyond the musical circles of Paris. The composer himself became utterly weary of them, and said on several occasions that such discussions, which were generally as shallow as they were prejudiced, served only to disturb and irritate those who were trying to create something. He believed that the old policy of allowing artists to mature in peace was far more conducive to good work. "A new composer scarcely appears nowadays" he told Calvocoressi "before people start writing essays about him and his work, and weigh his music down with ambitious definitions. They do far greater harm than even the fiercest detractors."

It was probably because of these tedious controversies that Debussy travelled so much during the years that preceded the Great War. Early in January 1907 he went to Brussels to superintend the production of *Pelléas et Mélisande*. During the final rehearsals he got almost into a panic, for it seemed impossible to him that everything could be got ready in time. His anxieties were all unfounded, however, for the opera opened on the appointed day, January 9th, and was a tremendous success. Georges Ekkhoud, the novelist, declared that Maeterlinck's beautiful drama should never again be performed without being imbued with the suave, subtle musical atmosphere provided by the French composer. A year later Toscanini directed its first production in Italy at the Scala in Milan. Hostile elements in the audience did their best to prevent the work being heard, but they were eventually silenced by the students of the Milan Conservatoire. Some time later, the opera was taken to Rome, where there was an ugly demonstration by certain members of the audience, although the critics all spoke highly of the production. *Pélleas* had by that time been introduced into Germany. It was well received, on the whole, at Frankfurt-on-Main, but at Munich and Berlin the opera-goers found difficulty in swallowing anything so typically French. New York heard it first in February 1908, when it was given a hearty welcome at the Manhattan Opera House under the general direction of Hammerstein. The conductor was Campanini, a sympathetic Italian who had fallen in love with the work when he first heard it in Paris in 1905.

Debussy's recognition in England was due chiefly to the work of T. J. Guéritte who founded the Société des concerts français in this country. The Quartet was first performed here in December 1907 under the auspices of this society, and in the following February, Debussy was invited to conduct *L'Après-midi d'un faune* and *La Mer* at the Queen's Hall. The former, by the way, had already been introduced to the London music-lovers by Sir Henry Wood in 1904. This was Debussy's first appearance at the Queen's Hall, and because of his lack of experience in conducting, he was extremely nervous. However, the concert was an outstanding success, and his work was warmly praised by the critics. A year later he was back in London again, conducting a programme that included his *Nocturnes*. After this he should have gone to Manchester and Edinburgh, but a severe illness—the first onslaught of the cancer that was to claim his life—

upset all his plans. He had been in great pain while conducting at the Queen's Hall, for in a letter to Durand, his publisher, he says that he was ready to drop. He then adds that he has to attend a reception : "What sort of figure shall I cut ? I shall look like a man condemned to death. I can't get out of it, apparently because of the Entente Cordiale and other sentimental conceptions most likely calculated to hasten the death of others."

Nevertheless, he was back in London again in May 1909 to supervise the rehearsals of his opera at Covent Garden. The principals were Bourbon, Marcoux, Rose Féart and Warnery ; and the conductor was Campanini. It seems that once again the composer became agitated during the final rehearsals, chiefly on account of a stage-manager from Marseilles. The dress rehearsal was really a distressing experience for everybody, but true to theatrical tradition when this happens, the *première* on May 21st was a remarkable triumph, although the composer himself was not present. He wrote to Durand just afterwards saying that the audience had called for him for a quarter of an hour, but he had been reposing peacefully at his hotel unconscious of the honour. "Cleofonte Campanini was twice recalled, and he telephoned me saying that the opera had been an enormous success, such as had rarely been known in England. He came to see me on the following morning to tell me all about it in his Punchinello manner, and he embraced me as if I were some medal blessed by the Pope." The importance attached to the production of this work in London stimulated widespread interest in Debussy. Edwin Evans gave a lecture on it at the Royal Academy of Music, and the musical journals devoted much of their space to articles on the composer who had liberated France from the domination of Wagner.

In France, Debussy was steadily gaining in prestige ; in fact during the same year he was appointed to membership of the Supreme Council of the Musical Section of the Paris Conservatoire. Gabriel Fauré was then one of his principal advocates. Despite his travels—he visited Vienna in 1910 and in the following year Turin, where he met Sir Edward Elgar, and Budapest—he was able to make progress with composition, and in 1912 finished his set of symphonic pieces known as *Images*. These three "pictures", *Gigues*, *Ibéria* and *Rondes de Printemps*, depict England, Spain and France respectively. The second and third were originally planned as works for two pianos in 1905.

His next major work was written when Gabriele d'Annunzio asked him to compose the music for his curious miracle play *Le Martyre de saint-Sébastien.* Debussy was particularly interested in this, and set aside the various minor works on which he was engaged so that he could devote the whole of his time to it. At just about that time he was interviewed by a journalist on the staff of the *Excelsior*, and the following quotation from the result of this discussion gives a useful sketch of the composer at the age of forty-nine :[1] "M. Claude Debussy, in his quest for light and silence, has withdrawn to a bright, secluded little corner, not far from the Bois de Boulogne. In his narrow study, which is most artistically decorated in fabrics of bronze and tawny hues, a deliberate simplicity reigns. The only objects that reveal the musician are a long Japanese kito and the bulky form of a small black piano.

"The composer of *Pelléas* has the dusky, golden countenance of an idol. His aspect is at once powerful, noble and unusual. His short beard and black hair help the illusion ; he looks like one of the Magi, who has strayed by mistake into our times. His gleaming forehead on which the light plays, is thrust forward in convex curves of unusual prominence, indicating violent impulses. He is slow to give his confidence. He has withdrawn within his mortal shell, into the domain of pure feeling, where he entertains all raptures. In these elegant surroundings, M. Debussy rolls a cigarette like any artisan, and speaks in a voice at first high-pitched and drawling which, as it increases in tone, becomes deep and pleasant."

Debussy explained to his interviewer that to write adequate music to this subtle, mysterious drama "in which the worship of Adonis is united with that of Christ", months of concentration would be required, so he felt obliged to limit himself to such music as would be worthy of the subject : probably a few choruses and incidental music, for he was compelled to have it ready by May of that year (1911) ; the month in which *Le Martyre de saint-Sébastien* was to be produced at the Théâtre du Châtelet. In discussing religious music with the journalist, Debussy said that the writing of sacred music had ceased in the sixteenth century, for only the beautiful, childlike souls of those days were capable of expressing their passionate, disinterested fervour in music that was free from all worldliness. "I do not practise religion in accordance with the sacred rites," the composer went on, "I have made mysterious Nature my religion. I do not believe that a man is any nearer to God for being clad in priestly garments, nor that one

1 Quoted from *Claude Debussy* by Léon Vallas, translated by Maire and Grace O'Brien. (Oxford University Press : 1933).

place in a town is better adapted to meditation than another. When I gaze at a sunset sky and spend hours contemplating its marvellous ever-changing beauty, an extraordinary emotion overwhelms me. Nature in all its vastness is truthfully reflected in my sincere though feeble soul. Around me are the trees stretching up their branches to the skies, the perfumed flowers gladdening the meadows, the gentle grass-carpeted earth, . . . and my hands unconsciously assume an attitude of adoration. . . . To feel the supreme and moving beauty of the spectacle to which Nature invites her ephemeral guests ! . . . that is what I call prayer . . .

"Who will discover the secret of musical composition ? The sound of the sea, the curve of the horizon, the wind in the leaves, the cry of a bird, register complex impressions within us. Then suddenly, without any deliberate consent on our part, one of these memories issues forth to express itself in the language of music. It bears its own harmony within it. By no effort of ours can we achieve anything more truthful or accurate. In this way only does a soul destined for music discover its most beautiful ideas. If I speak thus, it is not in order to prove that I have none. I detest doctrines and their impertinent implications. And for that reason I wish to write down my musical dreams in a spirit of utter self-detachment. I wish to sing of my interior visions with the naïve candour of a child. No doubt, this simple musical grammar will jar on some people. It is bound to offend the partisans of deceit and artifice. I foresee that and rejoice at it. I shall do nothing to create adversaries, but neither shall I do anything to turn enmities into friendships. I must endeavour to be a great artist, so that I may dare to be myself and suffer for my faith, Those who feel as I do, will only appreciate me the more. The others will shun and hate me. I shall make no effort to conciliate them. On that distant day—I trust it is still very far off—when I shall no longer be a cause of strife, I shall feel bitter self-reproach. For that odious hypocrisy which enables one to please all mankind will inevitably have prevailed in those last works."

Ill-health did not prevent Debussy from working at great speed on the score of *Le Martyre de saint-Sébastien*, but he was unable to do the whole of it himself, and entrusted the orchestration to André Caplet, who was to be the conductor. Shortly before its production the Archbishop of Paris declared the work to be offensive to Christian consciences, and forbad all Catholics to attend.

At the orchestral rehearsal, the composer was so moved by the music that he was in tears before the end, but the *première* was a disappointment partly on account of a misunderstanding between the conductor and the stage manager, and partly because of the poor interpretation of the principal rôle by the foreign dancer Ida Rubinstein, who had commissioned the work. The production narrowly escaped failure, and as usual, the criticisms were very mixed. Some reports were very enthusiastic, some caustic, and one journalist wondered if the whole thing had been intended as a practical joke. On the whole, far more criticism was directed against d'Annunzio than Debussy. Robert Brussel, in *Figaro*, said that for the first time in the history of melodrama the music had been intimately united and identified with the poem : it heightened and prolonged the effect without in any way altering the atmosphere, except to intensify it. "The four preludes, the choruses and soli, will undoubtedly be numbered among Debussy's most perfect works. Without indulging in the slightest imitation of antique forms, he has managed to interpret Saint-Sébastien most appropriately, in a simple lyrical style full of natural emotion. The orchestral writing, the tier-like disposition of the voices in the choruses, the manner in which he regulates their entries, the softness or brilliance of their effects, their rhythm, their vigour or subordination, all go to form a work that is self-sufficing, and which possesses a significance and beauty of its own."

Gaston Carraud concluded an enthusiastic report in *La Liberté* with : "It impressed me as being one of the finest things M. Debussy has ever written. Despite the sumptuous colouring and the fanciful originality and the marvellous diversity of the instrumental combinations, the emotion in the essential parts of the work remains intensely spiritual, and of a rare purity. There are moments of ecstasy and pain when the emotional atmosphere of *Le Martyre de saint-Sébastien* recalls that of *Parsifal*, although the works are so dissimilar in feeling and style."

Le Martyre de saint-Sébastien was never given much support as a dramatic work, but concert versions were given in June 1912, and André Caplet afterwards arranged it as a symphonic suite without choruses in an effort to make it more popular. Most people agreed, however, that without the drama it lost its significance. It was revived in its original form at the Opéra in 1922 and again in 1924, but without much success.

In 1913 Debussy gave permission for several of his compositions to be adapted for ballet purposes. Nijinsky, the dancer, handled the *Prélude à l'Après-midi d'un faune* in a manner that aroused the indignation of most music-lovers. Debussy described his method in a letter : "The man adds up demisemiquavers with his feet and proves the result with his arms. Then, as if he were suddenly stricken with partial paralysis, he stands listening to the music with a most baleful eye . . . " Nevertheless, when this dancer planned a ballet—entitled *Jeux*—on the subject of "a plastic vindication of the man of 1913", Debussy consented to write the music for it. The first performance of it took place at the Théâtre des Champs-Élysées on May 15th 1913, but it was not particularly successful. A concert version was given at the Concerts Colonne a year later, but it had a mixed reception.

Debussy started writing the music for another ballet in 1913. A painter who specialized in writing and illustrating children's books, André Hellé, asked him to collaborate in a dramatic version of his *Boîte à Joujoux*, in which a ballet was to be included. The composer wrote the greater part of this, but for some reason it was laid aside, and was uncompleted at his death. It was eventually finished by André Caplet and produced in Paris in 1919 with great success.

During the same year (1913) Debussy wrote a group of songs called *Trois Poèmes de Stéphane Mallarmé*. They are among the least known of his minor works, but are unusual for their subtlety. In December of that year he visited Moscow and St. Petersburg, and was given a truly wonderful reception. He conducted his own works played by Koussevitzky's superbly-trained orchestra in both cities, and was rewarded by tumultuous applause.

Various reasons have been suggested for the exceptional amount of travelling he did during the two or three years preceding the Great War, but the most reasonable is that his great love of luxury and extravagance compelled him to accept engagements to conduct his own works, and to play his own compositions for the piano, even when he was in poor health. He was an excellent pianist, but his conducting never rose above mediocre time-beating. Early in 1914 he visited Rome, Amsterdam and The Hague.

VIII

For some months after the outbreak of the Great War, Debussy could write nothing. His deep love of France and of her culture made him all the more sensitive to the onslaught of the "German barbarians" :

he had always protested against German domination in music ; now he felt all the more bitter as their armed forces ravaged his native land. To sit down and compose music while his fellow countrymen were dying seemed futile and unthinkable, but a man of fifty-two firmly in the grip of an incurable disease could do very little. We find him writing letters deploring his inability to handle a rifle, envying Satie who as a corporal was going to the defence of Paris, and saying that if to save France another face had to be bashed in, he would offer his with alacrity.

It cannot be over-emphasized that Debussy's patriotism was absolutely sincere, yet jingoism was repugnant to him. He wanted to write a *Marche Héroïque*, but to him it seemed insincere "to indulge in heroism, in all tranquillity, well out of reach of the bullets." A very discreet work on lines something similar, *Berceuse Héroïque*, was his "tribute of homage" to King Albert of Belgium and the soldiers of that country. In this work the Belgian national anthem is embodied into a realistic picture of the terrible fields of Flanders and of the battle-weary soldiers. A symphonic version was played at the amalgamated Concerts Colonne et Lamoureux, but owing to its restraint, a large number of people did not seem to grasp its significance.

Debussy's chief work during the first year of the Great War was the editing of the works of Chopin for his publisher, in place of the German editions. In June 1915, while he was staying at Pourville, near Dieppe, he felt an inclination to compose again, and produced the *Douze Études* for piano, *En blanc et noir* (pieces for two pianos), and two Sonatas, one for 'cello and piano and the other for flute, viola and harp.

The two Sonatas are important, for they are the result of his sudden decision, made during that summer of 1915, to return to "pure" music in the traditional form. His only quartet, it will be recalled, was written in 1893. A third sonata was completed in 1917, but he did not live to write the other three that he had planned.

These sonatas were a tribute to the many thousands of young Frenchmen who at that time were being slaughtered by the advancing enemy, indeed the composer declared that they were written not for his own sake but to prove, in a small way, that even if the Boches had succeeded in degrading French thought during the years of peace, thirty million of them could not destroy it. He signed these works : "Claude Debussy, musicien français".

In the late autumn of 1915 he returned to Paris and had to undergo a serious operation, but managed first to write that beautiful, pathetic little song *Le Noël des enfants qui n'ont plus de maisons*, in which the hungry, terror-stricken children of the devastated regions address a simple little prayer to Santa Claus.

At about that time he wrote to Arthur Hartmann, the violinist, explaining that illness had now brought to a close a good spell of work. His morphine injections had turned him into a walking corpse : "If I gave you a detailed account of my misfortunes, you would be reduced to tears . . . "

Throughout 1916 he was so weak, and bore so much pain, that composition was almost impossible. He wrote to his publisher in June saying that life had become too hard, and that as he was unable to write music, he could see no reason for continuing his existence. Most of that summer was spent at Le Moulleau-Arcachon, where he made an almost superhuman effort to ignore his disease and to write something. His last work, the Sonata for piano and violin was started, but it was not ready for performance until the following spring, and even then he delayed its first performance to give a concert in aid of army charities. Eventually its *première* took place at the Salle Gaveau on May 5th, 1917. Gaston Poulet was the violinist, and Debussy played the piano part himself, thus making his farewell appearance to the music-lovers of Paris. He was seen in the audience at a Franco-Italian concert given in June, when Molinari conducted a fine performance of *La Mer*, but soon afterwards was rarely able to leave his house.

Early in June he went to stay for a while at Saint-Jean-de-Luz, and although he had planned to write several more works, he found himself overwhelmed with a sense of fatigue. His correspondence at that time was full of despair. While he was at Saint-Jean-de-Luz he made his last appearance in public, for on a September day he and Poulet gave another performance of the Sonata for piano and violin. It was very well received, and an encore was demanded, but the composer could not give it.

The return to Paris was made in October. He showed Alfred Bruneau a few sheets of manuscript paper upon which he had scribbled some musical ideas that had recently occurred to him, and sighed : "I can compose no more."

His pain then increased daily, and he was confined to his bed. But he had to bear more than physical pain. The position of France became more and more alarming, and with the last great German offensive, it looked as if her armies would be defeated. Fate decreed that Debussy's last few days should be the bitterest of his life, for on Saturday March 23rd the Germans began the bombardment of Paris by long-range artillery. He was so weak that it was impossible to move his bed down to the cellar, and he was compelled to lie there while the shells exploded in the streets of the city he loved. Two days later, on Monday March 25th 1918, he died at ten o'clock in the evening.

The funeral took place on the Thursday. The *cortège*, led by the Minister of Education, had to make its way right across Paris, from west to east, accompanied by the incessant rumble of the distant guns. The two eminent conductors of the leading philharmonic societies, Camille Chevillard and Gabriel Pierné, walked in silence side by side followed by various other musicians, most of them in army uniforms. It was a dismal, wintry day. Here and there little groups of war-weary people looked on pensively as the simple procession made its way past the columns of army trucks that lined the streets, past the avenues of trees whose leafless branches waved a silent farewell, to the cemetery of Père-Lachaise. At the grave-side, one short oration was made, and then the mourners hurriedly dispersed. Sometime afterwards, Debussy's remains were transferred to the cemetery at Passy.

The gravity of the military situation precluded the holding of any memorial concerts, and it was left to the world's journalists to pay tribute to one of the greatest composers in the history of French music.

The Principal Works of Debussy

In many ways, Debussy's music is a reflection of his own personality : it is chiefly of a voluptuary and fastidious nature that is an intensification of the characteristics revealed in the story of his life. In the history of music it forms an important landmark, as it were, for apart from being the founder of the impressionist school in music, Debussy led the way for the atonalists of the nineteen-twenties, thirties, and of the present decade. He was one of the earlier composers to use the whole-tone scale—but certainly not the first—and to employ unresolved dissonances. The modes, which even today have not been fully exploited, were of special interest to him : he frequently experimented with the Phrygian, Dorian and Aeolian, and so too were the combinations of the higher overtones, chords of the ninth, and so forth. We have already seen how his love of "ungrammatical" progressions brought him the censure of the pundits : few composers of his period cared to use consecutive fifths as he did, if at all.

His uses of rhythm also foreshadowed the rhythmic freedom of our contemporaries, and to a lesser extent perhaps, his orchestration anticipated the "clever" instrumentation of today. He was very sensitive of the individuality of the instruments he employed, and rarely allowed their individual timbres to be lost by massing them. The grandiose scoring of Berlioz did not appeal to him ; he never tried to use a panoramic canvas. His fastidiousness can be seen over and over again in his scoring for the wood-wind—a section of the orchestra that always delighted him—almost everything he wrote for them was superbly done. Mention might also be made of his use of the harp : in several of his scores there are passages that contrast strikingly with the unimaginative use made of this instrument by other composers.

Prélude à l'Après-midi d'un faune

Mallarmé's *Aprés-midi d'un faune* is a poem full of obscurities which the average Englishman, particularly if he were trying to read it in French, would dismiss with one word—tripe. However, an excellent translation, made with infinite patience by Mr. Alexander Cohen, was published in the *Musical Opinion* in September 1935. It tells of a faun who wakes from a dream and meditates upon two nymphs ; one has eyes "cold as tearful spring", and the other is like "Breath in the fire of noon." The "bite of love's mysteries" fills him with desire, which he describes thus :

> Passion, thou know'st at purple's ripening
> The granate[1] bursts for bees' fierce murmuring ;
> Our blood, ere caught to be encaptured fain
> Flows too for vibrant swarming of love's pain.

In his feverish imagination he captures two water-nymphs :

> I seize them, severing not, and swiftly hie
> To rose-bed that the wanton shadows fly—
> Its perfume all outpouréd to the skies—
> Rosy our frolic be as day dies.

His excessive ardour frightens them, and they struggle to get away. One succeeds, and the illusion fades. He pursues a vision of Venus, and finally stretches out on the sand to sleep.

Albert Thibaudet has described the poem as "the violent love of an adolescent exploited in poetry by a sad, disappointed man."[2]

[1] pomegranate.

[2] *La Poésie de Mallarmé.*

Debussy's prelude, which does not adhere strictly to the poem, is one of the most exquisite and charming pieces of orchestral music ever written. There are two principal themes which are subtly woven throughout the work with a pleasing variety of rhythms. The freedom of the harmony is all the more noticeable because of the light scoring : it requires only a light symphony orchestra without trumpets or trombones.

Nocturnes

This is a symphonic triptych ; the three panels being *Nuages*, *Fêtes* and *Sirènes*. • The composer's own notes on this give us the best description : "The title *Nocturnes* is to be interpreted here in a general and, more particularly, in a decorative sense. Therefore, it is not meant to designate the usual form of the Nocturne, but rather all the various impressions and the special effects of light that the word suggests. *Nuages* renders the immutable aspect of the sky and the slow, solemn motion of the clouds, fading away in grey tones lightly tinged with white. *Fêtes* gives us the vibrating, dancing rhythm of the atmosphere with sudden flashes of light. There is also the episode of the procession (a dazzling fantastic vision) which passes through the festive scene and becomes merged in it. But the background remains persistently the same : the festival with its blending of music and luminous dust participating in the cosmic rhythm. *Sirènes* depicts the sea and its countless rhythms and presently, amongst the waves silvered by the moonlight, is heard the mysterious song of the sirens as they laugh and pass on."[1]

The theme of the first panel has apparently been borrowed from Mussorgsky's song *The noisy day has sped its flight*, one of the *Sunless* cycle. This movement is particularly beautiful because of the remarkable variety of nuances employed in the portrayal of the clouds. *Fêtes* is a delightful, scintillating movement, and in *Sirènes* a choir of female voices is introduced to take the flowing melody while the orchestra paints a seascape. The third movement does not come quite up to the standard of the other two, and is sometimes omitted altogether.

La Mer

This work, which is in a form more classical than most of Debussy's compositions for the orchestra, consists of three symphonic sketches : *De l'aube à midi sur la mer*, *Jeux de vagues*, and *Dialogue du vent et de la*

[1] Translated by Maire and Grace O'Brien in *Claude Debussy* (Léon Vallas).

mer. It tends to be superficial in that the essential characteristics of the sea are inadequately expressed, yet this work has great charm and grandeur. There are some very fine effects : the thunder of waves crashing into a rocky shore, silvery spray gleaming in the sunlight, the mist that hangs above the foam, the swirling backwash, and suchlike. Shimmering colours are adroitly woven into a polyphonic work rich in fantasy and full of vitality. The themes are vividly contrasted, and the scoring is typical of Debussy, except for some very impressive sonorities in which he uses the brass on a heavier scale than usual.

Images

Here is another symphonic triptych of which the three pictures are *Rondes de Printemps* (France), *Ibéria* (Spain) and *Gigues* (England). The first of these was described very neatly by Louis Laloy when he said that "great audacity is shown in the development of the single idea which glides, and then runs, through light fronds of melody till it joins in a breathless dance, whirls wildly for a moment, then grows calm and vanishes in the clear air. And the orchestra, having rejected the flamboyant brass, achieves with more luminous tints, all the clear, yet hazy, charm of a Corot landscape."

Ibéria is in three parts : *Par les rues et par les chemins*, *Parfums de la nuit*, and *Au matin d'un jour de fête*, which are related by the repetition of certain themes. The second and third are played without a break. *Ibéria* gives us a vivid picture of the sunny Spanish villages, tells us of the intoxicating spell of Andalusian nights, whirls us into the midst of the excited dancers, and then in the morning brings us out into the glorious sunshine.

The last picture, *Gigues*, was finished by André Caplet, who described it thus : "the portrait of a soul in pain, uttering its slow, lingering lamentation on the reed of an oboe d'amore. A wounded soul, so reticent that it dreads and shuns all lyrical effusions, and quickly hides its sobs behind the mask and the angular gestures of a grotesque marionette. Again, it suddenly wraps itself in a mantle of the most phlegmatic indifference. The ever-changing moods, the rapidity with which they emerge, clash and separate to unite once more, make the interpretation of this work very difficult. . . . Underneath the convulsive shudderings, the sudden efforts at restraint, the pitiful grimaces, which serve as a sort of disguise, we recognize the soul of our dear, great Claude Debussy. We find there the spirit of sadness, infinite sadness, lying stretched as in the bed of a river whose flow, constantly augmented from new sources, increases inevitably, mercilessly." This movement was originally entitled *Gigues tristes*, and it is a pity that the adjective was dropped. It is rarely performed, and when the other two *Images* are played on their own, their order is often reversed.

Jeux

This ballet is set in a garden, where three tennis players, a young man and two girls, are looking for a lost ball. It is dusk, and the lights throw fantastic shadows that suggest a game of hide-and-seek. They try to catch one another, they quarrel and sulk, but the charm of the warm evening stirs their emotions, and they embrace. Then they are suddenly disturbed by another tennis ball thrown at them by a mischievous hand, and they disappear into the more secluded parts of the garden. Debussy's music is appropriately full of broken rhythms, nimble little passages and other fragments, but this work has never been very popular.

La Damoiselle élue

This cantata for solo voices, chorus and orchestra reveals the influence of Wagner, Massenet and César Franck, and is therefore not Debussy at his best, though it is pleasant enough if the effeminate qualities of D. G. Rossetti's text do not offend the listener. There are some very attractive passages in the choral parts, and the orchestration is dainty. It is built on three principal themes which go through various stages of harmonic development.

Le Martyre de saint-Sébastien

The incidental music to d'Annunzio's mystery play is another composition for solo voices, chorus and orchestra. Considering the speed at which this music was written—it was sent to the theatre page by page, corrected in pencil—it is a powerful work, full of rich effects and strong counterpoint. Excellent use has been made of Gregorian modes, and the whole conception is on a high plane. The final choruses, especially, are very beautiful, and its atmosphere generally is very much in sympathy with religious thought, for there are passages of solemn melody and places conducive to serene meditation. At the same time, there are plenty of harmonic subtleties typical of the composer. The first prelude, in which the wood-wind produce splendid organ effects, the various interludes, and the "Magic Chamber" music, are all very effective.

Pelléas et Mélisande

The following is a synopsis of the opera :
The action takes place in a purely fictitous state called Allemonde ; a kingdom of long ago.

ACT I. The opening scene is a forest, where Golaud (Baritone), a grandson of King Arkel of Allemonde, discovers Mélisande (Soprano) weeping by a well. He approaches her, but because he is tall and strongly built she is afraid of him, and forbids him to touch her. She will not tell him the cause of her sorrow, but eventually agrees to accompany him. They leave the stage together.

The second scene is the hall in the King's castle. Golaud's mother, Geneviève (Contralto), reads to King Arkel (Bass) a letter in which her son tells of his marriage to Mélisande. The King is acceding to Golaud's request that he should be allowed to bring his wife to the castle when Pelléas (Tenor), Golaud's half-brother, enters.

In the third scene we see Mélisande with Pelléas in the gardens outside the castle. She dislikes the forbidding gloom of her new home.

ACT II. Mélisande is talking with Pelléas beside a fountain in the park, and loses her wedding ring in the water, by throwing it up in the light of the sun.

In the second scene we learn that Golaud was thrown from his horse in the wood at precisely the same time as Mélisande lost her ring. When she bursts into tears he asks earnestly if anybody has upset her. He notices that she is not wearing her ring and although it had been her intention to tell him the truth, she says that she lost it in a cave by the sea. He tells her to ask Pelléas to help her find it.

The third scene is the cave, but three beggars there frighten Mélisande and the two do not stay.

ACT III. Mélisande is combing her hair at the window of her room in a tower of the castle, when Pelléas passes by and greets her. As she leans out of the window and gives him her hand, her long hair falls down over his head and shoulders. He speaks of his love for her with great passion while doves come out from the tower and fly about them in the darkness. Golaud suddenly enters and laughing nervously admonishes them for behaving like silly children.

The second scene is a very brief one in the vaults beneath the castle, where Golaud shows his half-brother a stagnant well from which comes an odour of death.

Then in the third scene, a terrace nearby, he warns Pelléas that there must be no more childish flirtation, and adds that Mélisande will shortly become a mother.

In the fourth scene, before the castle, the anxious Golaud questions his little son (of his first wife), but the boy Yniold (soprano) is too frightened to tell very much about the relations between Pelléas and Mélisande.

ACT IV. In the first scene Pelléas asks Mélisande in a room in the castle to meet him for a last farewell by the fountain.

The second scene is in the same room, and the King is asking Mélisande why she is so sad. He is very fond of her. "An old man feels the need now and then just to touch with his lips the brow of a maiden or the cheek of a child, so that he may continue to trust in the freshness of life and drive away for a moment the menace of death." The jealous Golaud breaks into this beautiful scene and announces that Pelléas is leaving that night. Mélisande approaches him, but he thrusts her aside angrily. His pent-up bitterness overflows. He draws the King's attention to her fine eyes, adding scornfully that he has seen them at work. In his rage he cries to her "Get away ! Your flesh disgusts me ! ". Then he seizes her by the hair and hysterically drags her about, until finally, when she is on her knees, King Arkel, who has been unable to interfere, closes the scene with the line : "If I were God I should have pity on the hearts of men."

The next scene is merely an interpolation to separate the last scene from the next. Yniold has been playing by the fountain in the park and has lost his ball beneath a stone. He tries in vain to lift the rock. Then he hears the bleating of sheep going to the fold.

The fourth scene is by the same fountain, where Pelléas and Mélisande declare their love and bid each other farewell. Golaud discovers them as they embrace. He draws his sword and kills his half-brother. Mélisande flees into the wood.

ACT V. This is in one scene only : a room in the castle. Mélisande has given birth to a child, but is dying. A physician (bass) tries to comfort Golaud by assuring him that his harsh treatment of her was in no way responsible for her condition. The distressed husband begs her forgiveness. She replies that she has forgiven him, although there was really nothing to forgive. Golaud then asks her for the truth about her love for Pelléas, but she is already sinking, and after looking at her child, passes away. The King, looking on sadly, laments : "Only a little peaceful soul that suffered and did not complain . . . a frail, mysterious being, like all humanity . . . "

The great skill with which Debussy applied his music to enhance the text and to create the right atmosphere in this opera—his master-piece—was first observed by Gaston Carraud when he reported its *première* in *La Liberté*. He wrote : " . . . everything has been subordinated to the words. Throughout the work the declamation, which is remarkable for its fluency and ease, is concerned entirely with accuracy of expression. It is more rapid and fluid than the Wagnerian declamation, more uniform and more intimately connected with the music. It has been faithfully modelled upon the simplicity of our gentle tongue. Though closely akin to the spoken word, it is quite tuneful and merges into the accompanying symphony, tinging it with the shimmering reflections of its harmonies and sonorities. The symphony itself is marvellously discreet and rich ; I hardly know how to describe it. The harmonic concatenations defy analysis, yet they sound natural and clear. The tonality is often impossible to determine, yet one gains the impression of tonality. The short, arresting, suggestive *motifs* are no sooner formulated, than they vanish to make way for others, and then flash back again for a moment. The musical subject-matter is subdivided to the utmost degree, yet nothing could be more uniform or consistent. This music makes not the slightest concession to tradition . . . it repudiates all that is hackneyed, showy or trite ; it seems to roam with the same vagabond freedom as thought itself ; yet it is well-proportioned and has a balance and progression of its own. It has a form that is subject to the laws of symmetry, as all music should be ; but this symmetry remains a secret : one is conscious of it without being able to ascertain its form . . . "

To those who are weary of the artificiality of operas with stylized, pompous recitatives and arias in which words have been strung haphazardly on to elaborate melodies, this remarkable work comes as a relief. The natural inflections of speech and the shades of every phrase have been scrupulously preserved. Few other composers have shown such respect for the gentle cadences of the French language, and therefore it is all the more essential that clumsy translations should be avoided.

Debussy's departure from tradition was the subject of many criticisms at the time, and he replied to them in a statement in which he said : "I have tried to obey a law of beauty that appears to have been singularly ignored in connection with dramatic music. The characters of this drama endeavour to sing like real persons, and not in an arbitrary language built upon antiquated traditions. Hence the reproach levelled at my alleged partiality for monotone declamation, in which there is no trace of melody . . .

"To begin with, this is untrue. Besides, the feelings of a character cannot be continually expressed in melody. Moreover, dramatic melody should be totally different from melody in general. . . . Those who listen to music at the theatre are, after all, much the same as those who gather around a street singer. . . . One even observes greater patience among them than is practised by many of the subscribers to our state-endowed theatres—even a desire to understand, which, one might go so far as to say, is completely lacking in the latter public.

"By a singular irony, this public, which cries out for something new, is the very one that shows alarm and scoffs whenever one tries to wean it from old habits and conventional humdrum noises. . . . I do not pretend to have discovered everything in *Pelléas*, but I have tried to trace a path that others may follow, broadening it with individual discoveries which will, perhaps, free dramatic music from the heavy yoke under which it has existed for so long."

The work is scored for a moderate-sized orchestra: the usual complement of strings, three flutes, two oboes, cor anglais, two clarinets, three bassoons, four horns, two trumpets, three trombones, tuba, two harps, timpani, cymbals and triangle. Throughout the work the orchestration is restrained, discreet and of great delicacy: the brass is used very lightly except in one or two isolated passages. As usual with Debussy's scoring, the wood-wind play an important, highly-effective part, but always preserving their own individuality. Very pleasing effects are obtained by *divisi* passages for the strings.

To give a detailed analysis of the work would be impossible without printing dozens of excerpts from the score for which no space can be spared in this book; the reader must therefore explore the score for himself and take note of the way in which the drama is developed in the orchestra while the voices bring out the full beauty of the words. The various themes used by the composer are on the whole unobtrusive, and do not require detailed examination, but the remarkable versatility of rhythm is worthy of careful attention.

The String Quartet

Debussy's Quartet, one of the finest specimens of French chamber music we possess, was admirably described by Paul Dukas[1] after a performance by the Guarnieri Quartet in Paris : "Everything is clearly and concisely drawn, yet the form is exceedingly free. The melodic essence of the work is concentrated, but is of a rich flavour. It impregnates the harmonic tissue with a deep, original poetic quality. The harmony itself, though greatly daring, is never rough or hard. M. Debussy takes a particular delight in successions of rich chords that are dissonant without being crude, and more harmonious in their complexity than any consonances could be. Over them, his melody proceeds as on a sumptuous, skilfully designed carpet of strange colouring that contains no violent or discordant tints. One single theme forms the basis of all the movements of the work. Some of the transformations it undergoes have an unexpected charm that is particularly fascinating : as, for example, the passage that occurs in the middle of the Scherzo. (This movement is simply an ingenious variation of the theme.) Nothing could be more charming than the very effective reappearance of the rhythmical theme to the accompaniment of the delicate quivering throbbings of the second violin and the viola, and the *pizzicato* of the 'cello. If I were called upon to say which of the four parts I like the best, I should pick out the first movement and the *Andante*, which are exquisitely poetical and most delicate in conception."

Sonata for 'Cello and Piano

Although the form of this sonata is almost on classical lines, its style and general character are far from being so. Debussy thought of calling it *Pierrot fâché avec la lune*, for its three short movements were suggested to him by the old Italian comedy. He seems to have modelled it to some extent on the sonatas of the seventeenth and eighteenth century French composers, but there is a lot of rather feeble *badinage* in the second movement that spoils the work as a whole. However, if we overlook this, and the rather unsuccessful attempt to introduce folksongs into the finale, we find various novelties in this sonata that make it worth playing.

Sonata for Flute, Viola and Harp

The composer originally scored this for flute, oboe and harp, but the substitution of the viola for the oboe was necessary to produce the

1 *Revue Hebdomadaire.*

sombre colouring he desired. It is rather beautiful in its sad, soulful way ; it has plenty of pleasing melodies, good rhythms, and effective harmonies. A suggestion of Gregorian chants and Troubadour songs adds to the general interest, and one cannot fail to be impressed by the composer's happy choice in usihg this particular combination of instruments.

Sonata for Violin and Piano

There is something pathetic about this sonata because it so obviously reflects a brilliant man's weary struggle against death : it is a pastiche in which fragments of folksong, oriental melodies and wistful allusions to one or two of his earlier works are jumbled together by a despondent man able to use his talent but too tired to derive any benefit from his genius. It has a certain amount of vitality, but there is a desperation about it that brings to mind the old broken-down comedian who in a third-rate music hall tries so hard to be funny, but who succeeds only in being embarrassingly pathetic. Still, for those who love the music of Debussy this sonata has a sentimental value.

Other Published Works

SOLO PIANO

Danse bohémienne
> (1880) This is the early piano work that Tchaikovsky criticised.

Deux Arabesques
> (1888) Both very delightful ; great favourites with most pianists.

Rêverie
> (1890) A pleasant work with unusual harmonies and orthodox counterpoint. Debussy himself disliked it.

Ballade
> (1890) The principal theme is slavonic, and the work has a definite Russian atmosphere.

Danse
> (1890) Originally entitled *Tarantelle styrienne*, this work is noteworthy chiefly for its rhythms, use of chords of the seventh and ninth, etc. It has been orchestrated by Ravel.

Valse romantique
> (1890) Not of great interest.

Nocturne
> (1890) Not to be confused with the orchestral *Nocturnes*. Suggestions of Franck, Fauré and Borodin.

Suite bergamasque
> (1890, but revised several times afterwards) Four movements : *Prélude*, *Menuet*, *Clair de Lune* and *Passepied*. An important and interesting suite, the third movement being a specimen of Debussy's best, as far as the piano is concerned. Elsewhere, touches of Massenet, Grieg and Godard.

Mazurka
> (1891) This is probably a relic of Debussy's student days. Rather commonplace.

Pour le piano
> (1896) Suite consisting of *Prélude*, *Sarabande* and *Toccata*. The middle movement suggests the impressionism of his greater works.

Estampes
> (1903) The three "prints" are :
> 1. *Pagodes*, with fragments of Cambodian and Javanese dances, employing a Chinese five-note scale and repeating its principal theme at different octaves in various rhythms.
> 2. *Soirée dans Grenade*, a most beautiful Spanish piece reminiscent of the Habanera (a slow Cuban dance very popular in Spain). Commenting on this in the *Revue Musicale* of December 1920, Manuel de Falla, the eminent Spanish composer, said that Debussy's descriptive skill was miraculous : "This is indeed Andalusia that he depicts for us : unauthentic truth, we might call it ; for not a single bar has been borrowed directly from Spanish folk-music, yet the entire piece, down to the smallest detail, is characteristically Spanish."
> 3. *Jardins sous la pluie*, a brilliant toccata based on two French songs : *Nous n'irons plus au bois* and *Do, do l'enfant do*. These are heard through arpeggios that suggest gentle showers of rain. This work is a great favourite with the virtuosi, as it is extremely effective when properly played (and that is not very often). Many critics consider it to be the finest of Debussy's compositions for the piano.

D'un cahier d'esquisses
(1903) A small work of no particular importance. Very little known.

Masques
(1904) Ditto.

L'Isle joyeuse
(1904) An extremely gay, vivacious piece inspired by Watteau's *Embarquement pour Cythère*. A fine piece for the virtuoso, but extremely difficult. It was orchestrated by Molinari.

Images (first set)
(1905)
1. *Reflets dans l'eau.*
   Very beautiful, impressionistic.
2. *Hommage à Rameau.*
   Solemn, with no definite suggestion of Rameau
3. *Mouvement.*
   Pleasant, but not of outstanding interest.

Images (second set)
(1907)
1. *Cloches à travers les feuilles.*
   Fine harmonic effects.
2. *Et la lune descend sur le temple qui fut.*
   A curious piece supposed to represent a calm, moonlit scene and using a simple melody. At one time some of the critics thought it was a practical joke.
3. *Poissons d'or.*
   This fantasy of gold fish is very popular with a large number of pianists who love its scintillating movement.

Children's Corner
(1906-8) This consists of six little pieces : *Doctor Gradus ad Parnassum, Jimbo's Lullaby, Serenade to the Doll, Snow is Dancing, The Little Shepherd, Golliwog's Cake-walk.* They are pretty little pieces, the fourth being exceptionally beautiful. *Jimbo* was a little stuffed elephant owned by Debussy's daughter, Chou-chou, to whom the work is affectionately dedicated.

Hommage à Haydn
(1909) Of no great importance.

La plus que lente
(1910) A waltz, which he later orchestrated "for the countless five o'clock tea parties frequented by beautiful listeners."

Douze Préludes (first book)
(1910)
1. *Danseuses de Delphes.*
   Supposed to represent three Greek Dancers doing a dignified dance.
2. *Voiles.*
   A fine little piece, particularly fascinating because of its use of contrasted thirds and fourths.
3. *Le Vent dans la plaine.*
   An excellent, lilting impressionistic piece, played at considerable speed.
4. *Les sons et les parfums tournent dans l'air du soir.*
   Inspired by poems of Beaudelaire.
5. *Les Collines d'Anacapri.*
   Very jolly ; a tarantella and a Neapolitian melody form its basis.

6. *Les pas sur la neige.*
   Debussy said of this that the rhythm should have the sonorous value of a melancholy, ice-bound landscape.
7. *Ce qu'a vu le vent d'ouest.*
   Rather weird.
8. *La Fille aux cheveux de lin.*
   Inspired by a *Chanson écossaise* by Lecomte de Lisle.
9. *La Sérénade interrompue.*
   A pleasant Spanish scene, with guitar effects.
10. *La Cathédrale engloutie.*
    This is one of the most popular of Debussy's works for the piano. Based on the Breton legend of the cathedral that had been "swallowed up" by the sea, it uses Gregorian tones with *Organum*[1] and various minor effects that make this a fine piece for the virtuoso. It was orchestrated by Henri Büsser, but strangely enough, lost much of its charm when played by a full orchestra.
11. *La Danse de Puck.*
    A fantastic little piece said to have been inspired by *A Midsummer Night's Dream.*
12. *Minstrels.*
    Suggested to the composer by a visit to a music-hall.

Douze Préludes (second book)

(1910-13)
1. *Brouillards.*
   Typical Debussy, but not of great interest.
2. *Feuilles mortes.*
   Ditto.
3. *La Puerta del Vino.*
   Another vivid glimpse of Spain. Said to have been written upon receipt of a gay picture post-card from that country.
4. *Les Fées sont d'exquises danseuses.*
   One of the most attractive pieces in the book.
5. *Bruyères.*
   Mediocre.
6. *General Lavine-eccentric.*
   Inspired by a character Debussy had seen on the stage. It must be played "as if the fellow had been made of wood." One of the best pieces in the book.
7. *La Terrasse des audiences au clair de lune.*
   This was inspired by the words "the terrace for moonlight audiences" in a letter by René Puaux the French author, whose works Debussy greatly admired.
8. *Ondine.*
   Mediocre.
9. *Hommage à S. Pickwick Esq., P.P.M.P.C.*
   The famous Dickens's character always amused Debussy, and so did the Englishman's love of sticking letters after his name.
10. *Canope.*
    Suggested to the composer by the antique urns used for the remains of cremated persons.
11. *Les Tierces alternées.*
    One of the most interesting of these preludes.
12. *Feux d'artifice.*
    Inspired by a patriotic festival in Paris.

---

[1] *Organum* : the medieval practice of singing plainsong a fifth or fourth below or above the unison, if it suited the voice so to do. The parallel melody thus formed the origin of the harmony.

La Boîte à jouioux

(1913) Composed with the confidential advice of "some of Chou-chou's old dolls." This children's ballet is based on a tragic love-story that takes place inside a toy box. The music makes use of various songs, parodies of tunes from the operas, the sounds of toy instruments, musical boxes, and suchlike. It is very charming, yet subtle and quite daring harmonically here and there. It was orchestrated partly by Debussy just before his death, and completed by André Caplet.

Berceuse héroïque pour rendre hommage à S. M. le Roi Albert.

(1914) A simple piano piece, orchestrated later. of no great interest today.

Douze Etudes (first book)

(1915) Little more than technical exercises, yet very attractive pieces. Each study helps the pianist to overcome some technical difficulty. The composer recommends that the player choose his own fingering.

1. *Pour les cinq doigts.*
2. *Pour les tierces.*
3. *Pour les quartes.*
4. *Pour les sixtes.*
5. *Pour les octaves.*
6. *Pour les huit doigts.*
   (second book).
1. *Pour les degrés chromatiques.*
2. *Pour les agréments.*
3. *Pour les notes répétées.*
4. *Pour les·sonoritiés opposées.*
5. *Pour les arpèges.*
6. *Pour les accords.*

PIANO DUET

Symphonie en si

(1880) One movement only. This and the following interlude were intended to be orchestral works.

Triomphe de Bacchus

(1883)

Petite suite

(1889) Consists of *En Bateau, Cortège, Menuet, Ballet.* It is a very pleasant suite, and still enjoys great popularity. It has also been orchestrated for small and full ensembles.

Marche écossaise sur un thème populaire

(1891) This is commonly known as the Earl of Ross March. It is based on the primitive tune played by the pipers of Clan Ross before battle. Orchestrated by the composer.

Six Epigraphes antiques

(1914) These were written from music sketched out fifteen years previously. They are colourful, with some very pleasing effects.

1. *Pour invoquer Pan, dieu du vent d'été.*
2. *Pour un tombeau sans nom.*
3. *Pour que la nuit soit propice.*
4. *Pour la danseuse aux crotales.*
5. *Pour l'égyptienne.*
6. *Pour remercier la pluie au matin.*

TWO PIANOS

Lindaraja

(1901) Of no great importance.

En blanc et noir
>(1915) This is a set of three caprices. The middle one is a war picture dedicated to the memory of a friend who was killed on March 3rd 1915.

CHAMBER MUSIC

Rapsodie for saxophone and piano.
>(1905) This was commissioned by a Mrs. Elisa Hall of Boston, Mass., who was studying the saxophone for the benefit of her health (!) This instrument had not, of course, been degraded in those days by the jazz merchants. Debussy delayed the completion of it for some time, and the accompaniment was later orchestrated by Roger Ducasse. It has some agreeable Spanish rhythms, and on the whole is not at all bad, but nobody seems keen to play it today.

Première Rapsodie for clarinet and piano.
>(1910) Written as a test-piece for students at the Conservatoire. A beautiful work that should not be neglected. The solo part is very fine, and the accompaniment contains some excellent writing.

Petite pièce for clarinet and piano.
>(1910) This, too, is quite charming and well written.

Syrinx for unaccompanied flute.
>(1912) A dainty little piece originally called *Flûte de Pan*. It formed part of the incidental music to *Psyché*, a drama by Gabriel Mourey.

SONGS

Nuit d'étoiles
>(1876) Words by Théodore de Banville.

Beau soir
>(1878) Words by Paul Bourget.

Fleur des blés
>(1878) Words by André Girod. These three songs are among the very earliest of Debussy's compositions. Quite pleasant.

La Belle au bois dormant
>Poem by Vincent Hypsa.

Voici que le printemps
>Poem by Paul Bourget.

Paysage sentimental
>Poem by Paul Bourget.
>These three songs were written between 1880 and 1883. They have rather more character than those above, and indicate the composer's rapid progress technically.

Zéphyr
>(1881) Words by Théodore de Banville.

Rondeau
>(1882) Words by Alfred de Musset.

Pantomime
>(1883) Words by Paul Verlaine.

Mandoline
>(1883) Words by Paul Verlaine.
>Both of these settings of Verlaine's poems are excellent little works.

Clair de lune

(1884) This must not be confused with another setting of this same poem by Verlaine written in 1892.

Pierrot

(1882-4) Words by Théodore de Banville.

Apparition

(1884) Words by Stéphane Mallarmé.

Cinq Poèmes de Baudelaire

These five songs.were written between 1887 and 1889. The main theme of No. 1 was taken from *La Damoiselle élue*. The influence of Wagner is strong in this set. They are all very attractive songs, No. 3 being the best.
1. *Le Balcon.*
2. *Harmonie du soir.*
3. *Le Jet d'eau.*
4. *Recueillement.*
5. *La Mort des amants.*

Ariettes oubliées

(1887-8) Delicate settings of Paul Verlaine. Typical of Debussy in their subtlety and feeling. *Green* and *C'est l'extase* are noteworthy. On the whole, a most beautiful set of songs.
1. *C'est l'extase.*
2. *Il pleure dans mon cœur.*
3. *L'ombre des arbres.*
4. *Chevaux de bois.*
5. *Green.*
6. *Spleen.*

Deux Romances

(1891) Words by Paul Bourget. Not of much interest.
Romance.
Les Cloches.

Les Angélus

(1891) Words by G. le Roy. Charming, chiefly because of the bell-harmonics.

Dans le jardin

(1891) Paul Gravelot's words. Very graceful and slightly reminiscent of passages in *Pelléas et Mélisande*.

Trois Mélodies

(1891) Paul Verlaine's poems.
1. *La mer est plus belle.*
2. *Le son du cor s'afflige.*
3. *L'échelonnement des haies.*

Fêtes galantes

(1892) Poems by Paul Verlaine. No 2 was written in the 1880-3 period. No. 3 must not be confused with the *Clair de lune* in the *Suite bergamasque* for piano. It is the most popular of the three songs.
First set :
1. *En Sourdine.*
2. *Fantoches.*
3. *Clair de lune.*

Proses lyriques

(1892-3) Debussy wrote the words himself, and they are not very good. Nor, for that matter, is the music.
1. *De rêve.*
2. *De grève.*
3. *De fleurs.*
4. *De soir.*

Chansons de Bilitis

1. *La Flute de Pan.*
2. *La Chevelure.*
3. *Le Tombeau des Naïades.*

(1897) What a contrast to the *Proses Lyriques* ! These three songs are considered by many critics to be Debussy's best. The poems are by Pierre Louÿs. (Bilitis was a fictitious hedonist of ancient Greece). No. 1 is based on a syrinx melody ; a charming, simple work, in which we find a "song of the green frogs" in *appoggiaturas*. No. 2 is rather curious, but very beautiful in parts, particularly at its close. No. 3 has a fine melody used with good effect against a background of continually moving pattern. A grand musical picture wedded to an excellent poem.

Fêtes galantes

Second set :
1. *Les Ingénus.*
2. *La Faune.*
3. *Colloque sentimental.*

(1904) Poems by Paul Verlaine. No. 1 is a scene of young love made up of old dance rhythms. No. 2 has an accompaniment suggesting a flute and tambourine to represent a dancing faun. In No. 3 there is a suggestion of disillusion and irony.

Trois Chansons de France

1. *Rondel: Le temps a laissé son manteau.*
2. *La Grotte.*
3. *Rondel: Pour ce que plaisance est morte.*

(1904) The first and third are to words by Charles d'Orleans ; the second uses lines from Tristan L'hermite's ode *Le Promenoir des deux amants.* They are all of some importance.

Le Promenoir des deux amants

1. *Auprès de cette grotte sombre.*
2. *Crois mon conseil.*
3. *Je tremble en voyant ton visage.*

(1904-10) These three songs use extracts from L'hermite's ode from which the set derives its name. No. 1 is the same as No. 3 of the above set. There is nothing outstanding about these three items.

Trois Ballades de François Villon

1. *Ballade de Villon à s'amye.*
2. *Ballade que Villon fit à la requête de sa mère pour prier Notre-Dame.*
3. *Ballade des femmes de Paris.*

(1910) These three songs, of contrasted types, are all of a high standard No. 1 is sombre and pensive ; the second is an extremely beautiful song using modal counterpoint ; and the third is as gay as the women of Paris it extols.

Trois Poèmes de Stéphane Mallarmé

1. *Soupir.*
2. *Placet futile.*
3. *Éventail.*

(1913) There is intense subtlety and a certain degree of scrappiness in these three settings of Mallarmé's abstruse poems. Therefore they are unlikely to be very popular. Admirers of Mallarmé's later work have accused Debussy of trying to paint the lilies.

Noël des enfants qui n'ont plus de maisons

(1915) Debussy wrote both the words and the music of this exquisite little work, which has already been described briefly in the biography. There is also an arrangement of it for a choir of children.

Fantasie for piano and orchestra

(1889) This early work is more or less a piano concerto, and more interesting than one would imagine, judging by the composer's own dissatisfaction with it.

Deux Danses

Danse sacrée for harp and strings.
Danse profane for harp and strings.
(1904) Both of these dances were commissioned by the firm of Pleyel for competitions at the Brussels Conservatoire. · They are rather vague and modal, but quite pleasant. ··

Printemps

(1887) This early orchestral work has already been described in the biography.

Incidental Music for 'King Lear' (Shakespeare)

(1904) Of no great importance.

Trois Chansons de Charles d'Orleans

1. Dieu ! qu'il fait bon regarder !
2. Quand j'ai ouy le tabourin.
3. Yver, vous n'estes qu'un villain.
(1908) Unaccompanied choral songs for S.A.T.B., using modern harmony but written in the old contrapuntal style.

Printemps

(1882) Early chorus for female voices with pianoforte accompaniment. Words by Comte de Ségur.

Invocation

(1883) Male voice chorus with pianoforte accompaniment. Of no importance. Lamartine's text.

L'Enfant prodigue

(1884) The Grand Prix cantata. See the biography. Text by Édouard Guinand.

Khamma

(1912) This ballet was only sketched out by Debussy, and orchestrated by Charles Koechlin. A poor effort.

Ode à la France

(1916-17) A large choral work sketched out by Debussy (libretto by Louis Laloy) but left unfinished at his death. Eventually completed by Marius-François Gaillard, but without success.

Scenes from Ravel's opera,

L'Heure espagnole

PLATE XVII

PLATE XVIII

Lipnitzki

MAURICE RAVEL

PLATE XIX

$\mathcal{R}$avel

I

AFTER the death of Debussy most musical authorities recognized Maurice Ravel as the greatest French composer of the early twentieth century. It is true that a small minority have never accepted this point of view, and their criticisms of this composer's work are not altogether unreasonable, but this is a matter that we shall be able to decide more easily in another twenty years or so. In any case, these claims and counter-claims to an individual's supremacy are not of any great importance. For the benefit of those who are making a general study of French music it should be added that Vincent d'Indy (1851-1931) and Gabriel Fauré (1845-1924)[1] both made a valuable contribution to the music of France in the period now under consideration, and such contemporaries as Milhaud, Honegger[2] and other members of "Les Six" were beginning to exert their influence.

Maurice Ravel was born on March 7th 1875 at 12 Quai de la Nivelle,[3] Cibourne, near Saint-Jean-de-Luz. This is in the south-west corner of France, the Basses-Pyrénées, a part of the country that he loved all his life and frequently revisited. His father, Joseph Ravel, was a mining engineer of Swiss origin ; a very keen amateur musician who originally intended to become a professional pianist, and who spent several years at the Geneva Conservatoire with that object in view. Maurice's mother was a Basque woman, daughter of a fisherman. One or two writers have suggested that there was a Jewish strain in Ravel's ancestry, but this is quite untrue.

When Maurice was a few months old, the little family moved to Paris and took an apartment in the rue des Martyrs ; a very modest abode, quite poorly furnished. Joseph Ravel spent most of his time working at his inventions, and his income was extremely precarious, for like so many small inventors, he lived chiefly on the hopes of tomorrow.

---

1 The original plan of this book included biographies of these two composers, but they had to be omitted on account of the paper shortage.
The lives and work of these contemporaries have been described in my *Composers Gallery* (1946).
3 Later renamed Quai Maurice Ravel.

The little boy was a frail lad, and rather small for his age. He possessed striking black curls which gave him a definite Basque appearance during his early years. A love of mechanical toys was obviously inherited from his father, and he was always fascinated by conjuring tricks. Mention might also be made of his almost insatiable passion for fairy stories. When he was three another boy, Edouard, was born.

Maurice started to learn to play the piano very early, and he was only seven when his father persuaded Henri Ghys, an accomplished Parisian musician, to take him as a pupil. Within a few 'months the boy was playing duets with his father, but unfortunately the paternal preference was for arrangements of such popular pieces as Wagner's *Tannhäuser* Overture, and it was not long before Maurice heartily disliked the endless repetition of excerpts from the operas.

When he was a little older he attended classes at the Lycée, and began studying harmony with Charles-René. He was not exceptionally brilliant at music as a boy—there was no chance of exploiting him as a child prodigy, for instance—but he made very satisfactory progress, and at the age of fourteen was admitted to the Conservatoire. He went at first into the preparatory piano class held by Eugène Anthiome, but in due course passed on to Charles de Bériot's class, and also took harmony and counterpoint, first with Emile Pessard, then with Gédalge, and eventually with Gabriel Fauré.

His first friendship at the Conservatoire—where he was to study for fifteen years—was with Ricardo Viñes, a clever young Spanish pianist of the same age as himself, who was to be a life-long companion and an enthusiastic performer of his works. The Ravel family had by that time moved to the rue Pigalle, and it was here that the two boys met for music-making.

Ravel was always secretly envious of his friend's extraordinary technique at the keyboard, and from time to time would work feverishly to become his equal. But these desultory periods of enthusiasm never produced the desired result, for although Ravel had considerable skill he frequently succumbed to moods of laziness, and Viñes always retained his superiority. At one time Ravel's mother was gravely concerned about these fits of idleness and would offer him thirty centimes an hour for diligent practice.

When the Universal Exposition was held in Paris in 1889, Rimsky-Korsakov, who was then almost unknown in the French capital, was invited to conduct some of his own compositions at one of the

Exposition concerts. Ravel was present, and was deeply impressed with the great Russian composer's works. At the same exhibition he heard a Javanese *gamelang* orchestra, and was fascinated by the strange Oriental music they played, its curious harmonies and complicated rhythms. This, too, was to influence him when he began to compose.

At about this time he also became acquainted with the colourful works of Chabrier : he and Viñes used to play the *Trois valses romantiques* as piano duets. It was Ravel who hit upon the idea of writing to Chabrier and asking if he would permit them to play the waltzes to him. They were only sixteen years of age at the time, and Viñes, always rather more shy than his companion, was afraid that the eminent composer would be annoyed when he discovered that they were only very young students. However, Chabrier received them kindly, and criticised their performance quite helpfully, though without any great enthusiasm for their "interpretation" of his music.

Ravel always worked assiduously for the competitions that were held· at the Conservatoire each year, though he did so more to please his parents than to satisfy himself. In 1891 he won the Première Medaille. Charles de Bériot had very high hopes for him as a pianist, but at times he became quite exasperated by the periods of laziness that from time to time impeded Ravel's progress. In the composition class he was a more satisfactory student, for his interest rarely flagged. Pessard was a good teacher for Ravel because he always encouraged originality in his students, though at times even this most tolerant professor must have felt bewildered when Ravel produced almost incomprehensible manuscripts and expected him to play them. Pessard would make one or two attempts and then say : "I can make nothing of this fantastic stuff : you'd better play it yourself." He was a good-natured man, and could see that the revolutionary youth possessed real talent, but continually urged him to exercise more control upon his musical thoughts, and to take fewer liberties with harmony. He generally concluded his criticisms of Ravel's efforts with a sigh and such a remark as : "Well, who knows, perhaps you will create a new style for us."[1]

Although Ravel rebelled against the rigid application of the rules of harmony, he was not prepared to overthrow the system altogether, for he could see that there had to be some general "rules of grammar," however much one intended to break them. Needless to say, he became notorious at the Conservatoire for his "advanced views" and was frequently censured for his extravagant harmonies.

[1] Quoted by Gustave Mouchet in *L'Echo des Concours.*

During his early years there he met Erik Satie, that whimsical eccentric of the musical world, and was captivated by his unique personality and ideas on music. After that first meeting in a café they were often seen together, and frequent discussions with the composer tended inevitably to make Ravel more interested in purely creative work than in preparation for a career as a virtuoso. He began writing seriously with an eye upon the music publishers, and it was not long before he began to receive some encouragement from them. Incidentally, he once took a few of Satie's pieces to the harmony class at the Conservatoire and played them to the other students before the lesson started. Pessard arrived and nearly had a fit. He solemnly warned Ravel that such trash must be left severely alone, for Satie, he declared, had no place in the world of true music! But the young student continued to believe in Satie's work.

At about this time he discovered the poems of such people as Baudelaire, Mallarmé and Verlaine, which had a definite effect upon his creative efforts. He also became interested in the writings of Edgar Allan Poe.

When he was nineteen, Ravel wrote his first song, *Ballade de la reine morte d'aimer*, using a poem by R. de Mares. This and a setting of Verlaine's *Un grand sommeil noir*, which followed shortly afterwards, revealed the impression that Satie's friendship had made upon the youth. Neither of them found a publisher, nor did his *Sérénade grotesque*, a piano solo written at about the same time.

II

THE first of Ravel's compositions to be published was the *Menuet antique* which he wrote in 1895 and dedicated to his friend Ricardo Viñes. Where the antiquity comes in is not at all clear, but this piece is rather more conventional than most of his other works.

He was still studying with Pessard when he wrote the *Habanera*, the first of the unpublished *Sites auriculaires*, which later became part of the *Rapsodie espagnole*.

In 1897 he entered Henri Gédalge's class for counterpoint and fugue, and began his advanced study of composition with Gabriel Fauré, who had just succeeded Massenet. Fauré was fully aware of Ravel's unusual ability, but was a severe critic. Roland-Manuel has related that on one occasion Fauré sharply censured one of Ravel's efforts, but came to the conclusion a day or two later that he had been too harsh in his condemnation of the young man's ideas. At the next lesson he asked Ravel to let him see that piece again, and when the youth expressed surprise he admitted : "I may have been mistaken".[1] This is typical of Fauré's modesty and willingness to admit his own mistakes : a quality not found very often in the professors of his day. Ravel's appreciation of his master is to be seen in the dedication of his String Quartet and *Jeux d'eau*, which is to "mon cher maître G. Fauré."

In 1898 the Société Nationale de Musique recognized Ravel by giving a public concert of his works. The programme included the *Sites auriculaires* for two pianos, which Viñes and Mlle Marthe Dron had agreed to play. Unfortunately, instead of using two pianos they played upon one of Pleyel's recently-invented dual pianos, which consisted of two pianos built into one rectangular instrument with a keyboard at each end. They had to play from the composer's manuscript, and therefore could not see each other on account of the position of the music rests. During *Entre cloches*, the second part, they came to grief in the complicated cross-rhythm section, and the alternate chords were played simultaneously, producing a most horrible noise. The audience, including the critics, all thought that the effect was intentional on the composer's part, and the work was mercilessly condemned. Ravel said not a word to the two pianists concerning the catastrophe, and got over the great disappointment by concentrating his attention upon another work.

Antoine Galland's translation of *The Arabian Nights* had come to his notice, and he thought of writing an opera based upon it. Owing to various difficulties he got no further than the Overture—*Shéhérazade* —which was never published. The Société Nationale de Musique invited him to conduct it at one of their concerts, but the audience showed little appreciation, indeed many people hissed and booed. Pierre Lalo, one of the critics who was present, wrote : "If this is what M. Ravel imagines to be an Overture 'constructed in the classical form,' we must admit that he has a great deal of imagination. In its structure, his style is reminiscent of Grieg, or even more so of Rimsky-Korsakov or Balakirev. There is the same incoherence in the general plan and in the relation of the tones ; but the characteristics already striking enough in the models are carried to excess by the pupil."[2]

As it happened, Ravel himself did not think very highly of this particular work : he told a friend that he had written so many

1 *A la gloire de Ravel.*
2 *Le Temps* : June 13th, 1899.

whole-tone scales in it that he had been put off them for the rest of his life. A few years later, in 1903, he used the title and some of the themes from it for a set of songs.

In 1889 he wrote what was to become his first great success, the *Pavane pour une Infante défunte*, a piano solo that was later orchestrated. The title has no special significance—Ravel admitted that he chose it merely because it sounded well—and all the ingenious "stories" that imaginative people have written about it are quite unauthentic. The composer did not put any great value upon this work himself : he said in later years that its faults were all too apparent to him, and he had some difficulty in appreciating the many virtues that other people said it possessed. It was first performed by Ricardo Viñes on April 5th 1902 at a Société Nationale Concert, and Ravel had the rare experience of seeing an audience in a really appreciative frame of mind. Another work first heard at this concert was *Jeux d'eau*, which with the *Pavane pour une Infante défunte* was to spread the composer's fame all over France and to establish his name on both sides of the Atlantic.

In 1901 Ravel decided to compete for the Grand Prix de Rome. He had been in Fauré's class for four years, and felt that he stood a good chance of winning. Moreover, he believed that four years at the Villa Medici, Rome, in the company of other highly-talented young men, particularly those pursuing the other arts, would be a most valuable experience at this stage of his career. The cantata to be written that year was a setting of Fernan Bessier's poem *Myrrha*. Ravel worked very hard at his entry, but for some reason foolishly delayed the orchestration until the time limit had almost been reached. Then he finished it in a spell of frenzied activity, and submitted it at the very last moment. The adjudicators had no difficulty in finding fault with the hastily-written orchestration, and this, coupled with the fact that Ravel had not taken certain verses very seriously, lost him the prize. André Caplet was the successful candidate, and Ravel received the second prize : a gold medal.

Fauré was quite convinced that the prize was well within the reach of Ravel, and persuaded him to try again in the following year. To everybody's amazement he failed again : his *Alcyone* made no impression whatever upon the jury.

Twelve months later he made a third attempt, but his setting of *Alyssa* stirred only the antagonism of the adjudicators, and once again he was passed over. Fauré was staggered, and protested indignantly with several other prominent musicians who shared his faith in the young composer, but without effect.

Meanwhile, Ravel had been working upon his String Quartet in F. It was completed early in 1904 and first performed on March 5th. Some idea of its success may be gained from Roland-Manuel's account of the concert :[1] "On March 5th 1904, at the Schola Cantorum, the Société Nationale revealed to an enthusiastic public the Quartet in F—a miracle of grace and tenderness, a marvellous jewel of polyphony which submitted to the requirements of the classical form without manifesting any of its restrictions . . . "

Ravel was now nearing the age limit for the Grand Prix de Rome, so he decided to make one more attempt for the award, not because he desired any sort of honour, but merely for the sake of the privileges that he still believed would be so helpful to him as a composer. To the astonishment of the entire musical community, in other countries as well as in France, he failed to pass even the preliminary test in which the more incompetent candidates were eliminated! Nobody would believe it at first. Was it a mistake ? No, the authorities solemnly proclaimed that M. Ravel's musicianship did not reach the standard set by the examiners.

Progressive musicians all over France revolted at this, and many of the greatest figures in French music attacked the Académie in indignation. This caused a sensation : the newspapers and intellectual journals took up Ravel's case and demanded justice. Romain Rolland declared :[2] "I am not a friend of Ravel. I may even say that I am not personally sympathetic towards his subtle and over-refined art. But what justice compels me to say is that Ravel is not only a student of promise, he is already one of the most outstanding of the younger Masters of our school, which does not have many such. I do not doubt for an instant the good faith of the judges ; . . . But this is rather a condemnation for all time of these juries ; and I cannot understand why one should persist in keeping a school in Rome if it is to close its doors to those rare artists who have originality—to a man like Ravel, who has established himself at the concerts of the Société Nationale through works of far greater importance than those required for an examination. Such a musician did honour to the competition : and even if by some unhappy chance (which I should find difficult to explain) his composition seemed inferior to those of the other

[1] *Maurice Ravel et son oeuvre.*
[2] Quoted by Marguerite Long in the *Revue Musicale*, December 1938.

contestants, he should nevertheless be received outside the *concours.*
It is a case rather analagous to that of Berlioz. Ravel comes to the
examen de Rome not as a pupil, but as a composer who has already
proved himself. I admire the composers who dared to judge him.
Who shall judge them in their turn ? "

Within a week or two the matter became a public scandal.
Pamphlets were printed drawing the attention of the educated sections
of the community to the spiteful attitude of the reactionary adjudi-
cators, and public feeling became so strong that Théodore Dubois, the
Director of the Conservatoire, felt obliged to resign his office. Gabriel
Fauré was appointed in his place.

So many distinguished musicians had taken Ravel's part in the
dispute that the young composer became quite a hero in the eyes of all
the French musicians of the younger school : a distinction that he did
not desire, for he had never made any comment himself upon the
attitude of the pundits. He had of course deeply resented the
humiliation, and it is significant that in later years when the French
Government tried to make amends by offering him an award of the
Legion of Honour he refused to accept it.

During the year 1905 Ravel tried to express himself by writing
poetry as well as music. One of his literary efforts was the charming
little poem *Le Noël des jouets*, which he set to music and dedicated to
Madame J. Cruppi. The accompaniment was orchestrated shortly
afterwards. In the same year he wrote his *Sonatine* for piano, which
was first played at Lyons on March 10th 1906 by Madame de Lestang.
This also was orchestrated at a later date.

III

In those days, even more than later in the century, Paris was a great
cultural centre in which all the younger devotees of art, music, sculpture
and literature met to follow their calling, to exchange views and to
enjoy their carefree lives in congenial company. Montmartre and the
Quartier Latin were full of restless young men and women with
revolutionary ideas about almost everything, and determined to be
original at any price. Ravel found stimulating company in the studio
of a young painter named Paul Sordes, where a group of young artists
and other intellectuals with advanced ideas used to plan their campaigns
against reaction. They represented the revolutionary element in all
the arts, and were therefore generally regarded as outlaws. For that

reason they called themselves the Société des Apaches. Ricardo Viñes was a member, and so were such people as Léon-Paul Fargue, writer and critic, Maurice Delage, who was later to become one of Ravel's pupils and closest friends, M. D. Calvocoressi, the eminent critic who was afterwards to become very well known in England, Florent Schmitt, Roger-Ducasse, André Caplet, Manuel de Falla and at a later date, Igor Stravinsky.

No wonder Ravel found himself drawn towards this studio! Actually, he was far less revolutionary in his ideas than most of them, and became noted more for his restraint than anything else. He was, as always, an elegant young man, faultlessly dressed, small and lean, with his thin face almost enveloped in a thick black beard.[1] Among his more outstanding characteristics were his unfailing source of energy, his lack of interest in women, and his love of long country walks : attributes that were not possessed to any great extent by his companions ! Roland-Manuel described him as "the complete type of dandy Baudelairien".

Ravel was a shy, fastidious young man, but he possessed a marked (though not unfailing) sense of humour. He was very fond of playing practical jokes upon his friends. As a pastime, dancing enchanted him, but he preferred to sit out and watch other people enjoying this form of recreation than to take part in it himself. His self-consciousness generally made him feel awkward on the dance-floor.

One evening just after midnight Paul Sordes delighted his fellow members of the Société des Apaches by producing a score of Borodin's Second Symphony arranged as a piano duet. It was hailed with great enthusiasm, and Sordes and Delage played it with such vigour that the whole neighbourhood was disturbed. The next two or three days were spent in making apologies to embittered residents in the vicinity of the studio. But the most important outcome of that evening was the adoption of the first eight notes of the symphony as a secret call sign. If, for instance, one member of the society wished to attract the attention of another in a café, or in the street, he would whistle :

One can well imagine the many useful and amusing purposes for which this little tune was employed.

1 The beard was shaved off in 1910.

Another secret of this society was the name Gomez de Riquet : a fictitious personality who had to be met without delay whenever a member was accosted by a bore. Of course it was not long before all sorts of queer things were attributed to poor M. Gomez de Riquet, and the unfortunate gentleman became the subject of all manner of jokes : drawing room and otherwise.

From 1904 onwards the Société des Apaches made their head-quarters at Maurice Delage's spacious studio in the rue de Civry at Auteuil. It was sparsely furnished but for the two pianos, and one had to have no qualms about sitting on the floor. There were no near neighbours, so the meetings often went on all night. The Apaches generally went home by the first train on the Ceinture at dawn. Delage's studio became quite a famous rendezvous in time, for apart from all the fun and purely recreational music-making, lengthy, serious discussions on art, music, literature and politics took place there between the most brilliant young intellectuals in France.

There was great excitement one evening in 1905 when Ravel arrived with the score of a new suite for the piano called *Miroirs*, which consisted of five pieces, each one dedicated to a member of the Apaches. *Noctuelles* was inscribed to Léon-Paul Fargue, *Oiseaux tristes* to Ricardo Viñes, *Une Barque sur l'océan* to Paul Sordes, *Alborada del Gracioso* to M. D. Calvocoressi, and *La Vallée des cloches* to Maurice Delage.

Another popular meeting place for many of the young artists and musicians was the drawing room of Ida and Cipa Godebski, a young Polish couple deeply interested in all cultural activity. Cipa Godebski's sister, Missia, married Alfred Edwards, who kindly placed his yacht *Aimée* at Ravel's disposal from time to time when the young composer wished to work undisturbed. It was on this vessel that he wrote the *Rapsodie espagnole*, in which he made use of the unpublished *Habanera*, and *L'Heure espagnole* ; both of which reflect his deep interest in Spanish music and life.

In 1907 Calvocoressi asked Ravel to harmonize five Greek melodies : a request that led to the composition of *Cinq mélodies populaires grecques* for voice and piano. The words of these songs were written by Calvocoressi. A sixth song, *Tripatos*, was added in 1909 but never published. The success of the five melodies encouraged Ravel to enter a competition held by the Maison du Lied of Moscow for the harmonization of folk-songs of various European countries. He wrote seven, but only four were published (in 1910) : *Chanson française*,

Chanson espagnole, Chanson italienne and *Chanson hébraïque*. The last of these was orchestrated.

The year 1907 is also notable for the first performance, on January 13th, of Ravel's *Histoires Naturelles* by Madame Bathori. These songs, whose words were written by Jules Renard, caused quite a sensation. The public completely failed to understand them : some of the audience were amused, but most of them were annoyed. With the exception of a few who praised Ravel's "gift of transmuting into music the most unmusical of subjects," the critics were abusive. But many of the leading musicians—chiefly members of the Société des Apaches—took up the matter in Ravel's defence, and with the help of a newspaper controversy succeeded in giving the new work a tremendous amount of publicity.

Ravel's *Rapsodie espagnole* was first performed on March 19th 1908 at one of the Concerts Colonne. On this occasion the Société des Apaches attended in force to see that the work got a fair hearing, but this precaution proved unnecessary, for under the able direction of Colonne the *Rapsodie espagnole* was well performed and the audience was most appreciative. All the same, a few critics wrote caustic notices accusing Ravel of "affectation."

It was the practice of many of the less intelligent critics to call Ravel an imitator of Debussy, but although the two great French composers both revolted against Wagnerian domination, and both felt unattracted by the César Franck school, and although there are certain similarities in their style, it cannot be said that Ravel copied Debussy any more than he can be accused of imitating Rimsky-Korsakov or Liszt, both of whom he admired. For many years Debussy and Ravel were close friends, but in later life the spirit of rivalry between them became more keen and bred a sense of antagonism. For all that, they never ceased to respect each other's works. Ravel used to say : "When I am dying I should like to hear *L'Après-midi d'un faune*," and he arranged this piece as a piano duet. In later years he also dedicated his Sonata for Violin and 'Cello "To the memory of Claude Debussy."

The comedy-opera *L'Heure espagnole* was based on Franc-Nohain's one-act play of that name, which impressed Ravel sufficiently to make him abandon an attempt to make an opera out of Gerhart Hauptmann's famous drama *The Sunken Bell*. When *L'Heure espagnole* was complete, Ravel took it to Franc-Nohain's house and played it over on the piano for the author's approval. Alas ! the writer had no taste for modern music, and when Ravel turned to him at the end for his comments, he merely drew his watch and exclaimed coldly "Fifty-six minutes. ! " Still, it was accepted by Albert Carré the director of the Opéra-Comique, though it had to wait until 1911 to be produced.

Ravel was extremely fond of children and it was a common sight to see him scampering around or crawling about on the floor with the two Godebski youngsters, Mimie and Jean. It was for them that he wrote the charming suite *Ma Mère l'Oye* : a set of duets based on their favourite stories. He hoped that Mimie and Jean would play the suite at a concert, but they were too frightened, and its *première* was given by two other children, Christine Verger, age six, and Germaine Duramy, age ten, at the first concert held by the Société Musicale Indépendante. This society had recently been formed by the younger musicians to present contemporary works neglected by the Société Nationale, which was by that time becoming rather conservative in its outlook.

In the same year—1908—Ravel wrote a Suite for Piano based on poems by Aloysius Bertrand, *Gaspard de la Nuit*. A note on this suite will be found at the end of this biography, but it should be said here that this is one of the finest examples of Ravel's genius as a composer for the piano. Alfred Cortot said :[1] "These three poems enrich the piano repertoire of our epoch with one of the most extraordinary examples of instrumental ingenuity that the industry of composers has ever produced."

The death of his father on October 13th 1908 upset Ravel's work for several months. Joseph Ravel had always taken a keen interest in his son's music and had given him every possible encouragement, so the loss of this devoted parent was a great blow to the young composer. Only one work appeared in the year that followed : *Menuet sur le nom d'Haydn*, for piano.

In those days the Comtesse de Saint-Marceaux, a great patroness of music, used to hold musical soirées on Wednesday evenings to which many of the greatest musicians of the day were invited. The wearing of evening dress was strictly forbidden—a rule that only a person very high in society would dare to make in those conventional times. A sumptuous dinner was served, and then the company would withdraw to the exquisitely furnished drawing room where two Pleyel pianos dominated a scene of luxury. Ravel became a popular and regular guest on these occasions and frequently introduced his latest compositions to the very select audience there.

Quoted by Roland-Manuel in *A la gloire de Ravel*.

IV

Diaghilev's Russian Ballet took Paris by storm in the year 1909, and it was through this that Ravel became acquainted with the works of Igor Stravinsky, who was soon to join the Apaches and become one of his closest friends. The Ballet naturally made a very great impression upon Ravel, and the young French composer lost no time in bringing his compositions to the attention of Diaghilev. In 1910 he received a commission to write a ballet on the Greek legend of *Daphnis and Chloe*. Michel Fokine, the choreographer, had to make various alterations in the libretto to suit Ravel, then the composer went to the Godebski's summer house at Valvins to prepare the score. The lovely forest of Fontainebleau nearby enabled him to go for long walks in solitude while he was seeking inspiration. He went to an amazing amount of trouble over this highly-polished score : the concluding Bacchanale, for instance, took a year to write.

Daphnis and Chloe was first produced at the Châtelet Théâtre on June 8th 1912. It was not particularly successful because in several places Ravel's music was too complicated for ballet purposes ; moreover during the rehearsals there had been several disputes between Fokine, Diaghilev and Ravel which did nothing to facilitate the necessary fusion of the arts. The parts of Daphnis and Chloe were taken by Nijinsky and Karsavina.

Many critics consider this to be the finest French ballet in existence, and it is certainly Ravel's masterpiece. As a ballet it has never been very successful, but as a symphonic work it is superb. The two fine orchestral suites that have been taken from it have extended Ravel's fame all over the world.

His next work was "a chain of waltzes after Schubert" called *Valses nobles et sentimentals*. These were first played by Louis Aubert at a concert given by the Société Musicale Indépendante at which all the items were presented anonymously so that the audience could guess the composers of them. The waltzes were not at all well received : there were boos, hisses and cat-calls, and Ravel had the unusual and highly disconcerting experience of hearing his best friends roundly condemning them and even appealing to him for his concurrence with their views ! The critics were most offensive, yet a little later when the identity of the composer became known, many of them changed their tune and began to discover outstanding merit in these waltzes. (By that time Ravel had become fairly well established, and many critics considered it dangerous to be too censorious about his works.) Shortly afterwards, at the request of Mlle Trouhanova, the waltzes were incorporated into a ballet : *Adélaïde ou le langage des fleurs*. This was first produced at the Châtelet Théâtre on April 22nd 1912. Ravel conducted, and it was a tremendous success.

This induced him to orchestrate the suite *Ma Mère l'Oye*, and this, too, he turned into a ballet, using the story of the Sleeping Beauty as the principal theme.

Ravel was at that time living with his mother and brother Edouard at 4 avenue Carnot, near the Arc de Triomphe, but in the summer of 1913 he stayed for a while with Stravinsky at Clarens, on the shore of Lake Geneva, to collaborate with him in re-orchestrating Mussorgsky's *Khovantchina*. While he was in Switzerland he set three of Mallarmé's poems to music. The summer of 1914 was spent on the Basque coast at Saint-Jean-de-Luz, and it was here that he wrote the Trio for piano, 'cello and violin.

Immediately after the declaration of the Great War, Ravel tried to enlist, despite the restraint of his friends and relations, for he had a strong sense of patriotism. He was rejected, however, on account of his poor physique ; so he volunteered to help in the care of the wounded. Then he tried for the French air force, but again was rejected. Finally, early in 1916, he was accepted as a lorry driver in the army. His many adventures with his vehicle, which he called Rosalie, cannot be recorded here, but as the war dragged on his health deteriorated, and he became disgusted at the futility of the wanton destruction he had to witness. He refused to lend his name in support of an organisation that tried to prevent the performance of contemporary German music in France, and was sharply criticised for it.

In 1916 he decided to compose another suite, each movement of which was to be in honour of a friend who had fallen on the field of battle, though at the same time the whole work was to be a tribute to Couperin. Illness then overtook him, and after several weeks spent at a hospital just behind the lines, he was sent back to Paris for convalescence.

The death of his mother in January 1917 was another blow to him, for he had always put her first in everything, and he began to suffer serious moods of depression. It was not long before he was sent forward again, this time to Châlons-sur-Marne, but his health grew steadily worse, and he was discharged in the early summer of that year.

He then went to Normandy and set to work on *Le Tombeau de Couperin*. Although this piano suite is a memorial, it is not a solemn work. It was to have been performed early in 1918, but the bombardment of Paris stopped all musical activity in the capital, and it was not heard until April 1919, when it was an overwhelming success. The composer afterwards orchestrated four of its movements.

V

THE Great War was a profound and shocking experience to Ravel, and it continued to affect him long after the armistice : he suffered from insomnia and fits of depression, and became a chain-smoker. He turned cynical and inclined to indulge in melancholy moods, while physically he seemed to have shrunk. For two years he felt disinclined to compose, and wrote very little.

In December 1919 he moved for a while to the village of Lapras, hoping that the change of air and environment would help him to recover his spirits. While he was there he was again offered a decoration of the Legion of Honour, but refused to accept it.

At Lapras he began work on a ballet in which he hoped to recapture the gay spirit of Vienna before the war had turned it into a city of disillusionment, and then to show the effect of the four years' conflict. The work was more or less commissioned by Diaghilev, who had asked Ravel to write another ballet for him two or three years previously. When it was finished Ravel sent it to Diaghilev, but to his great surprise, the eminent impresario refused it. *La Valse*, as it was called, had already been performed with great success as an orchestral work at one of the Concerts Lamoureux, and Ravel was deeply offended by Diaghilev's attitude. They never spoke to each other again. In 1925 they met accidentally, and Diaghilev, hoping that the composer had forgotten the incident, held out his hand. Ravel refused it, and the impresario was so furious that he challenged the composer to a duel. Fortunately their friends managed to dissuade them.

The greater part of the next two years was spent in travelling. He visited almost all the countries of Europe, including England, where he was delighted at the very cordial welcome given to him in the concert halls. Much of his time in England was spent in trying to avoid the "fans" who wanted to meet him : he had no desire to become a public idol.

At that time he was working on his Sonata for violin and 'cello, which was first performed at the London residence of Madame Alvar by Hans Kindler and Jelly d'Aranyi. This work became very popular in fashionable circles : it was played at Lady Rothermere's house shortly afterwards, and Ravel received several requests for further performances.

In 1922 Ravel decided that he could work better in the country than in Paris, and began searching for a small property in the district of the forest of Rambouillet. He found a pleasant little villa in the picturesque village of Mountfort-L'Amaury, just under thirty miles from Paris. It had always been his desire to have a small place of his own, and this hillside villa with its pretty garden was ideal, despite the smallness of its rooms. He immediately began planning its renovation : a modernized bathroom and kitchen had to be installed, and he decorated all the rooms himself by stencilling designs in black upon the light walls. He renamed the property "Le Belvédère," and engaged a servant, Madame Reveleau, to reside there permanently. She served him faithfully until the end of his life.

Ravel's study, which was almost filled by his Erard grand piano, had grey walls and very dark curtains that enhanced the fine view from the window. He could look out across the orchards to the fringe of the forest.

The *salon* contained most of the various objets d'art he had collected in former years, including his most treasured possession : a mechanical nightingale in a gilded cage that would sing and flutter its wings when wound up. It was presented to him by Léon Leyritz, the sculptor. Ravel's dining room had a pleasant little balcony overlooking the garden—a miniature garden containing a pool, flagged walks and dwarf trees, that he planned himself. The most attractive feature of it was perhaps the Japanese garden.

He was fond of entertaining, and therefore one usually found two or three of his friends at "Le Belvédère." There were gay parties at which various Apaches would be invited to take part in discussions on music and art, to be followed by long evening walks in the forest. They would stroll along with "Rara" (as Ravel was known to his friends) telling anecdotes and producing his extraordinarily clever imitations of bird songs and animal cries. He often used these imitations to answer people who tried to flatter him.

Ravel possessed a great many imitations of rare prints, porcelains and other precious articles. He would display them proudly to his

MAURICE RAVEL at the Piano

PLATE XX

Scene from Ravel's *L'Enfant et les sortileges*

PLATE XXI

friends, and then when they had expressed their admiration, would tell them that he had bought them for next to nothing at a local store.

He lived a quiet, unexciting life, with no great emotional disturbances. One of his closest friends was Madame Hélène Jourdan-Morhange, a very talented violinist whose career was cut short by an injury to one of her hands. He indicated his esteem by dedicating his Violin sonata to her. At one time many people expected a wedding announcement, but Madame Jourdan-Morhange had lost her husband in the Great War and did not wish to marry again.

Ravel's attitude towards women generally may be summed up in his own words : "I prefer a beautiful locomotive to a beautiful woman". His mother used to say that no woman would ever tolerate his irregular habits : he generally got up very late, worked all day in his pyjamas, then dressed and went out in the evening. He rarely returned before midnight.

In speaking of Ravel's friends one must not overlook the family of Siamese cats that enjoyed both permanent residence at the villa and the continual devotion of their master. They were the only living creatures that he liked to have near him when he was composing.

Describing him in *Les Cahiers d'aujourd 'hui*,[1] Emile Vuillermoz has written : "Neither critics nor photographers have been able to arrive at any but contradictory and inaccurate portrayals. His audacious nose, thin lips, hermetic mouth, eyes gay and cruel, his face in which a wood-engraver has notched the wrinkles too energetically, the profile of his skull which a sculptor has modelled with a daring hand ; the severe, parched lines of his thin, mechanical body with its slightly tanned skin like that of a retired sailor,—all these form a disconcerting whole.

"One sees in him, as a rule, isolated details that do not go well together. He is a child and an old man. The merest trifle amuses him, and yet his ravaged face often takes on a severe and reserved expression. He passes without transition from childish heedlessness to painful gravity. He often looks as if he were suffering. His tormented features and frowning brow reveals one knows not what dark conflict . . .

"His look of a worried young fox or a mouse scenting traps everywhere is surprising in an artist so lucid, spontaneous and precise, who has nothing to fear from life."

1 No. 10 : 1922.

Ravel's attitude towards his own music was quite impersonal. He would rarely listen to his own compositions, and at concerts generally went outside for a cigarette when they were being played. Success did not attract him, and he never thought or spoke of his "career" in music. He was satisfied that his music brought him sufficient income upon which to live modestly. He took a few pupils if they interested him—the more distinguished of whom were Manuel Rosenthal, Roland-Manuel, R. Vaughan Williams and Maurice Delage—but heartily disliked taking money from them. He would generally accept a fee only under pressure. He followed the careers of talented young musicians with great interest and did everything he could to help them. "You are quite as clever as I am" he would say, "therefore you can do just as well as I have done if you try." A piece of advice frequently given to young composers was : "Take a model and imitate it. If you have nothing to say, you have nothing better to do than to copy. If you have something to say, your personality will never be more evident than in your unconscious infidelity."

VI

It took a great deal of persuasion to induce Ravel to visit America. He received several pressing invitations from "Pro Musica" (formerly the Franco-American Society) to appear at concerts of his own works, but he invariably objected that he hated being exhibited like something in a circus. Assurances that vast fortunes awaited him in the United States usually produced merely a shrug of the shoulders.

However, a definite offer of a minimum of ten thousand dollars for a three months' tour eventually tempted him, and he arrived in New York on January 4th 1928 completely bewildered by the crazy welcome that music lovers had prepared for him, though he could not help being impressed by the kindness of everybody. He was the answer to the American journalist's prayer, for without thinking of the "story" it would make, he admitted that he had brought twenty pairs of pyjamas, fifty-seven evening ties, about two dozen waistcoats and innumerable shirts of the rather gay type he had always favoured. Still, when that "sensation" had subsided, he was able to find great pleasure in exploring the "mechanized civilization" of America, the gadgets and whatnot.

He appeared at thirty-one concerts in the United States, and on several occasions acted as guest-conductor of various leading symphony orchestras   Mrs. Coolidge, the great American patroness of music, commissioned him to compose a work for one of her chamber music concerts, and the result was the quartet *Chansons madécasses* for voice, piano, flute and 'cello.   It consists of three songs, of which the second was first performed at a gala concert held by Mrs. Coolidge at the Hotel Majestic, Paris, in October 1925.   Ravel played the piano, Hans Kindler the 'cello, Fleury the flute, and Madame Bathori was the singer.   The other two songs were not finished in time.

Soon after his return from America Ravel wrote the famous *Bolero*, which helped enormously in popularizing his works.   It was first heard on November 20th 1928, and when the composer was congratulated upon its amazing success, he shrugged his shoulders and said : "Oh ! c'est la mode, simplement ! "

Then followed a great deal more travel, and mention might be made of his visit to Oxford in 1931 to receive the honorary degree of Doctor of Music.   But travel and a recently-acquired craze for spending half of the night at dances and in night-clubs did not improve his health, and he complained more and more of fatigue and insomnia.

In 1931 he also planned another American tour, and wrote a piano concerto to play with the great American orchestras—*Concerto en trois parties* in G, which was first performed on November 11th 1931 at the Salle Pleyel, Paris, by Madame Marguerite Long under the direction of the composer.

Soon after he had started writing this concerto he received a request for another concerto from Paul Wittgenstein, the Austrian pianist who had lost his right arm in the Great War.   He therefore wrote them both at the same time, and the *Concerto pour main gauche*, dedicated to ·Wittgenstein, was introduced to the public by that pianist on November 27th 1931 in Vienna.

Writing about these works, Ravel said : "It was an interesting experiment to conceive and to realize simultaneously the two Concertos.   The first, in which I shall figure as an executant, is a concerto in the most exact sense of the term, and is written in the spirit of Mozart and Saint-Saëns.   I believe that the music of a concerto can be gay and brilliant, and that it need not pretend to depths of emotion nor aim at dramatic effects. . . .   At the beginning I thought of calling the work a *Divertissement* ; but I reflected that this was not necessary, the title "Concerto" explaining the character of the music sufficiently. From a certain viewpoint my Concerto (in G) has some resemblances to the Violin Sonata.   It includes some elements borrowed from jazz, but only in moderation.

"The Concerto for the left hand alone is of a rather different character, and in one movement only, with many jazz effects, and the writing is not so simple. In a work of this kind it is essential to create the effect not cf light, delicate texture, but of a partition written for both hands . . . "

Late in 1932 a film company asked Ravel to write some songs for a film on the subject of *Don Quixote*. He did, but they were not accepted for the simple reason that his script was sent in much too late. These three songs, *Don Quichotte à Dulcinée*, were his last works, for soon after their completion he was involved in a cab accident and received a blow on the head which probably accelerated his last illness.

Several months passed during which his sense of fatigue and depression was much worse, and he experienced the greatest difficulty in making certain movements : he found it required very great effort to write and speak, in fact there were symptoms that suggested a partial paralysis. A slight improvement induced him to start work on two new compositions, but they had to be abandoned. In 1934 he was appointed director of the American Conservatoire of Music at Fontainbleau, but was too ill to take any active part in the work of that institution.

During the ensuing year he decided to try the effect of a holiday, and travelled through Spain and Morocco. He certainly derived some slight benefit from this, but it was not long before he was suffering again. He rarely spoke of his condition to his friends, who believed that he had a tumour on the brain. The real cause of his illness was described as "affaissement du cerveau"—shrinking of the brain.

In the summer of 1937 he attended a gala performance of *Daphnis et Chloé*, but in the car on the way home he burst into a fit of weeping. After this he retired to his villa at Mountfort-L'Amaury, and spent his last few months wandering quietly through the forest of Rambouillet. When these walks became impossible, he spent most of his time sitting on the little balcony overlooking the garden.

He retained his mental faculties until December 19th of that year, when Dr. Clovis Vincent, the Parisian brain specialist, performed an operation. Ravel went to sleep when the anaesthetic was administered and never regained consciousness. He died in the hospital in the early morning of December 28th 1937, aged sixty-two.

His brother Edouard arranged the modest funeral—Ravel had not wished for a pompous ceremony—and he was buried at the cemetery of Levallois-Perret. A large number of musicians stood at the graveside while Jean Zay, the Minister of National Education pronounced an oration. Memorial concerts were held in most countries during the months that followed.

THE PRINCIPAL WORKS OF RAVEL

As we have already observed, Ravel shared Debussy's dislike of German domination in music, particularly the irrational worship of Wagner, and it must be admitted that the two composers resemble each other in minor details of their works, but fundamentally, there are considerable differences. In Ravel's music, for instance, there is not much trace of that "dreamy emotionalism" that one associates with Debussy : there is not the same erotic tendency. The emotion in Ravel's works is not easily perceived.

Ravel was more of a classicist, and his precise and restrained style is in many ways quite different from Debussy's voluptuousness Although one can trace the influence of Rimsky-Korsakov, Liszt, Saint-Saëns, Debussy, Chabrier, Satie, and, of course, the Symbolist poets, no one can deny that Ravel's music possesses both originality and marked individuality—and these two qualities are not as synonymous as some people seem to imagine.

Whereas Debussy exploited the chord of the ninth, Ravel not only used this but exploited the chord of the eleventh harmonic also, but he did not stray far into the fields of atonality. His piano music is of special importance, for few composers exploited the resources of this instrument so ably as he without writing purely superficial "virtuoso music".

Much could be said about Ravel's brilliant orchestration : his genius for clarity and vividness, richness and individuality. In *Le Mercure de France*,[1] Jean Marnold declared that he had created an orchestral language that was exclusively his own. "Its extreme subtlety seems by its style to achieve simplicity through a natural unfolding of the infinite resources of each instrument. The basis of this complete mastery is his adequate and profound understanding of those resources."

Ravel's orchestration was altogether more vigorous and virile than Debussy's, and it must be remembered that Debussy was a master of this particular branch of the art.

Ravel orchestrated not only a large number of his own piano works, but compositions by several other composers : Debussy, Satie,

[1] August 16th, 1917.

Mussorgsky, Chabrier, Chopin and Schumann. Perhaps the most famous of all was his treatment of Mussorgsky's *Pictures at an Exhibition.*

In passing, a word should be added about his interest in jazz. He believed that it made an important contribution to modern art, and whether one liked it or not, it was bound to influence the future course of music. It is interesting to note that many of our contemporary composers now hold or incline towards this point of view.

L'Heure espagnole

Ravel called this one-act *comédie musical* a "conversation in music," and it is rather like an Italian *opera-buffa*, for it is not on classical lines. One might almost call it an opera in miniature, but it gives the impression of being more natural than an opera. The orchestral part, though extremely effective, is not obtrusive. The scene is a clockmaker's shop in Toledo during the eighteenth century.

After the Overture, "a chorus of the little voices of the clocks," Ramiro, a muleteer, enters with a watch to be repaired. It is the day on which Torquemada, the clockmaker, has to go around the town winding the government clocks, and Concepcion, his wife, hopes to receive her lover, the poet Gonzalve, during his absence. But Ramiro decides to wait until Torquemada's return, and it looks as if he will spoil the fun. She therefore decides to set him to work lifting heavy clocks for her, and he carries one of them upstairs just as Gonzalve arrives. Concepcion hides the poet inside a large grandfather clock. A little later, another of her lovers, Don Inigo Gomez also arrives, for it was he who got Torquemada the government contract so that the clockmaker would be away from home at a definite time each week. She hides him in a clock too, and both lovers are in their respective timepieces when Torquemada returns. To allay his suspicions they both pretend to be extremely interested in the clocks, and the shrewd Concepcion hits upon the idea of making both of them pay heavily for the privileges they have enjoyed with her by selling them the timepieces at several times their proper price. The opera ends with amusing efforts to get the stout Don Inigo out of his clock, and then they all join in a pleasant quintet

Its *première* was given at the Opéra-Comique on May 19th 1911, with Massenet's *Thérèse.* The critics could not agree upon its artistic value : one called it "pornographic vaudeville", and others praised it very highly, making special mention of the excellent orchestration.

Daphnis et Chloé

This magnificent ballet in three scenes is known to most music-lovers only as a fine concert piece, but to enjoy this properly one should know the story.

It opens with a scene at the edge of a sacred wood, where the young Greek maidens and shepherds dance in honour of the great god Pan. Daphnis and Chloe arrive, and Dorcon, a cow-man, tries to embrace Chloe but is angrily pushed aside by Daphnis. The two men then engage in a dance contest : Daphnis performs very gracefully and is rewarded with a kiss from Chloe, Dorcon is very clumsy and grotesque. Chloe and the others depart, leaving Daphnis asleep in the shade of a tree. Lycenion, who, it now appears, has not gone with the other maidens, then tries to tempt him by doing a particularly voluptuous dance, abandoning her veil in the course of it. But Daphnis hears a cry, and discovers that a band of pirates are pursuing the shepherdesses, and fearing for Chloe's safety, rushes off to protect her. Soon after his departure she comes on the scene from another direction altogether, and falls exhausted before the altar of Pan. The pirates arrive, find her and take her away. Daphnis returns, discovers one of her sandals, guesses that she has been captured and swoons with horror. While he is unconscious, three nymphs appear and dance around him invoking the aid of Pan.

The second scene depicts the pirates' camp. The leader gives orders for Chloe to be brought in, and commands her to dance before him. She refuses, and tries to escape, but he seizes her roughly. Suddenly, a huge and terrifying shadow appears on the side of the mountain : Pan has come to her rescue, and the pirates flee in disorder.

The third scene is the same as the first. Daphnis lies sleeping. It is dawn, and birds are beginning to sing : the forest stirs to life. Chloe appears with the shepherds and shepherdesses, and the whole company join in a great act of thanksgiving. Daphnis and Chloe embrace.

This is a work of great beauty, and it is surprising that no better effort has been made to produce it successfully in its proper form. The coming of dawn in the third scene is one of the loveliest things in the whole realm of music, and the dance of the three nymphs while Daphnis is unconscious is perfectly exquisite. Very fine, too, is the extraordinary effect produced by the orchestra when the shadow appears on the side of the mountain in the second scene. A first-rate company could work wonders with this ballet, despite the admitted difficulties.

Ma Mère l'Oye

Both the orchestral suite and the ballet of this name were adapted from the original piano suite.

The suite contains five movements, each illustrating a fairy tale. The first, *Pavane de la Belle au bois dormant*, is very brief, and consists of the slow dance performed by the courtiers while the Princess is asleep. It is in two-part counterpoint.

The second, *Petit Poucet*, tells the story of the woodcutter's son, Hop o' my thumb, who believed he could find his way back through the wood by dropping a trail of bread-crumbs. Alas! the hungry birds eat them, and the boy and his brothers are lost. This is an exquisite movement, the twittering of the birds being particularly effective.

The third, *Laideronnette, Impératrice des Pagodes*, is a miniature Chinese scene in which is told a tale about the Empress of the Pagodas. "She laid aside her robes and entered the bath. At once the pagodas began to sing and play: some had lutes made from nutshell, others used viols made from almond-shell; for the size of the instruments had to be in proportion to the size of the players."[1] The music is delightful, and includes a jolly piccolo tune in the Chinese pentatonic scale, which is afterwards taken up by the flute.

The fourth, *La Belle et la Bête*, is a conversation between a young princess and a prince who has been turned into an ugly beast. She speaks of his kind heart, and when she agrees to become his wife, he is transformed back into a handsome young man. In this, the bassoon takes the beast's part, and his entreaties are echoed in the coda by the solo violin, after the transformation has been delightfully portrayed by the harp *glissando*.

The last, *Le Jardin féerique*, is a lovely musical picture of the enchanted garden, in which the Sleeping Beauty is awakened by Prince Charming with a kiss.

This work is scored for two flutes and piccolo, two oboes with cor anglais, two clarinets, two bassoons with double bassoon, two horns, timpani, triangle, cymbals, bass drum, gong, xylophone, bells, celesta, harp and the usual strings. It is an orchestral masterpiece, taking slightly less than twenty minutes to perform.

The ballet of this name follows the suite fairly closely, though a prelude and certain interludes have been added. The second, third

[1] *Serpentin vert*: Mme. D'Aulnoy.

and fourth movements of the suite are here portrayed as the dream of the Princess, and very clever use is made of an inner stage for this purpose.

Adélaïde ou le langage des fleurs

The scene of this ballet, adapted from the *Valses nobles et sentimentales*, is set in the *salon* of a beautiful courtesan, who likes to express her emotions with flowers. A few couples are dancing, but the hostess is admiring her flowers : she is going from vase to vase inhaling their fragrance.

As the second waltz starts, Lorédan, an elegant young man, appears and offers her first a ranunculus to express admiration, then hawthorn blossom to indicate hope. But she chooses a white syringa to signify fraternal love and offers it to him. He refuses it, and seizes a scarlet iris to express his burning passion. She accepts it, and presents him with a black iris, an admission of deep love. He falls at her feet and presents a heliotrope, a symbol of love. But she replies with a marguerite, suggesting that she will consider the matter.

During the third waltz Adélaïde pulls the petals off the marguerite one by one, and discovers thereby that Lorédan's love is true. She is about to yield to him when a wealthy Duke arrives and gives her a bouquet of sunflowers, which represents a promise of great riches, and a diamond necklace. Adélaïde then dances with him while Lorédan looks on bitterly. In the epilogue the other guests have retired, and the Duke hopes that she will give him permission to stay with her, but she presents him with a branch of acacia, the symbol of only platonic love, and he departs. Lorédan then tries to woo her, but she gives him a poppy to express forgetfulness, and he retires. Adélaïde is then seen alone on her balcony, but Lorédan appears on the balcony of a neighbouring house. He displays a marigold and a bunch of cypress to signify despair, and then draws a pistol which he raises to his head. Adélaïde immediately repents, and throws him a red rose. He leaps across to her and the ballet ends with the usual embrace.

As we have already observed in the biography, this ballet was a tremendous success, and one cannot help wondering why it is not produced more often these days. Like Ravel's other ballets, it offers wonderful scope for fine choreography and *décor*.

L'Enfant et les sortilèges

The libretto of this ballet was written by Colette at the request of Jacques Rouché, the Director of the Paris Opéra, and bearing its original title *Ballet pour ma fille* it was sent to Ravel with a request that he should set it to music. He said that as he hadn't a daughter it seemed silly to write a ballet with that title, so it was renamed. It is really an operetta-ballet.

The scene is an old Norman house. A tea kettle is singing on the hob, and a black cat sits purring before the fire. A small boy is seated at a table rebelliously contemplating his school-books, and then he starts to sing that he doesn't want to work : he wants to play, to eat all the cakes, to pull the cat's tail, and so forth. His mother enters and reprimands him for slacking, but he merely puts his tongue out at her. For this he is made to have tea without sugar and nothing but dry bread to eat. He flies into a rage, smashes the tea-pot and cup on the floor, tears up his books, pulls the cat's tail, upsets the kettle of water and drags out the pendulum of the clock. He then gets tired and goes to sit in a chair, but the chair gets up and walks away from him, and dances with the armchair to celebrate its freedom from "that terrible child." The tea-pot asks the broken cup in English : "How's your mug ? " "Rotten" comes the reply, and then they both dance. The boy then feels cold and goes to the fire, but it leaps out and burns him, and he starts to cry. A fairy princess arises from the pages of one of his torn books and asks what will become of her now that the books have been destroyed. Old Arithmetic arises from another with his digits, which dance around the boy until his head is whirling. The cat sees its lover in the garden and leaps to the window ledge, where the two cats sing a duet.

The scene changes to the garden, where we hear a chorus of frogs and the voices of bats, moths, squirrels and suchlike all crying for vengeance for the ill-treatment they have suffered at the boy's hands. But he is now repentant and cries "Maman ! " Then he observes that a little squirrel is hurt and tries to bandage its wound. A complete silence conveys the animals' wonder at the sudden change in the boy ; then they see that he, too, is hurt, and help him by joining in his cry "Maman ! " The night is now passing, and with the dawn the mother appears and takes the child into her arms.

Many pages could be written about this very amusing ballet, but there is space for only a brief reference to its most striking feature : the wonderful effect of the chorus of animals in the last scene. The music here is really remarkable, and equally impressive is the sudden silence when all the little creatures are spellbound by the boy's change of heart.

Pavane pour une Infante défunte

The various arrangements of this, of which the orchestral is of course the most popular, were all made from the original piano piece. It is in Rondo form, and need not be described here in detail. It should suffice to say that with all the faults that clever sterile people have found with it, this early work of Ravel is very pleasant and deserves the great popularity it enjoys. The influence of Chabrier is obvious, but this is no way detrimental.

Rapsodie espagnole

This is in four parts. The first, *Prélude à la nuit*, is quiet and contemplative ; the second, *Malaguena*, is a very vivid movement in which the theme of the *Prélude* forms the basis of a dance ; the third, *Habanera*, is the slow Cuban dance he wrote in 1895 well orchestrated ; and the last, *Feria*, is a most exhilarating, colourful dance that increases in intensity until it reaches an extremely effective climax. As a whole, the work is a pleasing and most useful suite.

Le Tombeau de Couperin

Available both as a piano and an orchestral suite, this work is in six movements. The first, *Prélude*, is in memory of Lieut. Jacques Charlot, and consists of a lively dance. This is followed by a fugue in memory of Lieut. Jean Cruppi.

The third movement, *Forlane*, in memory of Lieut. Gabriel Deluc, is an Italian dance of the early eighteenth century. Then comes a *Rigaudon*, an old Provençal dance in memory of Jean Dreyfus ; followed by the very beautiful *Menuet*, dedicated to Pierre and Pascal Gaudin. The suite concludes with a Toccata, a memorial to Capt. Jean de Marliave.

It should be noted that in the orchestral suite, the Fugue and Toccata have been omitted.

La Valse

The composer has described the scene of this *poème choréographique* thus : "*Mouvement de Valse Viennoise*: Drifting clouds give glimpses through rifts, of waltzing couples. The clouds gradually scatter, and an immense hall can be seen, filled with a whirling crowd. The scene gradually becomes illuminated : the light of the chandeliers bursts forth. An Imperial Court about 1855."

The ballet opens with a curious orchestral effect supposed to represent the drifting clouds, through which the waltz rhythm slowly penetrates. This in time becomes a typical waltz of the Johann Strauss type, but later, harsh chords begin to change the character of it, and it becomes more intense and frenzied, filled with fear and anguish, until it reaches the final climax. This is undoubtedly one of Ravel's best compositions.

The Two Piano Concertos

Ravel's own notes on these have been quoted in the biography. No. 1 in G is a most entertaining work, gay and spirited, except for the tender, graceful middle movement. The finale, *presto*, uses jazz rhythms, and unless he is an exceptionally capable pianist, the soloist is likely to experience some difficulty in keeping pace with the orchestra. Speaking generally, the concerto is brilliant and elegant, but somewhat superficial.

About the Concerto for the left hand, it may be said that anybody who can play it properly with one hand is a very, very clever executant. Ravel was going to play it himself in Paris on one occasion, but decided to pass the privilege on to Madame Marguerite Long.[1] It is in one movement, based on a rather lugubrious sarabande, and the piano maintains the strong rhythm right through to the end.

String Quartet in F

In his description of this, Roland-Manuel referred to it as " . . . the ardent, splendid effort of youth confident of its force." It is a subtle work in four movements rich in delicately woven themes. Special mention should be made of the last movement for its great vigour and passion.

Although it was dedicated to him, Fauré sharply criticized it : he thought it was too short and disjointed. Ravel was inclined to revise it on this account, but Debussy stopped him, saying : "In the name of the gods of music and of my own, do not touch a note of your Quartet."

Jeux d'Eau

This was inspired by a verse from a poem by H. de Régnier that starts : "Dieu fluvial riant de l'eau qui le chatouille". It is one of the finest of Ravel's compositions for the piano : a brilliant picture of

---

[1] When Paul Wittgenstein played it he made certain modifications that infuriated the composer

splashing fountains, waterfalls and rippling streams. The piece is in sonata form and exploits the chord of the major seventh and ninth very prettily. There must be few pianists who would not find *Jeux d'eau* a source of great delight and interest.

Miroirs

Some details of this suite for the piano have already been given in the biography, but a few words should be added here about one or two of the movements. *Oiseaux tristes* was Ravel's favourite : it is supposed to represent "birds lost in a dark forest during the hottest hours of summer." The most successful, perhaps, is *Alborada del gracioso*, a brilliant piece that with *Une Barque sur l'océan* was later orchestrated. The latter is a kaleidoscopic affair, very colourful and vivacious but a trifle confusing. This suite is a mature work, and unusually attractive because of its rich harmonies.

Gaspard de la Nuit

Inspired by poems of Aloysius Bertrand, this splendid suite for piano is in three sections. The first, *Ondine*, is a remarkable and most unusual musical picture of showers of water. As a contrast, the second, *Le Gibet*, is a dismal landscape in which we hear the tolling of a bell. The pianist Gil-Marchex once said that this piece required no less than twenty-seven different methods of touch. Finally, *Scarbo* is a veritable whirlwind of a scherzo ; one of the most amazing virtuoso pieces we possess. The whole suite, but the third movement in particular, is full of interest for the more accomplished pianist.

Histoires naturelles

This set of songs originally had piano accompaniment, but it was later orchestrated by Manuel Rosenthal. The poems are by Jules Renard. *Le Paon* tells the story of a very vain peacock about to be married. His fiancée, however, lets him down and we get a delightful impression of his haughty gesture as he spreads his beautiful tail and struts away. *Le Grillon* depicts a moonlit landscape into which a cricket wanders, winds his watch and retires for the night. *Le Cygne* sails along apparently watching the clouds, but suddenly dives and digs with its beak in the mud for worms, which make it "as fat as a goose". *Le Martin-Pêcheur* is an exquisite portrayal of the birds at evening, and *La Pintade* is a sketch of the guinea fowl whose shrill voice stabs the air unmistakably in the music.

Chansons madecasses

A quartet for voice, piano, flute and 'cello consisting of three songs with words by Evareste Parny. *Nadanhove* is a syncopated berceuse that tells of a woman whose kisses reach the very soul of her lover ; *Aoua* ! is a slave's song of revolt against the tyranny of the white races, in which the piano provides some curious tom-tom effects ; and *Il est doux* is a nocturne containing a dialogue between the flute and voice, in which the 'cello enjoys some interesting pizzicato passages and the piano does its best to imitate a gong. When *Aoua* ! was first heard in Paris it caused a disturbance among the audience, for the French were then having trouble in Morocco, and the performance of this song was considered to be an act of great indiscretion.

RAVEL

OTHER PUBLISHED WORKS

Menuet Antique
   (1895) Piano solo.
Un grand sommeil noir
   (1895) Song with words by Verlaine.
Sainte
   (1896) Song with words by Mallarmé.
Deux epigrammes de Clement Marot
   (1896) Two songs : *D'Anne jouent de l'épinette*, and *D'Anne qui me jecta de la neige*.
Manteau de Fleurs
   (1903) Song with words by Gravollet.
Shéhérazade
   (1903) Three songs with piano or orchestral accompaniment : *Asie, La Flute enchantée* and *L'Indifférent*. Words by Tristan Klingsor. The orchestration is remarkable for its variety and delicate shading, indeed the orchestra is responsible for most of the "atmosphere"
Le Noël des Jouets
   (1905) Song with the composer's own words.
Sonatine
   (1905) This is a masterly little work for the piano in sonata form. It was later orchestrated : a great favourite with many of Ravel's friends.
Introduction and Allegro
   (1906) This is a septet for harp, string quartet, flute and clarinet ; rather like a harp concerto. An excellent work, with some very gay passages.
Les Grands Vents venus d'Outre-mer
   (1906) Song with words by H. de Requier.
Cinq mélodies populaires grecque
   (1907) Five songs on Greek melodies : *Le Reveil de la mariée ; Là-bas, vers l'église ; Quel galant ; Chanson des cueilleuses de lentisque ;* and *Tout gai.*
Sur l'herbe
   (1907) Song with words by Verlaine, in which the composer anticipated jazz rhythms. It tells of an old Abbé who is much too fond of the wine of Cyprus.
Vocalise en forme d'Habanera
   (1907) Song based on the Habanera.
Une Barque sur l'Océan
   (1908) An orchestral work from *Miroirs*, the piano suite.
Menuet sue le nom d'Haydn
   (1909) A piano solo.
Quatre chants populaires
   (1910) Four of the songs written for the competition held by the Maison du Lied of Moscow : *Chanson française, Chanson espagnole, Chanson italienne, Chanson hébraïque.* No. 4 has been orchestrated.
Valses nobles et sentimentales
   (1911) The composer called these a "chain of waltzes after Schubert." There are seven short waltzes of considerable feeling and colour, and an epilogue using various themes already introduced.

Elborada del Gracioso
(1912)   An orchestral work from *Miroirs*.

Prélude
(1913)   This is a piano prelude

A la manière de . . . Borodine, Chabrier
(1913)   For piano.

Trois poèmes de Mallarmé
(1913)   Three poèms for female voices, piano, string quartet, two flutes and two clarinets. These are of considerable importance, and may be numbered among the finest of Ravel's works.

Deux melodies hébraïques
(1914)   Two songs : *Kaddisch* and *L'Enigme éternelle*. Orchestral or piano accompaniment.

Piano Trio in A minor
(1915)   In four movements, for piano, violin and 'cello. The second movement is extremely vivacious and uses a fine tune. Then there is a good contrast in the dignified, pensive third movement. The concluding movement is stimulating but complicated.

Trois Chansons
(1916)   These three songs are for mixed choir, unaccompanied. They use the composer's own words.

Sonata for violin and 'cello
(1920-2)   This is in four movements. Ravel's love of making a work of art out of a very small amount of material is to be seen here. It is a charming work of great delicacy.

Sur le nom de Gabrielle Fauré
(1922)   This is a piano work.

Ronsard à son âme
(1924)   This song was written to commemorate the four-hundredth anniversary of the birth of Ronsard.

Tzigane
(1924)   This rhapsody for violin and piano was originally written for a lute accompaniment. It opens with a long recitative for the violin, but its *tempo* gradually increases until the soloist has to be more of a musical magician than a mere performer. It was later orchestrated and dedicated to Jelly d'Aranyi.

Sonata for violin and piano
(1927)   This sonata is in three movements, and is very difficult to perform. It contains many suggestions of *L'Enfant et les sortilèges* on which Ravel was working when this sonata was written.

Rêves
(1927)   This is a fine setting of Léon-Paul Fargue's poem, for voice and piano. The accompaniment is in three-part counterpoint.

Boléro
(1928)   This is so well known that little need be said, except that it is available as a piano solo, orchestral ballet, and in various other arrangements. It is one of the least important of Ravel's works, and ought to be given a rest.

Don Quichotte à Dulcinée
(1932)   Settings of three poems by Paul Morand for baritone and small orchestra. *Chanson romantique, Chanson épique,* and *Chanson à boire.* They are based on Spanish and Basque melodies. No. 3 is a very jolly serenade in *jota* rhythm.